FEEDING CHILAPA

FEEDING CHILAPA

The Birth, Life, and Death of a Mexican Region

Chris Kyle

UNIVERSITY OF OKLAHOMA PRESS : NORMAN

Library of Congress Cataloging-in-Publication Data
Kyle, Chris, 1962–
Feeding Chilapa : the birth, life, and death of a Mexican region / Chris Kyle. — 1st ed.
p. cm.
Includes bibliographical references and index.
ISBN 978-0-8061-3920-3 (hardcover : alk. paper) — ISBN 978-0-8061-3921-0
(pbk. : alk. paper) 1. Food supply — Mexico — Chilapa de Alvarez Region — History.
2. Chilapa de Alvarez Region (Mexico) — Economic conditions. 3. Chilapa de Alvarez
Region (Mexico) — History. I. Title.
HD9014.M63C464 2008
330.972'73 — dc22

2007044649

CONTENTS

ILLUSTRATIONS

FIGURES

TABLES

MAPS

PREFACE AND ACKNOWLEDGMENTS

This book is a case study of the birth, life, and death of an economic region in a remote valley in southern Mexico. It is in many respects a historical study but one that is informed by extensive familiarity with the landscape and its contemporary inhabitants. I am a cultural anthropologist by training and disposition, and the research that forms the basis of the book was fairly evenly split between archival and ethnographic investigations. Not being a historian, I felt unconstrained by the temporal boundaries that conventionally divide Mexican historiography into separate areas of specialized study. My focus is on the life cycle of a socioeconomic institution, a region, and on the place where the drama of its existence was played out. The region's life cycle spanned six or more commonly demarcated historical periods, and thus I touch on issues that can properly be considered to be the special intellectual province of several groups of scholars. Indeed, my study moves seamlessly into the present, and in the approach I enter topical terrain covered by geographers, economists, and political scientists as well as anthropologists and historians. I have done what I could to familiarize myself with the research findings of those working on the issues relevant to my study. Still, there is an immense body of extremely high quality literature to deal with, and I would be surprised if scholars from all of the pertinent disciplines and subdisciplines were uniformly satisfied with my coverage of their efforts. All I can do is offer my deepest apology and my assurance that any oversight was neither deliberate nor intended as a slight.

This book is in many respects a historical study of a single remote region, but it is not so historical, and the region not so remote and unique, that my arguments and conclusions have no relevance to some of the more pressing issues of our times. I am thinking here of two issues in particular — neoliberalism and international migration — that my study bears on (directly in the first case and a bit more obliquely in the second). Though both are matters of impassioned interest on either side of the U.S.-Mexican border, passions seem to run higher about neoliberalism to the south and migration to the north. It is precisely because my study is so deeply historical that the perspective seems to me somewhat different than is generally found among those for whom the issues count as a primary research or occupational concern.

Neoliberalism refers to a set of economic policy prescriptions that many Latin American governments, Mexico's among them, implemented in the past couple of decades. Assessments of neoliberalism's success at fostering constructive economic change range along a continuum from unabashed delight to anger and disgust. Certain components of neoliberalism are discussed in later chapters in the book, and I need not dwell upon the issues here. I would merely alert readers to a few themes that I hope I have made clear. Perhaps the broadest point to be made here is that there often is a great gulf between the rhetoric issued by both scholars and policymakers who deal in abstract propositions or macroeconomic principles and the economic realities that confront living human creatures. As an example, take the notion that the application of neoliberalism entails a withdrawal of government from intervention in an economy. From the perspective of people living in the region addressed in this book, neoliberalism has entailed nothing of the sort. Similarly, neoliberalism's supporters and detractors alike generally rest their case on a carefully constructed image of the existing world where the policies are to be or have been applied. It is a constructed image that often has very little time depth and equally little connection to the lived experiences of actual people. The exact content of the constructed world varies depending in no small part upon whether one wishes to support or condemn neoliberalism (or, for that matter, any other government program or policy), but what supporters and detractors seem to share is an underlying assumption that government policies actually matter and that they matter in the manner intended by their architects. In the chapters that follow, I have occasion to challenge both of these assumptions.

International migration presents a somewhat different set of concerns. In the overheated rhetoric heard north of the border, the story began sometime in the distant past when a trickle of Mexicans flowed into the United States seeking jobs. The trickle continued and has now become a flood, the border apparently doing nothing to stem the tide. Building a wall and even building and staffing military fortifications are seen by some as reasonable measures to "defend" the sovereignty of the United States. Frustrated that the government will not do more, vigilante groups now patrol sections of the border with the tacit and sometimes overt approval of powerful politicians. Immigrants have been driven deeper into the shadows, where they often fall victim to violent and exploitative human smuggling groups, among others. Meanwhile, immigrant rights supporters have been reduced to watching in horror as poor and vulnerable migrants are abused and assaulted, if not quite openly hunted.

This book is not about international migration, but it bears on the issue by offering perspective on the processes operating in Mexico to produce labor mobility. Over the course of the twentieth century, Mexican regions of the sort featured in this book successively had their internal structure first altered and eventually destroyed by the progressive expansion of industrialization. The exact pattern and timing of decline varied from one region to another. In the best of circumstances, regions were not so much destroyed by industrialization as they were transformed, with new economic sectors opening at a pace sufficient to absorb the refugees created by the decline of outmoded economic activities. Far more often, however, regions simply declined and disappeared while the refugees thus created were cast to the winds. They moved wherever they had to in order to survive. They went to cities in Mexico, to industrial work sites along the northern border, and across the border into the United States.

At the risk of venturing a bit beyond my data, I think it likely that Mexico is now in the final phases of exterminating the surviving remnants of preindustrial economic life in the country. It is at this point that neoliberal policies and international migration need to be viewed as parts of a single process. Far from representing a reduced role of government in the Mexican economy, neoliberal policies in Mexico seem to me to mark an extremely aggressive and robust effort at state intervention with the aim of expanding industrialization into the final unsullied pockets of the country. The consequence has been population movements of historic proportion. Viewed from the U.S. border, there has been a fairly massive wave of migration. Yet if I am correct, then neoliberalism has created something more akin to a tsunami than the steadily rising flood of migrants envisioned by pundits and policymakers in the United States. Certainly all industrialized societies have very high rates of labor mobility, and Mexico is no exception. But I think that Mexico has recently experienced something different. Time will tell, but my bet is that pressure on the U.S.-Mexican border will soon subside, if it has not already done so, as Mexicans newly displaced by the onslaught of neoliberalism settle in to their new industrialized lives.

Outline of the Book

The bulk of this book addresses the Atempa basin region's preindustrial political economy, ending with the region's ongoing industrial transformation and attendant dismemberment. Following a short introduction to the Atempa basin region in chapter 1, I begin, in chapter 2, with a consideration of the growth and development of Chilapa's urban economy. In addition to presenting a broad economic history of the city, this chapter has two central goals. The first is to convey a sense of the size and composition of the non–food producing, market-dependent population at various points in time. As will be seen, there evolved in the region no later than the early nineteenth century a spatially concentrated pocket of intense market demand, otherwise known as a city. While much of what was consumed within this pocket could be taken or left, as fancy or circumstances dictated, this was not the case with basic foodstuffs. Chilapa, as with any city, was utterly intolerant of disruptions in the timely delivery of food. My consideration of the size and composition of the market-dependent population is thus aimed at developing estimates of the amounts of basic foodstuffs that were needed for the city to survive as such. The second goal of this chapter is related to the first. Once food left the hands of producing households, it entered market networks. The chapter includes a survey of the shifting employment offerings that formed a part of these networks.

I then turn to the rural hinterland, the source of the foodstuffs consumed in the urban center. Chapter 3 begins with a brief survey of the agricultural resources of the region, including the physical environment and agricultural production techniques and technologies. Mostly this chapter addresses the early efforts to organize these resources into a rural supply network for the newly emerged city. Those involved in the effort met stiff resistance, which they attempted to overcome using physical violence to liberate food from rural households for delivery to the city. It was a misguided effort that roundly failed and, in the 1840s, plunged the city and the region into chaos. Deliberate attempts at organizing a hinterland having failed, Chilapa was obliged to fall back on the only force it had left: market demand. The second attempt at organizing a rural hinterland, particularly its political dimensions, forms the subject of chapter 4. Here I show that once the market was left to do the work, a coherent economic region crystallized almost overnight. The region thus created proved to be both stable and resilient, maintaining similar contours and content through the mid-twentieth century.

Chapters 5 and 6 pick up the story in the early twentieth century and continue into the present day. At the beginning of this period, life in the Atempa basin could be and was sustained with a minimum of interaction with the outside world. In chapter 5, I show how pressures building from within combined with intensifying pressure from without to undermine and ultimately destroy the preindustrial order. This serves as a prelude to a brief consideration of the economic aftermath, presented in chapter 6. Finally, a concluding chapter considers general economic and political implications of the shift from an agrarian to an industrial production system and the insights to be gained in viewing the process from a regional perspective.

A Note on Methods

This book is based on information collected using the eclectic blend of observational techniques that are characteristic of contemporary anthropology. Over the course of the past seventeen years, I have spent about three years conducting participant observation in and around Chilapa, including a seventeen-month stint from April 1990 to September 1991. My students, including a doctoral candidate (in 1999–2000) and participants in two ethnographic field schools for undergraduates (in 2002 and 2004), have also made substantial contributions to my understanding of the region. In addition to ethnographic research, I have done a fair amount of work with archival sources, particularly with documents held by the Archivo General de la Nación (AGN) in Mexico City and by civil and ecclesiastical authorities in Chilapa. Insofar as I have departed from the norm in anthropology, it is because my research addresses a region rather than a single community. I have not conducted a complete house-to-house survey, for example, but instead have relied more on government censuses and surveys than is typical. I have conducted sampling surveys of various sorts, most notably on land use, agricultural yields, transportation, and retail commerce, each discussed as relevant in the following chapters. Practically all of my data that have any sort of spatial dimension has been entered into a GIS database, using ArcGIS 9.1. Years ago, before this technology existed, I measured distances, calculated areas, made maps, and counted people, households, towns, fields, and much more the hard way, by pacing, shooting compass points, triangulating, and crunching numbers with a calculator or spreadsheet. Using aerial photographs, digitized maps, and GIS software, I have since recalculated many of my earlier counts and measures. There will be occasions on which I touch on topics about which I have previously published, and careful scrutiny will reveal that in some such occasions there are small numerical discrepancies. These are artifacts of the techniques and technologies used in recording and analyzing data; fortunately, none of the amended measurements differ in magnitude to an extent sufficient to significantly alter conclusions.

Much of my knowledge of the region derives from unstructured and semistructured interviews, from simply talking to people and from getting to know as much as I can about their everyday activities. While in the field, I often engaged in specific and narrowly targeted data collection activities, but I also regularly set aside days in which I would venture into the streets of Chilapa or into the surrounding countryside without definite purpose, to observe and talk to people as they engaged in living. If the work I found people doing was not too technical, I frequently volunteered to assist in exchange for permission to take photos and to have my questions answered; as a result, I have helped plant, weed, and fertilize more maize fields than I care to recount. Other production activities required a level of skill that I do not possess. Fortunately, Mexicans relish companionship, and thus I was generally tolerated as I observed and asked probing questions of people engaged in their everyday routines. In this way, I have had the opportunity to observe and collect at least some information from producers of rebozos, sugar, pottery, candles, fireworks, mescal, baskets, bread, brooms, and a number of other relics of the preindustrial era.

At the end of most days, I would review my activities with any of a number of key informants who lived in or near Chilapa. They were drawn from many walks of life and included a schoolteacher, a doctor, a farmer, a merchant, a government agronomist, an urban homemaker, and a British expatriate (a one-time aerospace engineer who retired into life as a preindustrial farmer). Early on, I learned that it was useful to regularly relate my experiences to one or more members of this group even when I thought I had a firm understanding of what it was I had been doing that day. Through these conversations (debriefing sessions, of a sort), I would almost always gain useful insights that otherwise might not have occurred to me; more than a few times, I had mistaken impressions corrected. Some of my most satisfying moments in conducting fieldwork came when my debriefer gently made me aware that I had not only interpreted one or another of my observations wrongly but had barely cracked the surface of something with much underlying complexity. All of this will, I think, be familiar to anyone who has conducted participant observation.

ACKNOWLEDGMENTS

A host of people have made contributions to the research and writing that went into this book. If I begin with contributions of an intellectual nature, Ross Hassig and Barbara Price clearly top the list. To me, the book is the logical outcome of applying Barbara's unflinching materialism and Ross's attentiveness to spatial matters to a particular body of data. Barbara and Ross also made substantive contributions through comments on unedited oral versions of sections and chapters, as well as on drafts in written form. Others who offered comments on the manuscript (or portions of it) include Brad Andrews, John Chance, John Monaghan, Matthew Painter, Steve Rubinstein, Monyka Salazar, Beth Warren, and William Yaworsky. Several of my students collected data that found its way into the book. I am grateful to John Pocus for assisting me in the Registro Civil in Chilapa and to Monyka Salazar for her work with late colonial period documents from the Archivo General de la Nación. William Yaworsky's research on modern nongovernmental organizations has greatly enhanced my understanding of recent economic changes in the Atempa basin. Students who participated in ethnographic field schools in 2002 and 2004 — including Mary Roca, Marianne McLaughlin, Charles Kelley, Damon Carter, Dominic Johnson, and others already named — exposed nooks and crannies of Chilapa that I had not known existed. In so doing, they made substantial, if unspecific, contributions to my understanding of the region.

I am also indebted to Alberto Sánchez Andraca and Emilio Silva Acevedo for helping me understand local agriculture and commerce, respectively. I do not know how to begin to characterize the debt I owe to José Díaz Navarro.

Turning to contributions more of a facilitative nature, my research in Mexico might have been possible but would have been far less pleasant were it not for Elena Navarro. Samuel Villela, Blanca Jiménez, and Marci Lane Rodríguez likewise offered logistical support at times when it was sorely needed. Officials of successive ayuntamiento administrations consistently removed obstacles and otherwise facilitated my research in the region. Working with the University of Oklahoma Press has been a wonder to behold. Alessandra Jacobi Tamulevich saw the manuscript to completion, Emmy Ezzell waited patiently while I learned to make maps, Julie Shilling ushered the book to production, and Sally Bennett gently and patiently lessoned me in the English language. Sally's indulgence has been exceeded only by that of Julie Gold and Alex Kyle, my partner and daughter, respectively. To all of you, I am grateful.

Acronyms

AGN	Archivo General de la Nación (National Archive)
BANRURAL	Banco de Crédito Rural (Rural Credit Bank)
CONAGUA	Comisión Nacional del Agua (National Water Commission)
CONASUPO	Companía Nacional de Subsistencias Populares (National Subsistence Good Company)
DEN	Departamento de la Estadística Nacional (National Statistics Department)
DGE	Dirección General de Estadística (General Statistics Directorate)
FERTIMEX	Fertilizantes de México (Fertilizers of Mexico)
FIDEPAL	Fideicomiso de la Palma (Palm Trust)
GEA	Grupo de Estudios Ambientales (Environmental Studies Group)
INEGI	Instituto Nacional de Estadística, Geografía, e Informatica (National Statistics, Geography, and Information Institute)
INI	Instituto Nacional Indigenista (National Indian Institute)
PEMEX	Petróleos Mexicanos (Mexican Petroleum)
PRONASOL	Programa Nacional de Solidaridad (National Solidarity Program)
SAM	Sistema Alimentario Mexicano (Mexican Food System)
SARH	Secretaría Agraria y Recursos Hidráulicos (Ministry of Agriculture and Water Resources)
SEDESOL	Secretaría de Desarrollo Social (Ministry of Social Development)

FEEDING CHILAPA

MEXICAN REGIONS

I have written this book to address what seems to me to be a void in the anthropological literature on regional development in Latin America, particularly in Mexico. There was a time in the early history of Latin American anthropology (most particularly in the interwar years) when anthropologists considered the region to be a fundamental unit of social structure that ranked alongside communities, neighborhoods, kin groups, households, patronage networks, and similar groupings in shaping the course and contours of social life. The preeminent example of a regional study is the Carnegie Institution of Washington's Maya Program, a sprawling research effort that went on for decades and involved researchers from a multitude of academic disciplines (Redfield 1941; Rubinstein 1991). Robert Redfield, as director of the ethnology portion of the project, oversaw the efforts of a dozen or more researchers. At the opposite extreme is Ralph Beals's three-month reconnaissance of the Mixe Highlands (1945), a shoestring operation funded by Elsie Clews Parsons. Other examples include the University of Chicago's Man in Nature Project and Ralph Beals's Sierra Tarascan Program (Rubín de la Borbolla and Beals 1940). Although the scale and theoretical orientation of these research efforts varied, they were united by a regional orientation. Researchers associated with many of these projects produced detailed community studies that are today considered classics in the discipline (e.g., Beals 1946; Foster 1948; Redfield and Villa 1934; Tax 1953). What is often overlooked by modern anthropologists is that these works were originally intended to be studies of intraregional variation. The ethnographies were never meant to be read alone, independent of the associated regional studies (e.g., McBryde 1945; Redfield 1941; West 1948) that were intended to provide background and contextual information.

This regional survey and community sampling approach to anthropological research disappeared, at least in Mexico, after the Second World

War. By the 1950s, the community study had become firmly entrenched as the signature mode of conducting ethnographic research, and the region as a unit of analysis was all but forgotten. Regions made a brief reappearance in the 1970s under the auspices of "regional analysis" (e.g., Smith 1976) but in such superbly abstract form that anthropologists, who were by then accustomed to rich ethnographic detail, mostly demurred. A full explanation of why anthropologists abandoned regional studies in the 1950s is a task I leave for another day. Suffice it to say here that the reasons had less to do with the intellectual merits than with funding issues within anthropology, with increased disciplinary specialization in the social sciences, and with the expectation among anthropologists that regional studies would be covered by geographers. Geographers proved to be an unbiddable lot, however. They too had set about refashioning their discipline, but they did so without apparent regard for the needs of anthropologists. And thus the regional study as an anthropological research strategy and as a genre of anthropological literature passed quietly into intellectual history.

There are a number of reasons why we should regret its passing and why a contemporary revisitation is warranted. Not the least of these is that regional studies could benefit from post–1950 theoretical developments within the discipline, particularly the maturation of ecological anthropology and the rise of materialist approaches to the study of political economy. Singly or, as in this book, jointly, these newer theoretical orientations provide a different basis for delineating regions, and for assessing the relative significance of social relationships within them, than the anthropological theory that was current in the 1930s and 1940s. Where earlier regions were defined based on linguistic and ethnic criteria, here they are understood to be ecological, economic, and political units. As such, they might crosscut linguistic boundaries or might encompass more than one ethnic group. Whereas the earlier regional studies mostly ignored urban centers and their Spanish-speaking residents, treating these as inconvenient European intrusions sprinkled across an otherwise interesting indigenous landscape, they cannot be so lightly dismissed when regions are defined based on patterns of resource flow.

What is perhaps more important, in hindsight it is now apparent that the decline in regional studies occurred at a pivotal historical moment, when the regions were poised on the cusp of fateful changes. In this, regions differ from communities, households, kin groups, and patronage networks. Households, kin groups, and patronage networks have certainly had their mettle tested and have had to be nimble to adapt to rapidly changing circumstances, but they nevertheless continue to play an essential role in structuring social life (e.g., Kyle and Yaworsky 2008; Wilk 1991). Communities have had a rockier ride. Some have survived and retained their structural integrity (e.g., Monaghan 1995), while others seem to have diminished in significance (e.g., Annis 1987; Cancian 1992). Still others have been transformed into novel transnational social entities (e.g., Cohen 1999, 2004; Kearney 1996). Regions always had a more precarious existence than these other social units and have proven far less resilient in adapting to the modern world. Most have, in fact, disappeared; in their place, one now finds much broader national and international social networks. Since the late 1960s, the emphasis in anthropology has understandably been placed on the local impact of these novel national and international economic and political linkages. But there seems not to be much recognition that the emergent social networks are often built on foundations laid by earlier regional relationships. In truth, the community study offers at best a difficult vantage point from which to achieve a meaningful perspective on the broad and shifting social forces that impinge from the outside on the smaller social groupings that are the staple of contemporary anthropological analysis. I make no claim that the regional study represents an analytical panacea in this regard. Yet I do feel that the regional study can offer a useful means of providing the broader perspective and context that is commonly and perhaps inevitably missing in the community study.

Let me illustrate with reference to the cases of Atzacoaloya and Ayahualulco, two southern Mexican towns of similar size and historical background and located within seven kilometers of one another. By local and historical standards, Atzacoaloya has emerged in the modern world as a veritable poster child of prosperity. As in days of old, its women make utilitarian pottery that remain preferred cooking vessels in the region. In recent years, women from Atzacoaloya have come to dominate retail trade in fresh produce in the regional market. The men have likewise been energetic in producing and marketing onion, garlic, and jicama, all agricultural specialties of long standing. Households have plowed their earnings into productive equipment, including irrigation pumps and trucks used to haul commodities to markets. Many have also sunk resources into the construction of new brick and concrete houses furnished with a growing inventory of modern consumer goods. And it is not only individuals and households who have benefited. The community too has managed to retain its integrity as a community, with a town government attentive to

Figure 1. Church in Atzacoaloya in 2004.

infrastructural and public health needs despite having very limited resources with which to work. Its women proudly wear a native costume that
announces their community of origin to all with whom they come into
contact. As for symbolism, it would be impossible to improve upon the
town's church as a vivid display of the vibrancy of community life (fig. 1).
The brightly painted structure (the color scheme changes every few years
— it is currently a very bold yellow with bright blue, green, pink, and
cream-colored trimmings) shelters lavish offerings of flowers, candles, and
attention directed at the town's protective santos (saints).

Ayahualulco cuts a very different image. Here idleness, strong drink,
and banditry compete with apparent success against the town's traditional
basket-weaving industry. Schoolteachers who commute to work have
learned from bitter experience to venture through the town's approaches
carrying nothing and wearing only the typical apparel of villagers lest they
be stripped naked (wearing shoes, as opposed to sandals, is especially
dangerous) and otherwise divested of detachable possessions. Vehicles
seen risking the journey, most notably a truck sent by a local bottling
company, bristle with weaponry to deter attack. The only recent infrastructural project to benefit the town was a drainage system built by outside

Figure 2. Church in Ayahualulco in 1991.

authorities as part of a broader (and successful) effort to contain a 1991
outbreak of cholera and to prevent the disease from leaping beyond the
town's immediate neighborhood. Once again, for symbolism one need
only glance at the town's church. Unpainted and unloved, the church stood
for years with one of its two towers unfinished and a robust crop of weeds
sprouting from the face of its crumbling facade (fig. 2). This condition
would likely persist today had a structural collapse in the late 1990s not
reduced the sorry edifice to a mound of rubble, which stood for a time in
the center of town as a fitting monument to the community's experience
with modernization.

Here, then, are two towns, separated by a mere seven kilometers and
sharing similar historical backgrounds. One is demonstrably thriving, the
other apparently in its death throes. The towns come close to exhibiting the
polar extremes of broader regional patterns. Both towns possessed idiosyncrasies in the manner in which they were inserted into the local region,
idiosyncrasies that proved decisive in conditioning the way each town
would come to be inserted into the modern global economy. But a community study of either one of these towns would get us next to nowhere in
understanding these processes and would instead run a very high risk of
leaving the anthropological world with a distorted image of rural Mexico.

These problems can be avoided, at least partially, by making the region the focal point of analysis. This allows one to examine the changing position of communities in their broader social context without simultaneously reducing the discussion to a consideration of charts and graphs representing the mysterious metrics of the modern economist.

Eric Hobsbawm (1994) recently argued that the late twentieth century will be remembered by future historians as the period when peasants, or preindustrial farmers, the world over disappeared under the onslaught of industrial capitalism. He might have added that similarly swept from the field were the characteristic forms of social organization that provided order and structure to preindustrial farmers' lives. In any event, the geographic expansion of an industrial mode of production has not been a smooth process but has instead proceeded in fits and starts, however foreordained the end result might have been (or, in some cases, might still be). Certainly this has been the experience of Mexico, whose industrial transformation has been an uneven process, punctuated by notable hiccups that have sometimes extended through the country as a whole while at other times have been confined to particular regions. More than most expanses of the earth's surface, Mexico is a land of regions that have only recently been patched together into a coherent national entity. This point was forcefully made by Lesley Byrd Simpson in his classic account of Mexican history, appropriately titled *Many Mexicos* (1966). As so many do in writing on Mexico, Simpson opened with a chapter describing Mexico's imposing physical landscape, arguing that an understanding of the country's history, culture, and society must begin with a healthy appreciation of the bewildering environmental diversity found within even small areas of the country. By picking a route carefully, one could take a dizzying adventure through tropical, temperate deciduous, and subalpine coniferous forests, semiarid steppe, and alpine tundra, all without traveling more than a few dozen miles.

Mexico's dominant physiographic feature is an enormous plateau, a huge slab of uplifted rock whose floor rises from about 1,500 meters above sea level at the U.S.-Mexican border to about 2,500 meters along its southern edge, just south of Mexico City. The uplifting is caused by the collision and subduction of the oceanic Cocos plate beneath the North American continental plate. Along with the uplifted plateau, two notable features have resulted from the subduction of the Cocos plate: the Acapulco Trench, a gaping chasm in the subduction zone just off the coast of southern Mexico, and a corresponding volcanic arc, known as the Transverse Neovolcanic Axis, along the southern edge of the plateau. Although the interior portion of the plateau surface has an abundance of relatively flat terrain, it also has its share of mountainous ridges and deeply incised canyons. In most places, the plateau is skirted by imposing mountain ranges, formed through volcanic activity along the edges of the uplifted rock, beyond which lie precipitous escarpments that plummet to narrow coastal plains on the east and west and into the Balsas Depression (and ultimately the Acapulco Trench) to the south. Between the Balsas Depression and the Acapulco Trench, the land rises again into Mexico's Southern Highlands, including the Sierra Madre del Sur in Guerrero and Oaxaca and the Chiapas Highlands in Chiapas. Simpson described the Southern Highlands, with only a bit of hyperbole, as a land "of planless mountains and deep depressions," "the wildest country imaginable" (1966:2), and "a forbidding and unmapped waste" (1966:4). Aside from portions of the central and northern plateau and the generally narrow coastal plains, the low-lying Isthmus of Tehuantepec and the comparatively featureless Yucatán Peninsula are the only parts of the country that offer sizable expanses of land that could be described as anything like flat. Mostly it is "a country set on edge; where straight lines and plane surfaces are virtually homeless" (Chase 1931:1).

Yet the complex physiography is not the only source of environmental diversity in Mexico. Rainfall, for example, is very irregularly distributed, both geographically and seasonally. Generally speaking, the amount of rain diminishes as one moves north, leaving the interior of the northern plateau among the driest deserts in the Americas. At the other extreme, portions of the state of Veracruz on the Gulf Coast are among the wettest locations in the Americas, often receiving well over three meters of annual rainfall. Except for southern Veracruz and environs, where rainfall is more or less continuous, the central and southern part of the country experiences a marked rainy season lasting from June to October, with practically no rain in other months. Even these generalizations are overly simplistic. Moisture-laden air masses that move inland from both the east and west coasts bathe windward slopes with sometimes-enormous amounts of rainfall while nearby leeward slopes and inland valleys receive considerably less. Thus, viewed from the Gulf Coast plain, the southeastern escarpment of the central plateau forms "a stupendous green wall nine thousand feet in height" (Simpson 1966:4), while a bit farther inland, parched valleys (e.g., the Tehuacán Valley) are carpeted with hardy desert vegetation.

Mexico's environmental diversity is a mixed blessing for its human inhabitants. On the one hand, the many varied environmental zones in close proximity to one another practically invite the development of complex regional exchange systems. Groups situated in particular locations are able to specialize in the production of locally favored goods, knowing that these will be exchangeable for items produced by neighbors living in other environmental zones. On the other hand, the rugged landscape creates physical impediments to transport and communication that impose sharp limits on the ability of groups to development complementary production and exchange networks. These constraints were especially acute prior to the mid-twentieth century, when the introduction of modern transport and communication systems greatly reduced the costs and the risks of conducting exchange.

This point warrants emphasis. It is often remarked that the growth of pre-Columbian civilizations in Mesoamerica was limited by the absence of domesticated animals that could be used for transport. Wheeled conveyances, which in preindustrial settings were powered by domesticated animals, were similarly absent prior to the Spanish conquest. Horses, mules, burros, and oxen, all introduced by the Spaniards in the sixteenth century, did relax the constraints on transporting goods (Hassig 1985), but the extent to which this removed impediments to interregional commerce is easy to exaggerate. Much interregional trade was conducted by mule train as recently as the mid-twentieth century, and much local trade relied on human portage even at the century's end. As for the wheel, prior to the mid-twentieth century, the use of wheeled vehicles was mostly limited to the flatter areas of the central and northern plateaus (Ortiz 1994). Only in the past fifty years have wheeled conveyances had a detectable impact on the lives of Mexicans outside of these areas.

As the title of Simpson's book implies, it would not be amiss to view Mexico prior to the mid-twentieth century as an aggregate of more or less isolated regions, each with its distinctive social and cultural character, rather than viewing it as a unified social entity. There were, of course, cultural features shared widely in Mexico and social linkages that to some extent bound regions together. These include pre-Columbian traits identified by Paul Kirchoff (1952) in defining Mesoamerica as a culture area, as well as traits introduced by Spaniards that are now widely distributed through Latin America (e.g., Foster 1960). Likewise, a central government based in Mexico City exerted a varying measure of political and economic control over outlying regions. Still, the characteristic forms of social, political, and economic association found in any given Mexican community were shaped as much by local integrative processes as by intercourse between regions.

In most cases, these regional political and economic systems consisted of a central urban settlement and a variable number of outlying agricultural settlements. The settlement pattern found in particular regions was conditioned in no small part by the productivity of agriculture, itself shaped by the distribution of water and of particular types of arable land. Expanses of deep, fertile soils on level surfaces were generally a prerequisite for significant urban development. Agricultural yields on sloping upland or plateau surfaces were lower and more erratic, and thus these areas were more likely to support only rural villages. In a few favored upland locations (e.g., the Sierra Zapotec and Mixe region in Oaxaca), a high overall settlement density fostered village specialization and the development of rural exchange networks that resembled, if on a smaller scale, those with an urban settlement at their core. Yet these were the exception; broad expanses of Mexico's uplands were too thinly settled to produce a level of market demand needed to support fixed marketplaces or even periodic markets. Unless villages were located within a reasonable distance of an urban settlement, villagers living in upland areas engaged in commerce only occasionally by trading with specialized itinerant merchants based in distant urban centers (e.g., Parsons 1936; Plattner 1975). A high degree of household self-sufficiency was essential under these circumstances.

Where sufficient rainfall or some other source of water that could be used for agriculture occurred together with sizable contiguous tracts of level surface and fertile soils, large population concentrations and complex regional exchange networks tended to develop (map 1). When measured in terms of settlement density, volume of production and exchange, or complexity of internal exchange relationships, the most important of these regional networks, from pre-Columbian times to the twentieth century, was the area centered in the Valley of Mexico (what is now Mexico City). A second regional system, almost as large, was found in an adjacent valley to the southeast and was centered first in pre-Columbian Cholula and later in colonial Puebla. Likewise, smaller but still substantial exchange networks were found in adjacent valleys west of the Valley of Mexico in the Valley of Toluca, south in the Valley of Morelos, and east of Puebla in the Valley of Tehuacán (Enge and Whitehead 1989). These regional systems are notable not only for their large geographic dimensions, high settlement density, and elaborate internal exchange relationships but also because, except for the Valley of Tehuacán, all of them were near enough to one another to

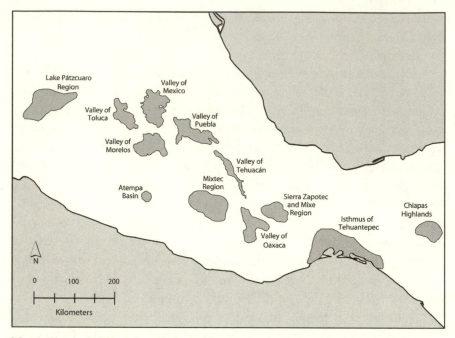

Map 1. The shaded areas show the approximate area of preindustrial economic regions once found in southern Mexico.

enable more-intensive interregional interaction than was the case else-where in Mexico (Sanders 1956). A somewhat smaller example of the same sort of thing occurred in the Valley of Oaxaca (Beals 1975). Interact-ing with the Oaxaca network, but clearly detached from it, were smaller marketing networks in the Mixteca to the west, the Isthmus of Tehuantepec to the east, and the Sierra Zapotec and Mixe region to the north (Beals 1945; Berg 1974). The Lake Pátzcuaro region of Michoacán (Kaplan 1965; West 1948) and the area around San Cristobal de las Casas in the Chiapas Highlands (Vogt 1969) were still-smaller and more-isolated instances of internally differentiated regional economies.

The regional systems mentioned above represent the best known and most commonly studied by anthropologists, mainly because they were the largest. But they are by no means the only parts of the mosaic referred to in the title of Simpson's book. Throughout the length and breadth of central and southern Mexico, pockets of comparatively dense settlement were found amid expanses of thinly settled "waste," as Simpson would have referred to land incapable of supporting large population centers or com-plex symbiotic exchange networks. Each of these pockets formed the center of an internally differentiated regional economy. Until recently, constraints on transport and communication left them mostly isolated from one another and largely autonomous in their internal development.

The hallmark of these regional systems was an internal division of labor and an associated regional market. The constituent households exhibited some measure of occupational specialization so that at least a portion of households' economic efforts centered on the production of goods or services that entered a local market. In turn, such households obtained from the market those goods and services that were essential to survival but the production of which they had forgone to concentrate on their particular specialized branch of activity. Beyond this, most regions were divided into two basic social components. The first, where the most highly specialized households were found, comprised the residents of an urban center. Most urban households produced very little (and in some cases nothing) that their members directly consumed, depending instead on market transactions to obtain needed goods and services. Of these needed goods and services, none was so pressing as food. This, together with fuel and related goods, had to be secured from a region's second great social component, the inhabitants of the surrounding countryside. From a regional standpoint, rural households consisted of specialized commercial farmers who contrasted with their urban counterparts in two fundamental respects: first, they tended to engage in a much broader range of productive activities; and, second, they often achieved a high degree of self-sufficiency. Indeed, coping with what a frustrated German merchant once called the "damned wantlessness" (*verdammte Bedürfnislosigkeit*) of rural Mexicans (cited in Chase 1931:313) was a central economic and political problem in a good number of Mexican regions. Quite simply, urban consumers commonly found that their need for goods produced by rural households was more compelling than any attraction rural households felt toward the goods and services controlled by the residents of an urban center. Even when an appropriate pecuniary sentiment was found among rural households, other issues could arise that interfered with efforts to supply an urban center. Demographic changes among either rural or urban populations could create imbalances in the ratio of agricultural producers to dependent consumers, and erratic agricultural yields in the countryside could frustrate even the most finely tuned production and distribution networks.

I should not leave the impression that Mexican regions were anywhere truly autonomous in the sense that they were wholly self-sustaining. None that I know of ever was. Salt, cotton, metal tools, and silver pesos top the list of commodities that most regions had to obtain from the outside, but an extensive inventory of nonessential goods regularly moved between regions as well. Furthermore, a sizable quantity of the commodities produced in urban centers was often, and perhaps always, aimed at remote consuming populations. Shifting patterns of supply and demand in remote markets made these commercial interactions chancy and put a premium on either diversifying or exploiting a competitive advantage that minimized potentially ruinous competition from rival suppliers.

Preindustrial regional economies were thus regularly bedeviled by two overriding concerns. First, urban centers had to be provisioned with foodstuffs and other essential resources that were produced in the surrounding countryside, sometimes with some difficulty or at considerable cost. These difficulties and costs could stem from the region's agricultural ecology or from supply-and-demand relationships that failed to stir a suitable commercial impulse among rural villagers. Second, distant markets had to present reliable commercial opportunities that allowed for the acquisition of goods that could not be obtained from local sources. Sustaining a regional economy required that a degree of equilibrium be maintained among these various intra- and interregional relationships. It was a balancing act that required constant recalibration; slight shifts in agricultural production costs, in urban demand, or in profit margins on external trade would reverberate through a regional economy and force compensatory responses throughout. More than a few regions confronted perturbations that no amount of recalibration could handle and suffered catastrophic failure as a result, their urban populations dispersing or reverting to an essentially self-contained agrarian existence.

Although many of the most fundamental social relationships within regions involved nothing more than individual households and the unfettered operation of supply-and-demand relationships in local markets, the complexity and the signal importance of the various commercial relationships upon which regional economies depended routinely gave rise to a need for various forms of centralized administrative attention. These administrative functions were concentrated in urban centers and created a division in urban populations between the broad working class and a smaller managerial elite. The statuses that constituted this managerial class crosscut the conventional categories of "public" and "private" sectors. Social actors such as factory managers, estate owners, and wholesale merchants performed administrative functions that were no less vital to a regional economy than, say, a tax collector or an official charged with adjudicating disputes involving weights and measures in a marketplace. In practice, the same individuals tended to drift back and forth across the public/private divide. As a species, what these positions had in common was that the incumbents bore responsibility for coordinating collective action among the households below them in the social hierarchy: they served as intermediaries between buyers and sellers; they saw to it that production rates were adjusted to approximate demand; they oversaw the construction and maintenance of marketplaces and other public facilities; they adjudicated disputes boiling up from the cauldron of social life; and they protected private property. It is true that members of this class were frequently able to command rewards far out of proportion to anything warranted by the magnitude of their exertions, but it is also true that the functions they performed were essential for a region to exist as a coherent social unit.

Although the exact timing has varied from one to the next, a complete survey would likely show that preindustrial Mexican regions all met extinction by the close of the twentieth century. The cause, in a word, was technology, particularly as applied to transportation. Within and between the regions centered on the great cities of the central Mexican highlands, modern transportation systems were introduced early and gradually, in much the same fashion as occurred in the developing industrial centers of Europe and North America. As a result, the economies of these regions experienced processes of internal restructuring and integration into global economic networks at a pace that reflected worldwide improvements in industrial production and transportation technologies. It was a tumultuous process, to be sure, but one through which most of the internally displaced were somehow reabsorbed even while room was made for newcomers from surrounding regions.

It was otherwise in Mexico's outlying regions. Through the southern states of Michoacán, Guerrero, Oaxaca, Quintana Roo, and Chiapas, and in isolated pockets of Puebla, México, Hidalgo, Veracruz, and Yucatán, the introduction of modern transportation systems was delayed into the latter half of the twentieth century. Although distant regions felt economic shock waves issuing from industrialization in the central highlands, while they remained connected to the central highlands by nothing more efficient than the venerable mule these waves were more distant rumblings than cataclysmic shocks. But road and rail construction proceeded apace, gradually rending the mountains and valleys that for millennia had served as protective ramparts. By the time roads finally wound their way into the valleys at the heart of remote economic regions, several decades of technological advances had substantially increased the efficiency and reduced the cost of motorized transportation. For regional economies, the result was devastating.

The first casualties were *arrieros* (muleteers), who disappeared instantly as interregional freight haulage shifted from mules to trucks and trains. Long-distance trade had always been a highly capitalized sector of regional economies, and this enabled a comparatively seamless transition to vehicular transportation. Trucks laden with the mass-produced tonnage of sophisticated late-twentieth-century manufacturing industries poured into regional market centers. Some of the imported products were purely new in the sense that they encountered in markets no locally produced functional equivalent. Other arriving imports competed directly with local products. Few preindustrial industries stood a chance against the onslaught. Local patterns of production and distribution worn smooth by the ages thus melted away as buses and trucks removed the friction of distance that had previously played a decisive part in structuring economic relationships.

The movement of goods and people within regions followed a different course. Trails were widened to handle newly arrived trucks and buses, but vehicles initially met stiff competition. Local haulage, using burros or tumplines, had been a part of the mixed portfolio of activities to which rural households had long attended without recourse to a region's cash economy. Rural households were practiced at limiting their commercial engagement in regional commodity and labor markets and could generally meet their limited haulage and other transportation needs well enough using resources that were readily available. Even where there was an incentive in the form of demand for additional haulage capacity, there was no pool of available capital that could be tapped to effect an immediate change to motorized transportation. To be sure, cars, buses, and trucks eventually displaced alternatives on local roads, but vehicles made inroads slowly, and for years one could witness the curious coexistence of cars, trucks, buses, horses, burros, and human porters. This was a transitory historical phase, however; a case could probably be made for using the relative share of a region's intraregional transport load that was handled by motor vehicles as an index of the destruction of the regional economy.

Rural producers did not have much use for vehicular transportation systems, but they did need urban consumers; this proved to be their downfall. Urban centers have come to be provisioned by distant suppliers, and rural producers have found that their efforts are no longer needed. This is not to say that rural households have become completely irrelevant or that people have made no effort to adapt to their changed circumstances. Almost everywhere, there was an initial attempt to stave off the tide of history by intensifying production. When this proved inadequate, households diversified into new branches of remunerative activity, adding, as opportunities presented themselves or as circumstances allowed, new forms of commodity production, petty commerce, or seasonal participation in distant labor markets. Not many of these efforts did more than postpone the inevitable. More than a few urban centers have been transformed into specialized relief centers, administering one or another form of state-subsidized support and assistance to the disenfranchised multitudes warehoused in the surrounding countryside. These are people that history forgot, useful only to the urban bureaucrats and others who make a living ministering to them.

This book tells of the birth, life, and death of one such regional economy, one of Simpson's many Mexicos. It is a region located deep in the heart of the "forbidding and unmapped waste" of Mexico's Southern Highlands that sprang into being in the late eighteenth century and survived for some two hundred years, almost to the present day. The core of the region consisted of the middle and upper reaches of the Río Atempa basin, a watershed on the north slope of Guerrero's Sierra Madre del Sur. The most prominent settlement was the small urban center of Chilapa. By Mexican standards, Chilapa was a small urban community, the hub of a comparatively modest marketing region. The Atempa basin's regional economy was also more isolated and self-contained than most, especially compared to those in the central highlands. At the same time, the economic and ecological relationships that traditionally linked communities in the Atempa basin to create a structured, internally differentiated regional economy were not unlike those through which countless other Mexican communities were integrated into their immediate social and economic environment. Likewise, the processes through which Chilapa was transformed from the center of a complex and vibrant regional society to a small, inconveniently located city situated amid one of Mexico's many impoverished backwaters were similar to those that have occurred elsewhere.

Most recent scholarly discussions of the political economy of southern Mexico have associated, either overtly or tacitly, the economic transformations of the late twentieth century with changing state economic programs and policies. Specifically, beginning in the early 1980s, the Mexican government began implementing a set of laissez faire economic policies that have come to be known as "neoliberalism," the general aim of which was to hasten Mexico's economic integration into international financial, commodity, and labor markets. Many of the changes were aimed squarely at the signature elements of Mexico's distinctive blend of free market and protectionist policies that had defined the country's postrevolutionary twentieth-century political economy. In 2000, only state control of the petroleum industry survived where a plethora of comparably aggressive state economic interventions had once existed. For example, restrictive international trade policies that had once made Mexico a proud model of a development strategy built around "import substitution" (Hansen 1971) were dismantled in the early 1990s and replaced by the rhetoric of "free trade," entry into the World Trade Organization, ratification of the North American Free Trade Agreement, and a generalized saturation of the Mexican marketplace by imported commodities. Perhaps the most startling change involved striking from the Mexican Constitution provisions for land redistribution under the *ejido* program, a program that was long thought to rank alongside the nationalization of the petroleum industry as a primary source of state political legitimacy and a guarantor of rural economic security.

Certainly, many of the applications of neoliberalism in Mexico have had a demonstrable impact on the lives of people in the Atempa basin. More generally, through the last quarter of the twentieth century, the state became the single most significant economic actor in the region. It became the region's principal employer, the source of unprecedented investments in basic industrial infrastructure, and a provider of both direct and indirect transfer payments that reached broad swathes of the region's population. Although the state's various juridical institutions and regulatory agencies have had less success in extending their writ into the region, even in this the beginnings of change are discernible (e.g., Kyle and Yaworsky 2008). The scope of state involvement in the region's economy has become so vast that any slight changes in the nature of its activities are bound to have some sort of impact.

That said, historically and empirically the actions of the state that most profoundly shaped (and that continue to shape) the region's economy were not necessarily those associated with either neoliberal reform or even with the package of postrevolutionary programs and policies for which Mexico is best known. Rather, the factors that have had the greatest demonstrable impact are far more mundane but less commonly analyzed or questioned elements of state economic intervention. Were I pressed to identify one action on the part of the state that had the most far-reaching consequences on daily life in the Atempa basin, I would not hesitate in pointing to the construction of Highway 93 (which links Chilapa to Chilpancingo, the state capital) in the early 1970s. Without cheap and timely access to the region, neither the state nor any other outside actor had the ability to fundamentally affect local economic and political relationships. Markets outside the Atempa basin, particularly those in the central Mexican highlands, had previously offered limited commercial possibilities to which producers and merchants in the Atempa basin opportunistically responded. But long-distance trade in luxury goods and other exotic consumer items notwithstanding, the region was largely insulated from direct intervention from the outside. The highway changed this by radically altering the commercial environment that conditioned economic decision making within the region. The highway effectively removed the obstacle of physical isolation that had previously protected the Atempa basin's preindustrial economy and society. Direct head-to-head competition pitting the region's preindustrial producers against outside industrial producers was thus inevitable, a competition whose outcome was predictable regardless of whether it was mediated through a package of neoliberal programs and policies.

Vehicles certainly allowed additional tonnage to flow through both inter- and intraregional commercial channels, but what undermined the regional economy in the Atempa basin had more to do with variety than with quantity. Specifically, the arrival in Chilapa of basic foodstuffs produced in the far-flung corners of the world is what has sealed the region's fate. These are commodities that are heavy and bulky relative to their market value, properties that sharply circumscribed the distance over which they could be moved before vehicles were introduced. The transport qualities of food, combined with the limited productivity of local agriculture, ensured that a substantial portion of the region's overall productive effort was traditionally devoted to the production and distribution of food. No branch of employment has yet appeared that can absorb more than a small fraction of the labor that has been freed by the shift to reliance on imported foodstuffs. While practitioners of the arts of candle making, weaving, tailoring, shoe making, and many more have also had a tough time competing against outside suppliers, even when combined, these occupational categories represent only a tiny minority of the region's population. Importing candles threatens the livelihood of perhaps a hundred people; importing food threatens tens of thousands.

Food is uniquely important to my analysis not only because its production involves such a large portion of the region's population but also because the indispensable role of food in sustaining life provides a consistent basis on which to assess the relative importance of particular behaviors and relationships. This brings me to a couple of definitional issues. The "economy," for the purpose of my analysis, involves a set of behaviors, technologies, and social institutions that collectively procure and distribute food among the region's households. Likewise, the "region" is here defined and delineated based on patterns of food production and distribution. Activities that might seem only remotely linked to agricultural production and distribution are significant in this study insofar as they can be shown to enable or otherwise facilitate the production or distribution of food to either rural or urban households. This book documents numerous economic changes in the Chilapa region, each of which involved, first, some sort of disruption to the pattern of food production or distribution and, second, a series of compensatory responses. Some of these disruptions were set in motion by changes originating outside the region, changes that altered the balance of interregional trade. Other disruptions were triggered by purely local processes. In either case, the responses they elicited were at times comparatively minor, requiring only minute adjustments in production patterns. At times, they impacted only a particular economic class or geographic subregion. In the most serious instances, they threatened or altered the region's food distribution network and thereby induced responses that had far-reaching economic and social consequences.

Centering this analysis on the urban food supply also casts light on the distribution of political power in the Chilapa region. The importance of basic foodstuffs to individuals and households has long made this particular class of goods a focal point of competition, in the Atempa basin as elsewhere. This competition has regularly and systematically resulted in differential access to at least portions of the region's food supply, something that conferred (and confers) upon some groups disproportionate economic leverage, or power, over others. At several points in the following chapters, I examine ways in which changes in patterns of food production and distribution have reshaped the possibilities for exercising political control as well as the uses to which such control could be put.

"No soy mozo de nadie" (I'm beholden to no one), a friend from La Ciénega, an agricultural neighborhood on the outskirts of Chilapa, once told me as he reflected on his life. This was in the late 1990s, at a time when La Ciénega was being engulfed by urban sprawl. He and his family were remnants of a nearly extinct group of households in the immediate environs of Chilapa that continued growing maize for autoconsumption using preindustrial agricultural techniques. His wife was the only woman I knew in Chilapa who ground corn using a metate (a grinding stone), patted tortillas by hand, and cooked over wood — techniques and technologies that others in the neighborhood had long since abandoned in favor of mills, tortilla presses, and gas stoves, respectively. My friend's initial attempt to explain his household's apparently anachronistic customs centered on the quality and wholesomeness of traditional foodstuffs and preparation methods. As the conversation developed, however, I could see that there was more going on than this. Although he had a hard time articulating the point, he clearly placed a value on household food production that transcended gustatory and nutritional considerations. Eventually, he issued the statement quoted above, which cuts straight to social and political aspects of obtaining food. Access to an autochthonous food supply gave the family more freedom of action than they would otherwise have had, giving household members the ability to drift in or out of the urban labor force without fear that the loss of any particular job might leave them without the resources they needed for survival. To be sure, the changing character of the local economy was pressing in around the family, forcing them to structure their lives as much around the schedule of the annual school year, if not around salaried or wage employment opportunities, as around the seasonal changes that shape the agricultural cycle. But insofar as he could, my friend avoided entering into social relationships that entailed subordinating his own priorities to those of another, be it an employer or anyone else. The family's effort to supply itself with food was thus as much a political act as an economic one.

My friend's observation about the political implications of food production is as applicable to the region as to his family. Mexico's complex topography once cast a protective shield over the landscape that only advanced industrial technologies have been able to overcome. The autonomy of local and regional networks of food production and distribution were in this fashion preserved longer here than in most parts of the Americas, perhaps in most parts of the world. Alas, the industrial era has arrived. And the reluctance of one household to embrace it has not been matched by many others either in the Atempa basin or elsewhere in Mexico. Theirs is a dying gasp of a "magnificent inertia" that the economist Stuart Chase found in rural Mexicans in the early 1930s (Chase 1931:318) but that has since mostly petered out. Households, communities, and entire regions have instead abandoned age-old patterns of living, yielded up their autonomy, and thrown in their lot with the industrialized world. Why? And with what political and economic consequences? This book is aimed at answering these questions.

ONE

A LAND OF OPPORTUNITIES

A "Land of Opportunities," or so proclaims a welcome sign that since the mid-1990s has spanned the road that a newcomer traveling to Chilapa would most likely traverse to get there. The road begins as an extension of a residential street on the east side of Chilpancingo. It is not easy to find for those unfamiliar with the neighborhood from which it emerges. Once one gets beyond the outermost residential areas of Chilpancingo and past the smoldering, illicit trash dumps that line the ravines on the outskirts of town, the road reveals itself as a narrow, winding highway through frightfully rugged terrain. Traveling on the road can be a heart-stopping affair for the uninitiated, so much so that I suspect to most people newly arriving in Chilapa the welcome sign's promise of "opportunities" is overwhelmed by a much more primordial sense of relief, of having just survived an unexpectedly harrowing adventure.

To discriminating travelers, this sense of relief would be short-lived, replaced not by an appreciation of the city's charm but rather by a sense of frustration at the quality of Chilapa's accommodations and confusion at the difficult choices these present. There are today at least two hotels that boast reliable hot water, toilets with seats, and enough water pressure to flush waste, but one of these is only a couple of years old and the other has dark, dank rooms that offset its few conveniences; prior to the completion of the new hotel, visitors with more than minimal expectations were generally unsatisfied, and sometimes downright shocked, at the city's spartan facilities.

To cite a specific example, in the summer of 1997 a film crew from Japanese NHK Television ventured to Chilapa to obtain footage for a documentary on jaguar motifs in Mexican art and ritual. Whereas Japanese custom places strong pressure on guests to subordinate their personal tastes to those of their hosts and to accept, without comment, whatever a host offers, one look at Chilapa's overnight facilities led the director to cast

aside a lifetime of cultural training and insist that the group return immediately to more satisfactory accommodations in Chilpancingo, from which
they would commute for the following week. Others in the group, while
deferring to the director's edict, privately groused that the three-hour round
trip on Highway 93 was a greater evil than Chilapa's hotels.

Other travelers are lured to Chilapa by unscrupulous tour guides based
in Acapulco and Zihuatenejo on the promise of an "authentic" Mexican
market. Judging from the glum expressions on their faces, authenticity is
generally a disappointment. The irony here is that Chilapa's weekly market
lives up to its billing; it caters to Indians, not to tourists. Had tour guides
told their gullible charges that the merchants selling such things as bolts of
polyester cloth, agricultural implements, replacement bicycle parts, and
cheap plastic shoes would have perhaps a thousand-to-one numerical edge
over sellers of finished tourist items, it seems unlikely that the travelers
would have bothered making the overnight trip up from the coast. The fact
that handicraft items produced by the region's artisans and sought by tourists are available in greater quantity and variety in retail outlets on the coast
(which, after all, is where consumers are located) could only heighten the
tourists' sense of having been duped.

There was a brief period in the late 1970s and early 1980s when two of
the most accessible villages near Chilapa — Acatlán and Zitlala — developed a bit of renown among Mexican urban intellectuals, particularly anthropologists. Certain fiestas and rituals practiced by the inhabitants of
these villages were advertised in *México Indígena,* a glossy, semiacademic
magazine that catered to urban elites with nationalistic inclinations. The
recent paving of the highway to Chilapa had greatly reduced the inconvenience of arriving in the region from Mexico City, and a small influx of
"culture tourists" was the result. Attending a fiesta in a nearby village
almost invariably entailed at least one overnight stay in Chilapa. Some of
the first to take advantage of the opportunity were rewarded not only by
witnessing apparently "authentic" and highly photogenic Indian rituals but
also with information gleaned from spending a few days chatting up the
natives, information that found its way in a couple of instances into that
most coveted intellectual prize, the scholarly article (e.g., Olivera 1979;
Suárez 1978). By the early 1980s, academics had largely moved on, following the road construction crews as they ventured eastward, pushing
beyond Chilapa into an area known as "la Montaña."

The Montaña is a region thickly populated by Indian farmers whose
villages cling precariously to hillsides or balance astride knife-edge ridges.

It turns out to be a tough place for anthropologists to work. The villages there lack even rudimentary facilities to accommodate visitors, and Chilapa is too far away to conveniently commute. In the end, few anthropologists have been willing or able to invest sufficient time or effort to get much out of research in the Montaña (Dehouve 1976 and Oettinger 1974 are notable exceptions), while villages within commuting distance of Chilapa came to be seen as too tainted by their proximity to urban mestizos (people of mixed European and Indian ancestry) to be satisfying. Chilapa itself, a small Spanish-speaking mestizo city, was mostly ignored through all of this. When not lambasted as home to elites who took advantage of downtrodden rural Indians (e.g., Matías 1997:91), it was dismissed as a somewhat inadequate gateway community that had to be endured, if only because there was nowhere else that offered gasoline, food, or overnight accommodations.

The absence of the familiar signposts of industrialized society — the corporate brand names, fast-food establishments, and convenience stores — is not all that would impress visitors to Chilapa from the industrialized world. Unless you know what you are doing, something as simple as finding prepared food can be a disorienting enterprise. Plenty of buildings scattered throughout Chilapa have the word "Restaurant" painted in faded lettering above or beside the door. The doors to such structures are generally closed, however, and the buildings (the promise implied in the faded paint jobs notwithstanding), indistinguishable from adjacent residential structures. A creeping uncertainty would persist even if one of their doors were suddenly cast open and the interior exposed to view; like the exterior, it would in most cases look as much like a residence as an eatery. Questioning a passerby or even a resident of the restaurant, most of which are in fact residences, could of course resolve the confusion, but not in a way that would inspire much confidence or offer much reassurance. Restaurants in Chilapa are generally open for business irregularly and only in the evenings. They serve a clientele from their immediate neighborhoods, people largely unbothered by the tyranny of calendars and clocks.

That said, a small but notable class of casual travelers who occasionally find their way to Chilapa come precisely because of the city's culinary traditions. Gastronomic tourists who venture to Chilapa can fairly pin blame for any dissatisfaction they derive from the experience on Diana Kennedy, who published a popular cookbook on Mexican foods in which she made a passing reference to Chilapa, dubbing it the "Lyons of Mexico" (Kennedy 1998:357–59). Poof! A single moment of literary license and Chilapa was transformed into a must-visit for English speakers with culinary pretensions, at least when these run to traditional Mexican food. Gastronomic pilgrimages to Chilapa involve an obligatory trip to the Casa Pilla. This is a restaurant in the center of town, one of the few that keeps regular hours, operated by doña Magdalena Casarrubias Guzman, a native of Chilapa who authored her own cookbook (in 1994) and has become something of an international sensation in Mexican cooking circles (if Internet discussion groups are any guide). A recent visitor from Chicago, lured to Chilapa by Kennedy's aside, reported that the town is indeed "one of the great gastronomic centers of Mexico." This is high praise, but the visitor diminished its effect by adding, gratuitously, that this great gastronomic center "is nothing more than a dusty town in the middle of nowhere."[1]

"Nowhere" is, of course, a relative idea; here lies the paradox in the town fathers' decision to mount a sign proclaiming Chilapa to be a "Land of Opportunities" over Highway 93. There was a time when both Chilapa and its hinterland offered abundant opportunities to those living there, but this has never really been the case for the outsiders arriving in the town by passing under the sign in question. If, many years ago, the sign and six or seven like it had been hoisted above the burro trails that converge on Chilapa, then the message would have had some resonance to a significant percentage of those passing under it. Travelers of these other thoroughfares once regularly found opportunities in the city. They found wholesale buyers of their products, merchandise for sale in retail outlets, and abundant commercial opportunities created by the modest purchasing power controlled by urban households. All of these and more were resources on which the lives and livelihoods of the region's inhabitants depended.

I suggest above that as a group, anthropologists found little in Chilapa that held their attention. Why the town held mine would thus seem to be a fair question. The short answer is that my research interests centered primarily on the political economy of a region that was undergoing the transition from a preindustrial to an industrial way of life. I was only secondarily interested in the more commonly analyzed aspects of social and cultural life that are unique to particular ethnic groups. Although I sought a region that had a deep human occupation history, the ethnic and linguistic affiliation of the region's inhabitants were largely unimportant to me. I was not convinced that ethnicity was an independent variable that acted to shape the economic and political structure of a regional economy, and nothing in my subsequent research has induced me to reconsider. The Atempa basin is home to both Spanish-speaking mestizos and Nahuatl-speaking Indians, but I did not choose to do my research in the region for this reason. Rather, I selected it because when I first arrived in Chilapa in the summer of 1987, one could clearly experience in the city and in its surrounding hinterland at least the vestiges of life as it was lived in the preindustrial world.

This point was first driven home to me when the power went out during my initial visit to Chilapa. Coming from New York City (where the great power outage of 1977 was the stuff of legend), I was surprised to find that when applied to Chilapa, this same phenomenon provoked a response that seemed to involve nothing whatsoever, at least among humans. Domesticated animals were moved to react. Once radios, televisions, and tape players were stilled, the airwaves were quickly claimed by the town's stock of dogs, burros, roosters, and pigs. Behind the scenes, there were a few dozen people for whom power outages were decidedly inconvenient, mainly butchers who had come to depend on refrigeration. Depending on its timing and duration, a blackout might also have induced *molineros* (mill operators) to shift to gas-powered mills or even compelled women to dust off their metates. A particularly sustained loss of power might eventually jeopardize a portion of the town's water supply, after tanks filled by electric pumps ran dry. But households and businesses were mostly equipped to function smoothly with or without electricity, and thus outages created little or no disruption to people's daily routines.

Power outages do not occur so often today, and with reliability has come dependence. New mills were introduced in the mid-1990s that have no backup power source. Many women have disposed of their metates, and the knowledge of how to use those that remain is fading with the generational change. A sustained outage would make eating a meal a challenge in many households. Buildings are today constructed with little or no regard for natural lighting, so even by day, an outage would plunge many into darkness. Where once an outage would engulf all but the dogs, burros, roosters, and pigs in an atmosphere of sublime tranquility, today portable generators and automobile engines fill any acoustic void that an outage would otherwise create. Dogs, roosters, and pigs get a chance to be heard, if at all, only in the wee hours of the morning; the burros are mostly gone.

Through the early years of my research in Chilapa, power outages were routine. They occurred at unpredictable intervals, though never more than a week apart, and lasted for unpredictable durations. More than a few people (and I count myself among these) held that the town was actually improved when the electricity went off. Certainly, nothing vital to life was threatened. Compared to later outages, my first was of modest duration. It lasted just long enough for me to see that it did practically nothing to alter the normal flow of daily life. More important, it lasted long enough to jolt me into recognizing that I had stumbled into exactly what I was looking for in a research site. I had found a town and a region that had moved only a narrow distance from its preindustrial past.

In the years that followed, I came to appreciate that even a narrow distance is still a distance. About a decade before my first visit to the Atempa basin, its peoples had unknowingly confronted and blithely crossed their Rubicon. Survival in the region had come to depend on access to the products of modern industry. This was in no way apparent at first glance, neither to me nor to anyone else. For the region's inhabitants, it hardly mattered. For all they could see, the modern world was an inviting place filled with job opportunities, affordable chicken, wristwatches, and, above all, sturdy shoes. There was no way for them to know that it was a trap, one whose destructive potential would only become evident when it was too late — at just about the time the sign went up over Highway 93. But these are points best argued in later chapters. First come with me on a quick tour of the region as I found it during my first trips in the summers of 1987 and 1988 and over a seventeen-month period in 1990 and 1991.

Chilapa is a city whose inner precincts reflect early-sixteenth-century Spanish colonial town design as renovated in the late eighteenth and nineteenth centuries; today a tremendous amount of urban sprawl lines its outskirts, but this has mostly arisen in the past decade and did not yet exist in the late 1980s. The urban core is a planned settlement laid out on a rectilinear grid, or *traza,* surrounding a central square, or zocalo. The south side of Chilapa's zocalo is bordered by the town's most prominent structure, an enormous cathedral that sits atop a site that was a cemetery until this was inundated and thence relocated outside of town during a devastating cholera epidemic in 1850. The original early colonial church still stands, just to the southeast of the cathedral, but its adjoining convent, atrium, orchards, and gardens were converted into residential lots when Augustinian friars surrendered the town to secular clergy in 1771. Today's cathedral, built in the 1940s after a fire destroyed an earlier effort, seems wildly out of proportion to the town (fig. 3). Early in the morning and late in the evening, the shadow cast by this building extends virtually to the edge of the town, or at least it did until the early 1990s, when the town crept up hills to the east and west. Facing the cathedral, at the north end of the zocalo, is the *palacio municipal,* the seat of local government, or *ayuntamiento.* This is a

Figure 3. Cathedral in Chilapa in 1988. The hillside in the background is today blanketed by urban development.

freestanding structure that appears to have been the brainchild of an enterprising colonial administrator of the early 1790s, one don Pascual José Portillo. At the time of his appointment, don Pascual and his administration were housed in more-conventional accommodations in a building on the north side of the zocalo, accommodations that were abandoned in favor of a newly constructed building that was boldly erected in the north end of the plaza itself (*Gazeta de México,* August 1791, cited in Andrade 1911:17). At least a portion of the site of the original *casa real* (the colonial forerunner to today's palacio municipal) was then converted into a daily market through which flowed most of the urban population's food supply.

To the east and west, the zocalo is lined by storefronts, several of which function also as workshops and residences. The streets that converge on the zocalo, the main arterials, are likewise commercial avenues, though here the overwhelming majority of stores are also residences (and sometimes workshops as well). Secondary streets are more purely residential, though small stores and workshops of various descriptions are found scattered through all areas of the town. The streets are today mostly paved in concrete, but until the 1990s, all but the arterials were either cobblestone or some mixture of dirt, dust, and mud, depending on the season.

The original early colonial period traza covered an area of about 40

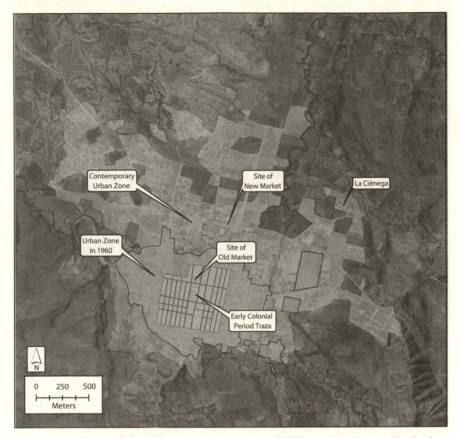

Map 2. Boundaries of the built-up settlement zone of Chilapa at various points in time (overlaid on an aerial photo taken in 1995 by the Instituto Nacional de Estadística, Geografía, e Informatica).

hectares (see map 2). It was expanded in the late nineteenth century by extending existing streets until they reached an impediment, such as a stream or a hill, adding about 65 hectares to the urban core. I did not realize this at the time, but my first visit to Chilapa turned out to have coincided with the very earliest phases of an explosive wave of urban expansion, one that has yet to run its course. Since the mid-1980s, well over 300 hectares have been added to Chilapa; the built-up urban zone now covers some 450 hectares. Both planned residential subdivisions and irregular squatter settlements now blanket the hills to the east, south, and west and the plain that extends to the north.

When I first systematically surveyed rural areas of the Atempa basin in the spring and summer of 1990, there were about eighty named commu-

Figure 4. El Jagüey in 1990. This is a fairly dispersed settlement with house compounds clustered around the church but also scattered amid agricultural fields.

nities in the area of central concern in this book.[2] Outside Chilapa, five communities illustrate the varying degrees of success that early colonial administrators had in their attempts to establish trazas of uniform design. These five include Acatlán, Atzacoaloya, Ayahualulco, Santa Catarina, and Zitlala. Together with Chilapa and San Jerónimo Palantla, where any effort to construct a traza roundly failed, all were sixteenth-century *congregaciones* (Torre Villar 1995:169–71), as settlements created through forced resettlement programs implemented in the early colonial period were known. The remaining seventy-some communities were patternless clusters of house compounds that were settled after 1603, the year of the final resettlement program. Some of the remaining communities have a reasonably compact footprint, others much less so (see figs. 4 and 5). Whatever the degree of nucleation, all named communities have a centrally positioned church or chapel, and many boast one or more of the following public or quasi-public buildings: a small primary school; a somewhat larger basketball court; a one-room clinic; the cavernous shell of an abandoned Fideicomiso de la Palma (FIDEPAL) warehouse (discussed in a later chapter); and a public meeting hall, known as a *comisaría*, often with a tiny attached jail cell.

I was not the first emissary from the industrialized world to venture

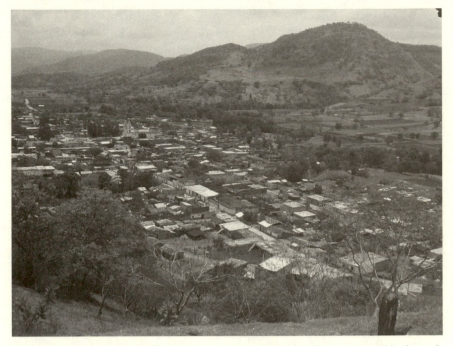

Figure 5. Atzacoaloya in 2002. This is a tightly nucleated settlement created in the early colonial congregaciones.

into villages of the Atempa basin. When I first entered La Mohonera, for example, I was greeted by a group of men who acted as though I were expected, even late in arriving. It turned out that they mistakenly thought I was the vanguard of a returning group of foreign *evangélicos* (Protestant missionaries). The first, they fondly recalled, had worked in their community a few years earlier and had promised to return. Surprised at the obvious affection and anticipation that the missionaries had left in their wake, I asked the men whether many from their community had been converted to Protestantism. This drew a series of puzzled looks, a bit of mumbling among themselves, and some awkward head-scratching before finally a spokesman emerged to gently explain that at some point in my upbringing I must have been misinformed. "Evangélicos," I then learned, were not interested in spreading a religious doctrine. It turned out that the only proselytizing the foreigners had done that had made an impression involved modern hygiene; they had come to dig latrines.

But an odd platoon of latrine-digging missionaries was not the region's only visitation from the outside. The schools, basketball courts, clinics, and FIDEPAL warehouses that I found in 1990, together with power lines that snaked into the most inaccessible areas, were all dead giveaways that others had preceded me. All of these structures were built of brick, concrete, and sheet metal, materials that could be moved to the site only using vehicles traveling over at least rudimentary roads. About three-quarters of the communities in the Atempa basin in 1990 were connected to Chilapa by a gravel road or a dirt track that could be traversed, though sometimes only seasonally, by motor vehicles. Most of these roads and tracks were originally constructed in association with combined electrification and school-building endeavors of the late 1960s and early 1970s; the clinics and FIDEPAL warehouses, built in the largest or most accessible villages that could serve as central places, were constructed later. Although the first attempt at rural electrification had left many communities with a streetlight or two, residential electric service was established much more slowly and was far from universal in 1990. A majority of houses in just over half of the region's communities had electricity, but in most cases it powered only a forty-watt light bulb or two and perhaps a radio. A fortunate few had refrigerators, an appliance that was invariably pressed into commercial service as the foundation around which was built a small *tienda*. The larger villages typically had several such commercial concerns, the smaller villages either one or none at all. The tiendas' inventory was predictable. It consisted of soda — Coca Cola's presence was felt even beyond the reach of electricity — and snack foods, cooking oil, mayonnaise, tins of pickled chiles, infant formula, small amounts of exotic (i.e., nonlocal) fruits, vegetables and spices, pediatric electrolyte replacement solution, ceramic cooking vessels, candles, light bulbs (if relevant to the neighborhood's circumstances), batteries, and hygienic products (including soap, toilet paper, sanitary napkins, and disposable diapers). In wandering the outskirts of villages, where household debris accumulated, one could find residual evidence of the consumption of most of these products along with the packaging of antibiotics and birth control pills, technologies that were distributed less visibly through the clinics that dotted the region.

All of these intrusions from the modern world I duly noted, but what was most striking was the lack of apparent change that any of it had effected in peoples' daily lives. Like the urban center, the countryside was teeming with activity. At first glance, the basic daily routine looked like something that had been worked out in its observable form untold centuries ago. Early in the morning, men, burros, and oxen fanned out into the surrounding fields (fig. 6). Women and girls hovered around their houses, tending to cooking fires, laundry, and infants and toddlers. Midmorning

Figure 6. Farmers planting maize fields in the countryside amid badly eroded and deforested slopes.

Figure 7. The Río Atempa at Acatlán. To the left is a boy on a burro returning to town from working in outlying maize fields. To the right are women and children bathing and laundering clothing. They are taking advantage of a deep pool in the river created by a small dam built to divert irrigation water onto adjacent fields.

and through early afternoon, streams of women (and occasionally men) ventured to or from brick-lined wells or stone-lined water storage reservoirs, where they collected water for domestic use. Still others assembled at springs or on gravel bars along perennial streams to launder clothes and bathe themselves and their young children (fig. 7). In midafternoon, food-bearing women began daily migrations out of villages into the surrounding fields, where they ate with the men, who to that point had spent their days toiling behind *yuntas* (ox teams) or wielding machetes and either wooden digging sticks or *palos* (metal rods used to break soil). After eating and spending a suitable interval lounging in the shade, women then closed out their working day in the fields alongside the men. In the empty spaces between all of these various activities, there were invariably young boys tending small herds of goats and honing their slinging skills. And everywhere, those above the age of about fifteen whose hands were otherwise unoccupied could be seen braiding strands of palm leaf into *cinta* (literally, string or rope), a raw material used in the region's complex palm industry. In late afternoon, the dispersed multitudes began their diurnal trek back to the villages to sleep, only to repeat the exercise the following day.

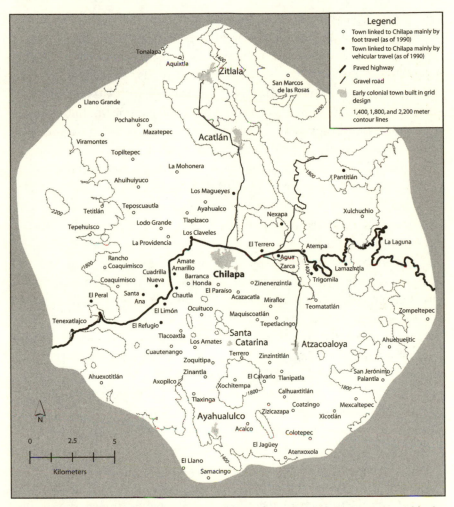

Map 3. Settlement distribution in the Atempa basin in 1990 relative to major vehicular transportation corridors.

Unless the following day was a Sunday or any of the dozens of fiesta days celebrated in a village or its immediate neighborhood. Far from being a day of rest, Sunday brought a great tide of humanity flowing over trails and roads to the weekly market, or *tianguis,* in Chilapa's zocalo (see map 3). Agricultural and domestic work did not stop entirely for the tianguis, but most households would dispatch at least one or two members from their ranks to join those crowding into the urban center to conduct trade. Fiesta days were something else altogether. Although market days had a gay spirit of sorts, a typical Sunday would not call for the full complement of festive elements that reached their fullest expression at a town's patron saint's day celebration. These elements included firework displays, religious processions and masses, carnival rides and games, theatrical dances, and gluttonous feasting. Itinerant vendors did big business at these events, especially sellers of fresh flowers, prepared foods, children's toys, and mescal, the local distillate. Hardly a day passed without such an event somewhere in the region. This could be located by simply mounting one of the region's loftier elevations and gazing out across the basin, scanning the sky for smoke trails and listening for the telltale report of skyrockets. Never have I encountered a people who so heartily welcomed disruptions to their daily routine. In my studies of daily life in the region, I had to be constantly vigilant because an occurrence as trifling as the unexpected appearance of a curious anthropologist could supply all the pretext that was needed to suspend normal activities and improvise a celebration.

Though roads extended to most villages in the late 1980s, the region's fleet of cars, trucks, and buses was nevertheless small and was mostly based in and around Chilapa's zocalo. The entire regional public transport system, including taxis (cars and trucks), vans, and buses, came to about fifty vehicles, nearly half of which were dedicated to interregional rather than intraregional traffic. Privately owned cars and trucks were more numerous and probably numbered around six hundred. With a regional population of just over 70,000, there was about one vehicle for every 110 residents. Vehicle operators exercised dominion over pack animals and pedestrians on only four roads, including Highway 93, a gravel road running twelve kilometers north from Chilapa to Zitlala, a seven-kilometer stretch of gravel between Highway 93 and Atzacoaloya, and a similar four-kilometer route between Highway 93 and Nexapa (fig. 8). Discounting comfort, access to each of these areas using public transportation was excellent, and this was the normal method of travel for residents of towns along these routes. But travelers to or from areas removed from these corridors were more likely to walk than not, even where an occasional bus or truck might lumber along a nearby road.

In the case of many villages, the completion of the electrification and school-building projects seemed to have exhausted the need for a road, and I saw several that had apparently reverted back to an original condition, usually a trail. Many of the small school buildings sat unused, and the FIDEPAL warehouses had been abandoned. Only the clinics were visibly operational on a regular basis, staffed one day a week by nurses and medical students based in Chilapa. Taken together, there were probably no more than a couple of hundred brick or concrete buildings outside of Chilapa;

Figure 8. Passenger truck on the road to Atzacoaloya en route to the tianguis in Chilapa.

most of these were in the towns frequented by vehicles. Most comisarías and practically all houses outside of the towns that were readily accessible by road were instead constructed of local materials, with walls of stone, adobe, or wattle and daub, and roofs of tile or palm thatching. From afar the villages blended into the landscape so thoroughly that many could be distinguished from the surrounding countryside only by identifying an isolated grove of shade trees or some other break in the maize fields, grasslands, or palm or deciduous thorn forests that cover most of the basin.

Of course, first impressions can be deceptive. It turned out that all of these apparently age-old activities and patterns of living survived in the Atempa basin only by the grace of the federal government and by means of a stiff infusion of subsidies. In the two years between my first visit to Chilapa and my first systematic survey of the region, I had done enough preparatory research with government statistics and various other sources to recognize that something was out of balance in the region. The 1980 census simply reported more people than could be sustained given what I knew, or thought I knew, about the productivity of preindustrial agriculture. The simple explanation was that substantial quantities of food, particularly maize, were being imported into the urban center to supplement the local supply. This raised questions about what exactly rural producers were doing to make a living, and these questions were what I had intended to investigate.

A starting point was to confirm my assumption about maize imports. I thought a logical place to begin would be to identify and interview merchants involved in trafficking grain. My inquiries quickly produced confusion. Finding a maize wholesaler had not been a problem. I began at a warehouse strategically situated along the main entrance to the zocalo where hired employees could be seen daily loading or unloading maize from cargo trucks. Upon interviewing the owner, I discovered that this particular gentleman made a living in part by buying maize in nearby villages and shipping it to Acapulco. This was not at all what I had expected, and initially I dismissed it as my first brush with the type of maddeningly discordant fact that I assumed all experienced scientists eventually learned to ignore. The man put me on the trail of a merchant who reputedly imported maize, a man I duly tracked down in the daily market. After chatting a bit, I finally got to the point and asked about imported maize. He directed me to the last of a half-dozen bins of maize, noting apologetically that it came from Arcelia (in northwest Guerrero), as though this explained everything, and that he was not asking much for it. Upon inspection I saw why; it was terribly infested with weevils and was suitable only to be fed to poultry and swine.

I turned then to the Companía Nacional de Subsistencias Populares (CONASUPO), a government institution that bought and sold staple foodstuffs at regulated prices. I thought that perhaps here I might find the missing maize supply. By this time, I had been in Chilapa long enough to appreciate that the urban food supply was mostly of local origin (fig. 9). When I approached CONASUPO, I was entertaining the idea that local farmers might be selling their high-quality grain in the city while consuming the much lower quality product imported by CONASUPO. I had not actually encountered anyone, in Chilapa or in rural villages, who admitted to eating CONASUPO maize, though I did hear stories of poor and starving Indians who had been reduced to this extreme. I considered these tales melodramatic but thought perhaps there was something to it. The local manager of the regional CONASUPO warehouse graciously opened his books to me, but the amounts of grain there recorded added up to no more than a small percentage of the total regional demand. I eventually concluded that the entire imported supply, from Arcelia and CONASUPO, came to an insignificant amount and that it was consumed almost entirely by the region's poultry flocks and swine herds. The earlier evidence that maize was being exported to Acapulco was beginning to look less discordant after all.

Figure 9. Maize vendor in the tianguis in Chilapa.

My first big break in identifying the origin of the missing food supply came in the fall of 1990, when I began measuring local crop yields. The procedure I used involved a complicated series of field measurements and mathematical equations, of the length and dry weight of grain from a sample of maize ears, of standing crop densities, average ear lengths, and so on. When the measurements began accumulating and I started making the relevant computations, the resulting yield estimates were far beyond anything that I had been prepared to accept. My expectations had been based in part on the anthropological literature, but they were reinforced also by discussions with (and a review of raw data collected by) local agronomists employed by the Secretaría Agraria y Recursos Hidráulicos (SARH). My findings were very different (by a factor of three or more) from the numbers these agronomists had been passing up the bureaucratic pipeline and into the government's aggregate published statistics, numbers ostensibly based on field studies using methods very similar, but not identical, to my own. The differences proved to be important. After much discussion and some comparative demonstrations of our respective methods, we finally determined that my measures had been accurate after all. It turned out that a quirk existed in the method used by the SARH agronomists that produced accurate results when applied to hybrid or genetically "improved" maize varieties but badly botched estimates when applied to the indigenous strains of maize that the region's farmers actually planted. Local grain yields were far higher than the local SARH office had been reporting and also higher than I had been led to expect from reviewing the relevant literature.

In the end, my dissertation (Kyle 1995) documented productivity gains far greater than any that had been reported in the anthropological literature and in either published or unpublished government statistics. Some of this material is important to the development of my arguments; accordingly, portions of my conclusions are summarized below. Rising food costs through the twentieth century had steadily choked economic growth in the Atempa basin region, which by midcentury was moving swiftly in the direction of a Malthusian dilemma that threatened to bring down the urban center and the regional economy. The region was kept afloat only by means of a string of lifelines in the form of government subsidies, the most decisive of which were ones that made large quantities of chemical fertilizers available to local farmers. Fertilizers lifted the productivity limitations on local agriculture and resulted in an immediate surge in grain production, urban economic growth, and the size of the region's population (birth control pills notwithstanding). This demographic surge carried the regional population well beyond the numbers that could be sustained absent industrial inputs. The gravel roads and tracks, which I had initially pegged as vestigial traces of an earlier generation of well-intended development experts, therefore served a vital function after all. Twice a year — once when fertilizers were hauled in, and later when maize was hauled out — vehicles were essential in sustaining the regional economy.

This was the state of affairs that I documented based on research done through 1991. In the years that followed, the government would come to reconsider its commitment to funding what had, however inadvertently, been made into a pseudo-preindustrial regional preserve. Without the slightest regard for the tremendous entertainment value that the communities within this and similar preserves have held for a couple of generations of anthropologists, the framers of Mexico's economic future came to the decision that this was no way to manage a country. The subsidies were accordingly withdrawn, or at least redirected, and the region was left once again to fend for itself. In Chilapa, people barely noticed. Merchants merely turned to outside suppliers and in so doing severed the city's most important link to its immediate hinterland. In the countryside, however, the enormity of the historical transition was immediately apparent. Almost overnight, tens of thousands of people became irrelevant to all but their loved ones. Viewed historically, this was a dramatic reversal of political and economic fortune. Control over the region's food supply had once placed rural people in a very strong bargaining position relative to their urban neighbors. Today, rural people are leaving in droves. Those who remain rely on alms, make-work projects, and similar services that are funneled through an urban center whose fate they once controlled. For these people, there is only cruel irony in the assertion that today's Chilapa represents a "Land of Opportunities."

I will pick up the discussion of the present-day circumstances of the Atempa basin region in a later chapter. For the next chapter, I turn to a different time, to the preindustrial past and to the years when the scattered settlements dotting the basin first coalesced into a coherent economic region.

TWO

THE CITY

Two hundred and fifty years ago, there was no regional economy in the Río Atempa basin. The basin was home to something under a dozen communities, and very little, apart from size, distinguished the economy of one from that of the next. Chilapa, with a population of about 3,500, was the largest; Acatlán and Zitlala weighed in at over 1,000 each; and at least two others, Atzacoaloya and Ayahualulco, easily topped 500. All of these and a handful of smaller communities were principally agricultural. In Chilapa and (to a lesser extent) Zitlala, there were small, nonagricultural contingents of civil and ecclesiastical authorities and a still smaller group of merchants specializing in long-distance trade, but these did little to intrude upon the overwhelmingly agrarian habits of the generality of the population. Fifty years later, Chilapa had grown into a regional colossus of over 10,000. Most of this growth occurred in a single decade, the 1790s, by which time a considerable percentage of the community's population had broken with the past and taken up commissions other than farming. By 1800, with only a small fraction of Chilapa's population engaged in agriculture, a division between city and country, and with this a regional economy, had been born. It was a transformation that should be placed high on any list of history's great modifiers of the manners and customs of the Atempa basin's population.

The early years were precarious ones for the new urban center. Chilapa's growth had been so explosive that the rural suppliers of the food needed to support it strained to keep up. They did not do so voluntarily, and the coercive pressures emanating from the city eventually erupted, in 1842, into a conflagration during which the city found itself under siege, sacked, occupied, and briefly abandoned until the whole violent mess was overwhelmed by a still more destructive event, a cholera epidemic that swept through the region in the summer of 1850. In the end, it was a bitter fight

and one the city lost. Chilapa would eventually recover but in defeat was
forced to temper its expectations through a substantial reduction in size.
From a peak population of nearly 14,000 in the early 1840s, Chilapa shrank
to about 6,500 in 1860. It would remain roughly this same size for the next
ninety years, until a combination of mounting ecological problems in the
countryside and stirrings of industrialization in the central highlands provoked a new round of disruption. Chilapa's is a history that is mostly
unwritten, and it squares uneasily with the familiar narrative of Mexican
history. There are shared elements, most notably an episode in which the
rural masses rose up against their oppressors and forced compromises in
the form of land, but the devil is in the details, which differ in fundamental
respects from the story taught in Mexican primary schools and foreign
universities alike.

In this and the following two chapters, I have twin goals. The first, and
most important, is to provide facts and figures in support of the many
sweeping statements I make regarding the character of the preindustrial
regions generally and the Atempa basin specifically. I focus particular
attention on three periods: the initial emergence of Chilapa as an urban
center in the 1790s (this chapter), the crisis in the countryside in the 1840s
(chapter 3), and the political relationships that emerged in the region in the
rebellion's aftermath (chapter 4). A second objective is to continue laying
the groundwork for a fresh evaluation of recent Mexican history. One
consequence of the myopic perspective on broad historical transformations
that results from an exclusive reliance on community studies is that researchers are apt to account for localized historical transformations with
reference to a standard narrative that was originally created to legitimate
the postrevolutionary Mexican government. This would not be so bad if the
stakes only involved what to tell schoolchildren about Mexican history, but
it is something else altogether when propaganda is uncritically accepted by
academics and allowed to form the basis around which research questions
and agendas are framed. The full development of this particular strand of
reasoning must await my conclusions, but certain building blocks essential
to the arguments are woven into the sections and chapters that follow.

PRE-URBAN CHILAPA

By the standards of the Americas, Chilapa is an old town. Precisely
how old is a subject of vigorous disagreement among Chilapa's surpris-

ingly large and passionate group of amateur historians, most of whom make a living as schoolteachers, doctors, and the like. There are those among this group who will tolerate no argument for a founding date other than the year 1458, when some early colonial accounts (e.g., Paso y Troncoso 1905a:177) report that the community was conquered, absorbed into the Aztec empire, and populated by at least a few Aztec colonists. Others prefer 1533, when a reluctant pair of Augustinian friars arrived and began the process of converting the resident population to Catholicism (Grijalva 1985:41). The Augustinians had found Chilapa's population living on (in the case of elites) and around (everyone else) Cerro Chilapantépetl, a hill just above La Ciénega that separates the lower Ajolotero valley from the middle Atempa valley. This site offers a commanding perspective of the surrounding valleys but has only as much fresh water as can be hauled 130 meters or more up the hill (or collected from rainfall at the site); partly for this reason, it was found to be incommodious by the Augustinians. Shortly after arriving, they persuaded the existing political authorities to help oversee the construction of a new town of European design. Chilapa in this way took a position alongside Totolapan and Ocuituco, both in contemporary Morelos, as one of the Augustinians' first three bases of operations in New Spain (Grijalva 1985), as the colony was then known. The construction of a church, convent, and traza began in the spring of 1534, which, a third faction among the historians argues, makes this year a more appropriate founding date than either 1458 or 1533. All of this may be true, retorts a fourth and final group, but the interests of historical accuracy demand that we recognize 1537 as the only reasonable possibility. An earthquake late in this year flattened the original church and convent. When construction began anew, it was at a site a few hundred meters west of the original location (Grijalva 1985:63–65). The inner portion of today's traza is a product of this second attempt at a town, work that began in late November or December 1537.

Against this backdrop, and with the weighty issue of when to celebrate the town's anniversary hanging in the balance,[1] it is with some hesitation (lest I lose friends) that I offer my own opinion, which is simply that all with an opinion take a deep breath and await word from archaeologists. Preliminary evidence suggests that there are both Early and Middle Formative period (3000 to 1000 B.C. and 1000 to 400 B.C., respectively) remains within the boundaries of today's Chilapa.[2] The human occupation of the site, if not a community known by its modern name, clearly predates the 1458 Aztec arrival by a wide margin. The archaeological evidence is likely to eventually show that some of the oldest agricultural settlements in the Americas were found at or near the site of today's Chilapa. Recent research by plant geneticists has confirmed what many archaeologists had long assumed, that maize was most likely domesticated nearby in the central Balsas region of Guerrero (Fedoroff 2003; Jaenicke-Després 2003; Matsuoka et al. 2002; Piperno and Flannery 2001). The well-watered Atempa basin was likely among the first areas into which this new means of making a living spread.

In any case, the early Spanish friars cleared the top of Cerro Chilapantépetl, gathered up the dispersed multitudes from the surrounding countryside, and moved the lot onto the plain below. As had the Aztec before them, the newly arrived Spaniards made Chilapa into a political center, a base of operations where directives from higher-level colonial authorities were received and sometimes implemented, where tribute was collected for shipment north, and where Crown and church officials were on hand to adjudicate petty disputes. By the late sixteenth century, it had become the *cabecera* (seat) of an *alcaldía mayor*, a province-level administrative unit, and of an Augustinian *doctrina*, the Mendicants' version of a parish (Gerhard 1993:111–14). Chilapa was thus home to both civil and ecclesiastical bureaucracies, both staffed by a handful of Spanish elites and minions. There were also a few (in 1582 they numbered perhaps four or five) Spanish merchants who engaged in long-distance trade in commodities that circulated through the broader colonial economy (Paso y Troncoso 1905a:181–82). And although these proper elements of Chilapa society grew slowly in the years leading into the late eighteenth century, they were nevertheless a distinct minority and did not in themselves provide a foundation for urban growth.

Most of Chilapa's early and middle colonial period inhabitants consisted instead of historically anonymous *indios* whose lifestyle was largely indistinguishable from that found in nearby settlements. I should perhaps note that the documentary record allows for only a rough reconstruction of this lifestyle. Those dictating to colonial scribes saw fit only to report facts that held some relevance to the administrative concerns of civil or ecclesiastical officials or to the commercial concerns of Spanish or mestizo merchants. Many features of the daily life of Indian households held no such relevance and are thus a blank in the archival records. While the description of the colonial economy offered here covers its known elements, I have indulged in a bit of speculation at certain junctures where the absence of information becomes intolerable.

Perhaps the most important point to make about the economy of early and middle colonial period Chilapa is what it did not involve, namely, nearby mines, huge public works projects, large agricultural estates, a major transportation corridor, a port, a major urban center, or any of the other landmarks that bled the life out of so many Indian communities of the day. In the middle and late sixteenth century, a few laborers might have been drawn from Chilapa to work in silver mines near Zumpango del Río, about seventy-five kilometers to the west.[3] Likewise, labor from Chilapa was occasionally directed to support troop movement on the *camino real* that linked Mexico City to Acapulco, a trail that passed over the Sierra Madre del Sur at Tixtla, some fifty kilometers to the west.[4] Yet these were exceptional occurrences rather than a regular feature of the local economy. As a general rule, Chilapa was too far east to be greatly bothered by either Zumpango's mines or the camino real. It was too far south to be affected by more-productive silver mines, such as those near Taxco in northern Guerrero. And it was too far west to have been involved in the cochineal and silk booms of Oaxaca. It was, instead, in a small pocket of territory that was just far enough away from the various strategic production and other activity centers of the early and middle colonial period to avoid wholesale participation in any of them.

This is not to say that Chilapa was completely spared from meddlesome colonial officials, only that its residents avoided the worst types of depredations visited on New Spain's Indians. As elsewhere in the colony, from the mid-sixteenth until the early nineteenth century, Chilapa's Indians were obliged to pay their tribute mostly in specie rather than in kind, as had earlier been the case.[5] Specie was also useful, though probably not absolutely vital, in ensuring that households were suitably provisioned with salt, cotton, and agricultural tools. Of these, salt was an essential nutrient that could be obtained through purchase from Spanish merchants or through an extensive indigenous trade network that connected the Atempa basin to salt-producing groups on the coastal plain to the south (Good 1995). Cotton was not, properly speaking, essential, though it was used so widely that it can be thought of as such. Raw cotton was obtained through commercial networks parallel to those involving salt. It was then spun into thread using spindle whorls and woven into cloth using the indigenous backstrap loom, technologies few households lacked (see AGN-H, vol. 122, exp. 2, fols. 38–43; Paso y Troncoso 1905a:181–82). The only goods that approached the status of essentials that Indians could acquire only from Spanish merchants were items made of metal, including machetes and sheaths to strengthen the tip of scratch plows. These items were useful, and many farmers undoubtedly bought them from time to time. But they could, and did, get by without such goods if necessary.

Indians did not need to purchase much, if anything, but the obligation to pay tribute in specie was enough to compel households to engage in activities that brought them into the grip of Spanish bureaucrats and merchants, the conduits through which specie entered the territory. One possible source of earnings, though apparently an insignificant one, involved the direct production of commodities such as silk (Paso y Troncoso 1905b:103) and cochineal (*grana silvestre*) (New York Public Library 1777:10) that were sold to Spanish merchants in Chilapa, who arranged for shipment north into the broader colonial export economy. More important sources of income included wage labor, some of which was conscripted (known as *repartimiento* drafts), some perhaps forced through debt peonage, and some ostensibly "free," and the rental of community lands to Spaniards. A final source of earnings involved direct participation in commercial networks that linked groups living on the coastal plain to the south to the central highlands. In the first decades following the Spanish conquest, Indians obtained gold from coastal groups (Paso y Troncoso 1905b:103). Gold was replaced by cacao by the mid- to late sixteenth century (Paso y Troncoso 1905a:181–82), and this was supplemented by cotton by the mid-eighteenth century (Villaseñor y Sánchez 1746:182).

A late-sixteenth-century document (Paso y Troncoso 1905a:181–82) describes this trade as follows: Chilapa's Indians hauled maize flour, chiles, chickens, woven palm products (especially *petates,* or mats), honey, and wax to coastal areas where it was exchanged for cacao, salt, and probably rice and dried fish. I will touch on the fate of salt, rice, and fish in just a moment. Here I am interested in the cacao, and cotton in later years, goods that were brought back to Chilapa and there sold to Spanish merchants in exchange for specie, especially silver *reales* and *medio reales* that were used to make purchases and to satisfy tribute obligations. In essence, Chilapa's merchants sat with a stock of imported currency and other exotic and sometimes useful (if not quite essential) commodities, trading these for cacao or cotton that the Indians obligingly gathered up from dispersed coastal producers and delivered to Chilapa. The cacao and cotton thus acquired by the Spanish merchants was shipped north into the central highlands and there exchanged for specie, some of which was then returned to the Atempa basin to purchase more cotton and cacao and to repeat the cycle. The specie that fell into Indian hands, after perhaps circulating momentarily through local commercial channels, eventually found its way into the clutches of the civil and ecclesiastical bureaucracies and was thereupon swept back to the north and into the royal coffers.

Although cacao was regularly sold to merchants for reales, there were chronic shortages of specie in colonial New Spain, and there simply were no denominations of minted currency small enough to handle day-to-day commercial transactions involving items of everyday use. For this reason, Indians almost certainly continued the pre-Columbian practice of using cacao beans as a currency in the local market well into the eighteenth and perhaps into the nineteenth century (Gibson 1964:358; Hamilton 1944:36; Seeger 1978:172–73). Regarding markets, a weekly tianguis that met in Chilapa's zocalo is mentioned in a sixteenth-century document (Paso y Troncoso 1905a:179), is hinted at elsewhere (Villaseñor y Sánchez 1746:182), and, in all likelihood, existed throughout the colonial period. Although some observers noted that households in Chilapa occasionally earned income from the local sale of fresh produce (e.g., Villaseñor y Sánchez 1746:182), such sales primarily involved Indians and were aimed at distributing secondary foodstuffs and other goods among largely self-supporting households. While this might have led to some circulation among households of the town's existing stock of specie, it would not have resulted in a net acquisition of new earnings, something that could only be achieved by importing cacao or cotton or by selling commodities or labor to the Spanish administrators and merchants who had access to imported reales. Most transactions in the tianguis would have involved values far lower than minted denominations of specie would allow; many were thus probably executed in kind, without any use of an all-purpose medium of exchange or using cacao beans as a currency.[6]

Goods that regularly appeared in the tianguis would have included grains (maize, wheat, rice, and *chia,* an amaranth), beans, fruits, vegetables, herbs, spices, sesame oil, salt, domesticated animals and animal products (including turkey, chickens, eggs, pork, lard, cattle, goats, and cheese), dried fish (some local, some imported from the coast), wax, candles, honey, *panela* (a type of unrefined sugar), *aguardiente* (cane alcohol), pottery, palm goods (including sombreros, petates, sandals, and serape-like capes known as *soyates*), wood, charcoal, raw cotton, and probably a whole lot more. Chilapa could, and likely did, achieve near-total self-sufficiency with regard to all of these goods except salt, rice, and cotton. These (and probably small amounts of other regional specialties, including dried fish) were obtained by Indians in their sojourns to the south. Some goods imported to

Chilapa by Spanish merchants — metal tools, for example — might have found their way into the tianguis but were more likely sold alongside other, less essential imports in fixed retail outlets in the center of Chilapa.

URBAN BEGINNINGS

Through the course of the eighteenth century, growth in the cotton industry in the central Mexican highlands led to a corresponding rise in the demand for cotton. In Chilapa, growth in cotton weaving in Puebla is what mattered most. Puebla's cotton spinners and weavers initially obtained raw cotton from Veracruz, but as demand expanded and outstripped the supply it stimulated an expansion of cotton cultivation through Guerrero's coastal plains (Amith 2005:362–82; Bazant 1964:67). For the first time in its history, Chilapa found itself situated atop an important trade route, one of two that most directly connected Puebla to the cotton production zones on the southern coast (map 4). The route was sufficiently important to attract the attention and resources of Spanish financiers, merchants, and professional arrieros. Mules needed both pasture and substantial quantities of grain, neither of which was readily available in Puebla. Investors instead sought to base freighting operations in towns at intermediate locations; the Atempa basin, which had all of the needed resources as well as a convenient location relative to the trail, was ideal for the purpose. Urbanization in Chilapa had its beginnings in this shift in patterns of provincial trade, when the town emerged as a specialized freighting center and transportation depot.

We are fortunate to have a detailed snapshot of the earliest phases of urbanism in Chilapa in the form of Viceroy Revillagigedo's census of 1791 (AGN-P, vol. 16, fols. 107–221).[7] Among the most glaring changes in Chilapa that is evident in this document is the near-complete disappearance of the Indian component of the community and its replacement by scores of Spaniards, *castizos*, mestizos (three groups known collectively as *gente de razón*, literally, people of reason), and *pardos* (Afro-Mexicans). In 1742 a count of Indian and non-Indian groups reported 447 and 139 households, respectively (Solano 1988:49; also Villaseñor y Sánchez 1746:178). In 1791 these numbers stood at 64 and 524, respectively. The overall population was effectively unchanged, at 586 households in 1742 and 588 in 1791, but the balance between Indians, pardos, and gente de razón had decisively shifted. Indians fell from about 75 percent of the population in

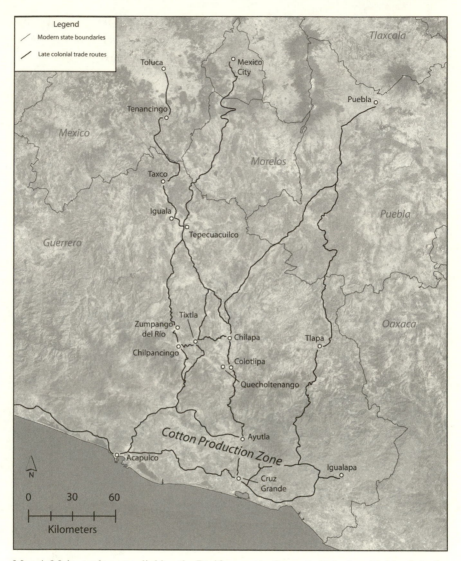

Map 4. Major trade routes linking the Pacific coast to the central Mexican highlands in the late colonial period.

1742 to about 10 percent in 1791. As I show in chapters 3 and 4, Chilapa's Indians did not go far and would soon return.

During their absence, Chilapa underwent a fundamental change that went well beyond a simple reconfiguration of the community's ethnic makeup. Ethnic categories had occupational implications in late colonial New Spain. Although Indians later became integrated into Chilapa's urban economy and would eventually disappear as a distinct group in the broader urban population, Indians in the Atempa basin in the late colonial period were farmers. They came in two basic varieties. The first were residents of "free" agricultural villages, or *comuneros,* who centered their productive efforts on subsistence and very secondarily on commerce. A second group comprised those who were somehow tethered to landholdings owned by Spaniards or mestizos, including *arrendatarios* (tenants or sharecroppers) and, more famously, wage-earning *peones.* It is not entirely clear into which of these categories Chilapa's Indians fell in 1742, but by 1791 most had become arrendatarios or hired peones on generally small but some respectably sized landholdings owned by Spaniards and mestizos.

In contrast to Indians, gente de razón and pardos were not principally farmers; those who did farm did so primarily as a commercial enterprise and only secondarily as part of an effort to supply food for consumption in their own households. Of 524 households headed by gente de razón and pardos in 1791, 63 were headed by landowning farmers (*labradores*) and 5 by owners of large agricultural estates (*hacendados*). Adding these together with the 64 households of Indians gives a total agricultural population of 132 households, about 22 percent of the total. Nearly 80 percent of households depended in whole or in substantial part on other forms of work. In this, much had changed since 1742, when all or nearly all of 447 Indian households had been headed by farmers. Many of the gente de razón and pardos living in the town in 1742 were likely labradores as well, such that the total number of farming households probably approached 500, in the neighborhood of 80–90 percent of the total. Numerically, arrieros and their assistants (*sirvientes de arrieros*) had replaced the various types of farmers as the most important occupational blocks in 1791, a reflection of the growing importance to the town's economy of commerce in general and the cotton trade in particular. The census recorded 85 arrieros and 264 sirvientes de arrieros drawn from 277 separate households, or 47 percent of the total. To these numbers one could add another 30 or 40 peddlers, merchants, shopkeepers, and other trade-related retainers. Taken together, well over half of Chilapa's households earned a significant portion of their income directly from the movement of cotton and other commodities through the region.

Unfortunately, no account of the life and times of an arriero in late colonial period Chilapa is known to have been preserved in the historical record. It is nevertheless worthwhile to piece together as much of a sketch as possible of this and of Chilapa's late colonial freighting industry because the town's transition to full-blown urban status grew from this foundation.

It was a foundation that had an enduring impact on the structure of the city — one that arguably remains visible to this day. Unless specifically referenced, the following paragraphs draw on studies of the late colonial economy of Guerrero (Amith 2005; Guardino 1996), of commerce in colonial provincial centers generally (especially Kicza 1983 and Stein 1997), and of arrieros elsewhere in New Spain (Boyer 1981; Suárez 1997; Super 1981). The essential points involve two features of the town's economic organization: its full-blown commercialization and its highly stratified class structure.

An Indian of the early or middle colonial period carried certain products of his household's efforts to the coastal plain in search of cacao and other regional specialties, carrying these using tumplines or the versatile household burro; Chilapa's arrieros of the late colonial period were muleteers who led sometimes vast mule trains, each mule capable of hauling 150 to 200 kilograms of goods at a rate of thirty or more kilometers a day over a sustained period of time (Hassig 1985:281–83; Suárez 1997:45). Arrieros were trained professionals, though rarely wealthy ones, who were introduced to the profession by patrons of some sort, either relatives or employers. After apprenticing and working as a sirviente for some years, an arriero would acquire his own team of mules.[8] Once established as an arriero, he would, in turn, hire sirvientes — often his own sons, who would later inherit his mules and eventually take over the family business.

Becoming an arriero required more than merely learning the appropriate skills. The high cost of purchasing even a single mule, much less the team of mules needed to make the enterprise profitable, generally made it necessary for an arriero to have a financial backer: perhaps a wealthier relative, a merchant with whom the prospective arriero had dealt while working as a sirviente, or a mule dealer who sold on credit.[9] At a cost of fifty to sixty-five pesos per animal (Amith 2005:332; Suárez 1997:57), this was no trifling matter. The 1791 census includes a count of the number of mules owned by seventy-nine of the town's eighty-five arrieros. The total comes to about 943 mules, an average of 12 mules per arriero.[10] Twelve *atajos,* or about 480 mules, were owned by just ten individuals. Another 463 mules were distributed among the remaining sixty-nine arrieros.[11] There was thus a group of ten arrieros (eight with one atajo and two with two atajos each) that had comparatively large teams of mules and another group that had far smaller numbers of animals. Even these small teams represented a significant investment. With tack, a team of 8 mules could easily cost four hundred pesos, more than an Indian would see in a lifetime;

this amount might have been sufficient to purchase, among other things, one of the small haciendas that were then spreading like noxious weeds into the countryside and making life miserable for nearby Indians. But I digress, touching on topics that properly belong in the following chapter. The essential point is that the freighting industry of the late colonial period was a much more monetized, capitalized, and socially differentiated affair than anything that had come before it.

The work of arrieros followed seasonal rhythms. Most activity was concentrated between January and June, the driest months of the year, when trails were free of mud, rivers fordable, and the risk of water damage to cargo low. The important trade events on the coast, the cotton harvest and the fair that accompanied the arrival of the Manila galleon in Aca-pulco, also occurred during these months. Congestion on the trails leading north and south from Chilapa would have been impressive, what in today's world would be bumper-to-bumper traffic. For example, during the height of the 1802 freighting season, mules passed through a customs house on the camino real near Tixtla at an average rate of one mule every two minutes for twelve solid hours; on the busiest days, this rose to a rate of more than one mule per minute (Amith 2005:319–20). Traffic on the trail through Chilapa might not have been quite as heavy, but it would have been substantial nevertheless. During the off season, and especially during the rainy summer months, most of the more-established arrieros (those with large mule teams) withdrew from the business, pasturing their animals and ceding the trails to more-humble arrieros, those who could neither afford to stop working nor find seasonal agricultural or other work in Chilapa.

An arriero intending to collect a load of cotton on the coast would begin the journey in Chilapa, where mules would be loaded with goods that could be sold either directly to cotton farmers or to cotton factors located in the principal regional centers. Arrieros would also carry specie with which to purchase cotton, but payment in kind or on credit was preferred owing to the rarity of coinage. Infrequently an arriero might have the resources needed to purchase the entirety of an outgoing cargo and to acquire a load of cotton on the coast, in which case he would become an itinerant merchant (*viandante*) and thus blur his occupational classification. More often, an arriero would be hired by a local merchant, hauling goods he did not own for either a fixed salary or a share in the profit accruing from the expedition. Even when hired, an arriero would do everything possible to supplement his performance of the contracted services with petty trading of his own accord, again blurring the distinction between arriero and viandante.

An arriero's outgoing cargo could include goods originating in the Atempa basin or ones imported from the central highlands. Of the goods produced in the environs of Chilapa, petates (used as a packing material for bales of raw cotton) and panela were the most common, but honey, wax, and a variety of other commodities might be loaded onto mules as well. Alternatively, or additionally, mules might be loaded with goods imported from the central highlands; here the possibilities included exotic fabrics (including muslin, lace, silk brocade — made of Asian and European silks — and French linens and woolens), finished textiles (including blouses, dresses, shirts, trousers, and English stockings), and miscellaneous notions (trimmings and ribbons, buttons, needles, and so on), belts, hats, fine ceramics, imported brandy, flour, cinnamon, tallow, cheese, iron bars, machetes, and other items that were regularly stocked by large wholesale trading firms in Mexico City and Puebla.

General stores, known as *tiendas mestizas,* were common in provincial centers such as Chilapa; these were linked through a variety of financing arrangements to the wholesale firms in the central highlands (Stein 1997:385–86; see also Kicza 1983). There were five or six tiendas mestizas in Chilapa in 1791. There also appear to have been at least two warehouse facilities, or *almacenes,* controlled by local wholesalers. The owners and managers of these facilities formed the core of those who contracted freighting services with Chilapa's arrieros, but a couple of other groups were probably involved as well. One was a small clutch of hacienda owners. Their participation in the cotton trade took a couple of different forms, depending on the character of the land they controlled. Two or three hacendados focused on panela, a commodity that was the functional equivalent of silver coinage in the context of the cotton trade (Amith 2005:357–58). An equal number controlled pasturage that was rented to arrieros. Both groups of hacendados probably played a prominent role in financing trading expeditions. A final group of elite participants in the cotton trade included five or six individuals who were counted as government officials in the 1791 census but also had commercial interests in the region. Their role would have been almost purely financial in nature.[12] In all, Chilapa's arrieros worked mostly at the behest of a group of some twenty individuals, some of whom were hired agents for commercial firms in Mexico City and Puebla, others who had partnership arrangements with these firms, and some who were wealthy and participated using their own stock of capital.

Upon arriving on the coastal plain, an arriero might proceed directly to a trade depot, such as Ayutla, Ometepec, or Igualapa, and purchase cotton from a bulking agent, or he might travel about the region from farm to farm to buy directly from cotton producers.[13] In either case, he would handle as many transactions as possible in kind rather than in specie, as specie was always in short supply. Again, panela in particular seems to have functioned almost as a currency for Chilapa's arrieros operating in cotton-producing zones. Once the outgoing cargo was sold and a load of cotton acquired, the arriero returned to Chilapa. Depending on the financing arrangement, he might sell the cotton to merchants in Chilapa or, if he was acting as a purchasing agent for the merchants, unload it in exchange for the agreed-upon payment for services rendered. Particularly when working on contract for merchants, an arriero might continue straight to Puebla before unloading. There he would exchange the cotton for a load of goods to be hauled back to Chilapa's almacenes and tiendas mestizas. It seems to me likely that there was a relatively sharp distinction in the customary patterning of trading expeditions by arrieros with and without a full atajos or more of mules. For an arriero guiding a train of forty to eighty mules, winding about the coastal countryside to purchase small quantities of cotton from individual cotton farmers would not have been a sound business strategy; if they traveled to the coast at all, they probably went no farther than Ayutla, a regional center on the edge of the coastal plain due south of Chilapa. Arrieros with smaller numbers of mules, however, could venture into the coastal hinterland with reasonable efficiency and could realize savings by avoiding middlemen and purchasing cotton directly from producers. It seems possible, even probable, that arrieros with small teams of mules specialized in collecting cotton and hauling it to Chilapa's warehouses. The arrieros with full atajos probably specialized in making the run from Chilapa to Puebla.

Whether operating on contract or independently, and whether traveling to the coast or to the central highlands, arrieros were thoroughly immersed in a web of commercial relationships that linked the Atempa basin to the broader colonial economy. In the years immediately following the 1791 census, those in Chilapa would find a way to reduce the intimacy of these linkages, but certain features of the region's economy were permanently altered. Central among these was the commercialization and monetization of the region. Although a shortage of specie forced merchants of the late colonial period to execute many transactions in kind or on credit, the standard of value was everywhere the silver real; at some point, arrieros received payment for their services in this medium. This was a sharp contrast to the weakly monetized subsistence economy of earlier years, when only small fragments of people's working lives involved commodity production or the payment or receipt of salaries or wages. Whereas a household of Indian farmers might have had an annual cash flow of no more than three or four pesos (nearly half to cover various tribute obligations, the other for clothing, tools, salt, and whatnot), a sirviente earned this amount in a month, while an arriero earned considerably more (Amith 2005:332–33). The growth of the freighting industry thus resulted in a very substantial increase both in the quantity of specie flowing through Chilapa and in the breadth of its distribution among households.

This increase in income earned either as specie or as commodities that were convertible into specie was a significant change and a prerequisite to the robust urban growth that would shortly occur. Even in 1791, the multiplier effect of the freighting industry on the town's occupational structure is evident. The earnings of arrieros and sirvientes created sufficient consumer demand to support households whose members specialized in an array of secondary manufacturing and service activities. At least forty occupational specialties were represented in Chilapa in 1791,[14] a number that was almost unchanged over a hundred years later when the town's occupational profile was next recorded, in the 1900 census (DGE 1905a:180–99). By 1791, Chilapa had clearly shed much agricultural work and had moved a significant distance from its agrarian past. Notably, much of the town's population had come to depend on a marketed supply of food and other essentials; it is no coincidence that don Pascual José Portillo, the head political official in Chilapa from 1790 to 1793, chose this historical moment to move the casa real into the zocalo and to free space in the center of town for the sine qua non of an urban settlement, a fixed, daily market. Like a fledgling, Chilapa was perched and ready for takeoff on an urban career.

It was a precarious perch, however, for there were sharp limits to the growth that could rest on the foundation of freighting services alone. Chilapa's merchants and arrieros had no control over the amount of cotton that was produced on the coast or consumed in Puebla's textile workshops. Once the transport capacity needed to move the available cotton from the coast to Puebla was in place, no additional investment in Chilapa could generate further economic expansion. Indeed, Chilapa's first steps toward urbanization might easily have been extinguished altogether, a common fate among Latin American cities that were caught short in marginal locations vis-à-vis shifting trade routes and population concentrations (Morse 1962). The regional economy depended on the health and stability of the cotton trade, which, it turned out, was about to be cast into utter turmoil by

the growth of the United States' plantation economy and the industrialization of England's textile industry. These developments depressed prices
for both cotton and textiles and had a progressively more devastating
impact on coastal cotton producers and Puebla's manufactures alike (Bazant 1964:68; Salvucci 1987:150–67; Thomson 1989). When combined
with disruptions in trade caused by the Mexican War of Independence
(1810–21) and the subsequent political turmoil in the newly created re-
public, the result was a decline in cotton production on the coast, in textile manufacturing in Puebla, in long-distance commerce in Mexico as a
whole, and thus in the demand for Chilapa's arrieros.

EXPLOSIVE URBAN GROWTH

That there was neither a general abandonment of Chilapa nor a reversion back to its agrarian origins is in part a testament to the resilience of the
economic structure of the community as this had evolved in tandem with
the cotton trade. Mostly it was a result of a fortuitous convergence of
circumstances, a simple case of good luck. Competition from cheap foreign imports and the substantial domestic output from Puebla's workshops
notwithstanding, households in Chilapa had ready access to raw cotton,
ample labor, a colonial economy with a prodigious demand for cotton
thread, and a local market that was hungry for affordable cloth. The result
was the altogether sudden and explosive growth of cotton spinning and
weaving industries in Chilapa.

Spinning cotton into thread and weaving it into cloth rather than simply hauling it through town must have occurred to at least some people in
Chilapa almost as soon as commercial cotton cultivation on the coast
began. Through the late colonial period, it was customary for shippers to
haul raw cotton, in bales, directly to Puebla, where the seed was removed
and the cotton carded and spun into thread by the urban and rural poor.
Because two-thirds of the weight of raw cotton is contained in the seed, any
effort to process it nearer to the site of cotton production would have
dramatically lowered transport costs. Furthermore, in addition to the savings that could be realized by substituting processed cotton on shipments
going north, at least some of the cotton that was hauled to Puebla eventually returned to Chilapa in the form of thread and cloth. Spinning thread
and weaving cloth in Chilapa would, and did, result in substantial savings
to consumers by eliminating all of this unnecessary to-ing and fro-ing.

Given that all of the needed ingredients for a local textile industry were present, the relative lack of evidence of cotton spinning and weaving in Chilapa in 1791 is surprising. Only six individuals were specialized spinners (*hiladores* or *torcedores*), and only thirty-three were weavers (*tejedores*). While the number of weavers is probably an accurate reflection of the circumstances, the spinners were almost certainly undercounted. Six spinners is simply not enough to produce the amount of thread that would have been needed to support the efforts of thirty-three weavers; had both spinners and weavers been working at full tilt, a ratio of at least five spinners to each weaver would have been needed (Burton 1984:26). Early in the industry's development, most of the thread used by weavers was either spun by rural Indians using spindle whorls or on wheels by gente de razón, for whom this was a secondary occupation that went mostly unrecorded in the 1791 census (Guardino 1996:21).

In the years immediately following the 1791 census, the circumstances of the industry changed dramatically. This is evident from an inventory of textile machinery in the year 1800 made by the *subdelegado* (the late colonial period successor to the earlier *alcalde mayor*).[15] The subdelegado's report states that of 1,951 households in Chilapa in that year, there were between one and eight spinning wheels in 1,740 households and looms in 142. Although the 1791 census did not include an equipment inventory, one can assume that all of the weavers had looms, and thus an increase from 33 households with looms in 1791 to 142 with looms in 1800 is reasonably clear. The increase in spinning wheels was even more spectacular. Though the six spinners recorded in Chilapa in 1791 likely had wheels, a note included in the 1800 inventory inaccurately but revealingly reports that Chilapa had neither spinning wheels nor looms until 1793. Both types of machinery were clearly present in Chilapa before this date but in comparatively insignificant numbers; 1793 instead marks the beginning of a brief but remarkable episode of growth in the community and its economy.

In 1800, Chilapa's textile workers produced thread, *manta* (a coarsely woven cloth used to make men's clothing), and a small number of finished articles of women's clothing, including skirts, blouses, and *rebozos* (shawls). The limited output of finished items for women was consumed mostly in Chilapa. Most women, including practically all of those living in rural communities, continued weaving their clothing using backstrap looms, though increasingly they used thread spun on wheels in Chilapa rather than by themselves using spindle whorls. This use of cotton thread by women in Chilapa and elsewhere created robust demand locally and throughout the surrounding regions. The demand was strong for manta as well. The subdelegado's report noted that until recently thread and manta had been imported from Puebla but that by 1800 Chilapa's producers had completely replaced imports and had begun exporting both products.[16] Manta woven in Chilapa and Puebla sold for roughly the same price in the cities where it was produced, 1.5 to 2 reales per *vara* (about a yard) in Chilapa and 1.5 to 3 reales per vara in Puebla,[17] but transport costs substantially increased the price of Puebla manta when sold in Chilapa. The savings that resulted from weaving manta in Chilapa were enormous and were sufficient to expand the pool of consumers to include Indians, whose continued use of homespun cloth and thread spun using spindle whorls must have looked steadily less sensible as raw cotton became increasingly commercialized, then scarce, even while the price of thread and manta in Chilapa declined.

The subdelegado's report of 1800 is notable not only for documenting the early explosive growth of Chilapa's textile industry, but also for indicating an equally explosive growth in population. From 588 households in 1791, the town swelled to 1,951 in 1800. Part of the increase was a result of a return of the Indians who a few decades earlier had moved (or been moved) into the surrounding countryside. The subdelegado reported that there were 968 households of Indians, up from 64 in 1791. If the size of these households was comparable to that of others documented in Chilapa in 1791 (5.5 persons per household), this would mean that the Indian population of about 320 grew to 5,324 in a single decade. The number of gente de razón also increased. The subdelegado reported the presence in Chilapa of 983 households of gente de razón in 1800. This works out to a population of some 5,406 people, up from the 3,242 who were counted in the 1791 census. Combining the numbers puts Chilapa's overall population at about 10,730 in the year 1800, up from 3,562 in 1791.

It is worth looking in as much detail as possible at the organization of the textile industry in its earliest years because the industry formed the foundation on which the city's economic and political structure would eventually come to rest.[18] The census takers of 1791 found weavers scattered throughout the town. They were not randomly distributed, however, but were clumped together into groups of two to four households. This clumping contrasts markedly with other occupational categories, which, except for government officials, merchants, and shopkeepers living around the zocalo, show no particular pattern of spatial concentration. Arrieros and sirvientes de arrieros, for example, the two dominant occupational categories in 1791, show only a slight concentration in the southeast and southwest quarters of the town. In a few cases, the clumping of weavers was a result of family connections, with separate households related through patrilineal kin ties (usually a group of brothers living near each other), but more often there is no apparent connection, aside from location, between the households.

In addition to the clustering of small groups of weavers, an equally striking spatial association can be seen between weavers and related occupational categories, including spinners and, especially, tailors (*sastres*). Although very few individuals cited spinning as a primary occupation, most of those who did resided very near a household of weavers. This residential association is more striking between weavers and tailors. Virtually all of the households of weavers were located near tailors, and virtually all tailors were located near weavers. In a couple of instances, there were family connections between spinners and weavers and between weavers and tailors, but far more often the practitioners of these various arts were related by nothing apparent beyond spatial proximity. The cumulative picture is one of an evolving industry that from its inception exhibited an impressive measure of vertical integration, though without much overarching or centralized organization. The vertical integration apparently arose spontaneously among clusters of households in working-class neighborhoods, each cluster containing all the necessary labor, capital, and expertise needed to obtain raw cotton and to convert it into either bolts of raw cloth or finished articles of clothing.

It is generally assumed that textile manufacturing in preindustrial Mexico operated on one of two models: sweatshops (*obrajes*), most common among producers of woolens; and a put-out system, found among cotton weavers (Salvucci 1987:45; cf. Thomson 1989:96–97). In a put-out system, merchants would advance raw materials to spinners, weavers, and tailors on credit or, in what amounts to the same thing, a partial advance payment of piece rates. The merchants would then collect the processed materials and repeat the exercise with those specialized in the next step in the production chain. In Chilapa it would go something like this: merchants would first hire arrieros to fetch cotton from the coast, then dole out the raw cotton and an advance sum of money to spinners in Chilapa, who would remove the seed, card the fiber, then spin it into thread. The spinners would return the thread to the merchants to expunge their debt and to collect any remaining wages due. The merchants might then sell a portion of the thread (in

Chilapa, Tixtla, Tlapa, Chilpancingo, or even Puebla), passing the balance, together with more advance wages, to Chilapa's weavers, who would convert it into bolts of raw cloth. This too would be recollected by merchants, who would sell a portion to consumers who preferred to cut and sew their own clothing, as many did, and deliver another portion to the tailors, who would make finished clothing that was sold in the merchants' tiendas mestizas to those who preferred their apparel and could afford store-bought. Put-out systems of production were notoriously degrading to the lion's share of producers, for whom indebtedness to the merchant overseers was a chronic condition. Wages were kept scandalously low lest laborers become distracted and allow production to slip below a rate of output equal to the possibilities allowed by the human body. The classic example of this system of production was found in eighteenth-century England (Hobsbawm 1968:29), but elements of it were present in Puebla (Bazant 1964; Salvucci 1987), and it has been suggested to have characterized production patterns in the Atempa basin as well (Guardino 1996:21).

Although elite merchants almost certainly had some hand in Chilapa's textile industry, my reading of the relevant documentation leads me to a somewhat different portrait of the industry as a whole. There was simply too much cotton flowing through Chilapa for the growing city's small elite merchant group to maintain the monopoly control over raw materials that a put-out system requires. Not only could cotton be supplied to spinners by itinerant merchants, the viandantes, but raw cotton also was readily available to arrieros who worked on a contractual basis for elite merchants. Arrieros (and even sirvientes) could obtain cotton through petty transactions that they conducted as a sideline to the performance of contracted services, or they might even receive payment for their contracted services at least partially in kind, which is to say in cotton, for the shortage of specie was a problem that afflicted rich and poor alike (Amith 2005:357–58). Textile producers existed amid a sea of arrieros; in more than a few cases, they lived in the same households.

The town, quite simply, was in the unusual position of being awash in raw cotton; for this reason, elite merchants were able to participate in the evolving textile industry only insofar as they behaved themselves and contained any exploitative impulses. Nothing could have reined in these impulses as effectively as a swarm of petty merchants who precipitated out of the warrens of spinners, weavers, and tailors and readily sold directly to consumers at a minimal markup. This is what Chilapa's elite merchants faced at every stage in the textile production chain. Most, accordingly, sat

on the sidelines and grumbled. In this they could be heard in the background of the subdelegado's 1800 report, complaining about the low quality of cloth produced by Chilapa's weavers and about the urgent need to
recruit master weavers and institute a guild organization that could impose
quality controls. Neither of these was a sound recommendation. The spinners' and weavers' determination to limit their output to thread and manta
that were consumed by the rural and urban masses was what had led to the
industry's development in the first place. The growing city's most compelling competitive advantages included easy access to cotton and robust
demand for both thread and cheap cloth. The first of these would have been
less compelling and the second lost entirely if the industry had concentrated on high-quality cloth that could be sold only by elite merchants
through their commercial connections in distant urban markets. In the end,
the elite merchants opted to keep their capital more profitably and (except
for that of the hacendados) more harmlessly invested in supplying raw cotton to Puebla, producing panela used to trade for cotton on the coast, or importing exotic merchandise from the central highlands.[19] Thread and manta
production and distribution, at least in the early years, were left to the small
artisan and petty merchant and only secondarily to elite merchants.

The textile industry's comparative autonomy from a monopolistic
merchant class goes some distance in explaining the phenomenal rate of
population growth that Chilapa experienced in the final decade of the
eighteenth century. Through the course of the eighteenth century, textile
producers in the Puebla region (as elsewhere in the central highlands) had
proliferated to such an extent that markets there were saturated with cheap
cloth even while there were acute shortages of raw and spun cotton (Salvucci 1987:9–32). Merchants had firm control over both raw cotton and
finished cloth, and they drove compensation rates for spinners and weavers
to or below subsistence levels. Making matters worse, guild officials collected annual membership dues and fees on spinning wheels and looms
while exerting annoying regulatory pressures that fell hard on the city's
many small-scale spinners and weavers (Bazant 1964:65–68; Thomson
1989:101–48). All of these problems could be avoided in Chilapa, where
cotton was cheap and abundant, elite merchants frustrated, guild officials
absent, and the local consumer market robust. Small wonder Chilapa grew
rapidly.

In the end, Chilapa's late colonial textile industry came to be embedded in a set of commercial networks that were only weakly linked to those
controlled by elite merchants. Although cotton continued to move through

the Atempa basin and on to Puebla, a portion of the cotton arriving in Chilapa was detached from the general northward flow and diverted into a rapidly growing slipstream of mundane consumer goods that circulated through the weekly tianguis and its urban counterpart, the daily market. The principal vendors in these venues consisted of both producers and legions of petty merchants who arose from the producers' ranks. The textile industry's biggest contribution to the region's economy, aside from the change created in patterns of work in the city, was to place Chilapa on a solid urban foundation that had strong commercial links to its surrounding hinterland. In this, the textile industry made a contribution that went far beyond anything created by the earlier freighting industry.

INDUSTRIAL COMPETITION AND PREINDUSTRIAL ACCOMMODATION

All was not entirely well, however, and Chilapa's rapid surge in demographic and economic growth soon encountered resistance from both near and far. Within the Atempa basin, Chilapa's emergence as an urban settlement had enormous implications for residents of the newly created rural hinterland (see chapter 3). Outside of the basin, a specter that haunted Chilapa's textile industry from its earliest days would have been apparent to anyone, even in the 1790s, who could achieve a global perspective on the times. Take 1793, the watershed year when all of the spinning wheels and looms were said to have arrived in Chilapa; in this same year, Eli Whitney was granted a patent on his cotton gin, a machine that revolutionized the work of seed removal and led to a practically instantaneous expansion of the plantation system of cotton production through the southeastern United States. This in turn enabled England's existing carding machines and spinning frames to shift from wool and underproduction to cotton thread production on a scale that might even have impressed even Sir Richard Arkwright, the father of England's industrial textile factories, had he lived to see it. By the 1830s, power looms that could keep pace with earlier improvements in thread production had been invented, and the Industrial Revolution was off and running. So too was the British Empire, which had to be expanded, reorganized, and in other ways made equal to the task of finding markets for the monstrous quantities of thread and cloth that issued from the mother country (Hobsbawm 1962:51–61, 1968:134–53). The result of all of this was a saturation of global markets with raw cotton from the United States and machine-made thread and cloth from England.

In Mexico, there were those who tried to keep up with the dizzying pace of innovation, but much more was lost than gained in the effort. Textile production in Puebla declined steadily through the early decades of the nineteenth century as the quantities of English cloth imported into the central highlands rose and cloth prices fell. Cotton production also declined as Mexican farmers found that they could not compete with U.S. plantations. By the 1840s, modern factories in Puebla had begun to produce machine-made thread and cloth, but they faced stiff competition from foreign manufacturers and the market was never fully reclaimed by domestic producers (Bazant 1964:68; Keremitsis 1987:12).

Given its distant location and the high cost of transportation, Chilapa's textile industry was for a time protected against the specific problem of competitive imports. Machine-made manta filtering south from the central highlands probably chipped away at the northern edges of Chilapa's market early in the nineteenth century, but there remained steady demand in central and southern Guerrero. In addition to increased competition, merchants traveling out of the Atempa basin ran risks associated with political instability. Assault and robbery were nearly constant hazards for long-distance traders for more than a century following the outbreak of the War of Independence in 1810.[20] Another problem was maintaining a supply of cotton. Although nineteenth-century cotton output in Guerrero is not as well documented as in Veracruz, where the decline was precipitous between 1810 and 1820 (Bazant 1964:68), a shift away from cotton to other cash crops or to ranching occurred in all of Mexico's production zones, and the days when bale upon bale of cotton passed through Chilapa became a distant memory. Furthermore, small farmers on the coast no longer produced sufficient quantities of cotton to allow arrieros to make purchases by traveling directly into agricultural zones. Chilapa's raw cotton supply came to be funneled through Ayutla's market, where it was under the firm control of elite merchants (Ravelo 1987:102). Cotton prices rose in all of this, to a level that eventually made machine-made thread imported through the central highlands competitive if not actually cheaper. These changes must have taken a tremendous toll on the profitability of Chilapa's spinning and weaving industries, which appear never to have recovered from the violence of the 1840s. Only a few *mantaleros* (manta weavers) were reported in the 1900 census (DGE 1905a:197), and these disappeared soon after, following the construction of two enormous textile factories on the coastal plain near Acapulco (Salazar 1987:38–39) that churned out cheap manta at a spectacular rate and undercut what remained of the demand for manta woven in Chilapa.

Chilapa's artisans did not sit passively in the face of these changes. After the turbulence of the 1840s, Chilapa's textile workers found in rebozos (shawls) a product that was unknown to British industry but in steady demand both locally and in surrounding regions. Rebozos were made in a variety of sizes and grades, but all of those made in Chilapa were apparently woven with machine-made thread.[21] Spinners lost work as a result, but rebozo manufacturing held a solution to this particular problem. Unlike manta, rebozos were woven of thread dyed through a painstaking resist-dyeing technique (also known as *ikat* or *jaspé* dyeing) that added a substantial amount of work to the production process. Once a length of rebozo fabric was woven, the piece was taken off the loom (fig. 10), leaving several feet (depending on the quality and size of the rebozo) of loose warp threads at either end; these were later hand-knotted into intricate designs by women known as *empuntadoras* (for a description of rebozo production techniques, see Davis 1991 and Ventura 2002). Together, dyeing and knotting were new types of work that offset the losses that accompanied the shift from local spinning to the use of machine-made thread.

Unfortunately, the documentary record offers only meager scraps of information relevant to Chilapa's nineteenth-century economy, including no information on the town's occupational structure that can be compared to the data contained in the censuses of 1791 and 1900. This makes it difficult to be especially precise in discussing the exact timing of or the sequence of steps involved in the shift from the production of manta to rebozos. I suspect that the change was relatively abrupt and that it occurred in the immediate aftermath of the 1840s uprisings. Several lines of indirect evidence lead me to this assumption. For example, shortly after these events, in 1857, a *rebocero* (rebozo weaver) from Chilapa founded a tienda and *rebocería* (a retail rebozo store) in San Luis Acatlán, a community on the edge of the coastal plain east of Ayutla (Giles 1953). By 1880 another rebocería, known as La Chilapeña, had appeared in Toluca, Mexico (Velázquez 1981:74).[22] No later than the 1880s, marketing efforts such as these had given Chilapa's reboceros an established national reputation and their rebozos a presence in markets in the central highlands as well as in the Atempa basin and surrounding regions.

A second line of evidence pointing to a 1850s takeoff point for rebozo production (every bit as indirect as the evidence of Chilapa's rebozos

Figure 10. Rebocero working at a loom in Chilapa in 1968. Photo by David Grove.

appearing in distant markets but no less suggestive for its indirectness)
involves the city's demography. At first glance, rebozo production appears
to have enabled Chilapa's textile producers to dodge the initial bullet fired
from modern industry, allowing them to adapt with reasonable grace to the
changed market conditions by substituting outmoded work (spinning) and
products (manta) with new work (dyeing and knotting) and a new product
(rebozos) that took advantage of industrially manufactured raw materials
(thread, and later dyestuffs) while avoiding direct competition with industrial producers. But scratch the surface and things look less rosy. Chilapa's
population grew spectacularly with the initial rise of the textile industry in

the 1790s, but these numbers could not be consistently maintained, and the size of the town gyrated wildly for several decades. From the previously cited population of about 10,730 in 1800, Chilapa dropped back to something near 6,000 in 1825, then ballooned to nearly 14,000 by 1840 before falling meteorically between 1844 and the late 1850s. Then it stabilized. Between 1860 and 1960, a full century, the population hovered around 7,000. Provisioning issues, addressed in the following chapter, played a central role in the instability of the early nineteenth century, but the inability of rebozo manufacturing to fully offset the loss of work that accompanied the decline in thread and manta production appears to have played a role as well. The reasons for this become apparent in looking more closely at patterns of consumption of the two products.

Thread and manta were used to make everyday apparel, which had a limited life expectancy when exposed to the rigors of regular use. Studies elsewhere in Mesoamerica (e.g., Keremitsis 1987:108; Tax 1953:158–63) report that the members of a typical farming household consumed one to two sets of clothing per person per year, an amount that is in accord with the limited data on this point reported in a study done in the Atempa basin in the mid-twentieth century (Díaz 1976:68–71; Muñoz 1963:130–31). Rebozos, in contrast, were used only by adult women; even if we assume that there was rough gender equity, the overall pool of rebozo consumers was something less than half of the population of thread and manta consumers. Moreover, even rebozos of low quality, known as *rebozos corrientes,* lasted for years, and those of higher quality (*rebozos finos*) could serve for a decade or more; a woman would generally consume well under a dozen in her lifetime. Thus, both the pool of consumers and the rate of consumption were lower for rebozos than for manta. Even the much higher unit price of rebozos could not offset the loss of sales volume.

Under these circumstances, it became incumbent upon producers to find market outlets beyond the Atempa basin if rebozo production was to replace manta as the underpinning of the urban economy. This meant manufacturing greater numbers of rebozos finos. The local demand for these more costly creations was very limited; they were instead aimed almost entirely at distant markets. Compared to rebozos corrientes (and even more so regarding manta), the greater value by weight and volume of rebozos finos allowed merchants to transport them over comparatively great distances with a lower per unit markup (lower relative to the item's total value) to cover the cost of transportation. But Chilapa's producers met stiff competition at every turn. To the west and east, they faced markets supplied by rebozo producers in the highlands of Michoacán and Oaxaca, respectively. Both of these areas had established trade linkages to Guerrero's coastal plain (Amith 2005), so even maintaining hegemony over the coastal market was problematic. Still more serious competition sprang from the rebozo-producing center of Tenancingo, located north of Taxco at the southern end of the Valley of Toluca (see Velázquez 1981). Tenancingo was better positioned than Chilapa to supply both northern Guerrero and the urban centers of the central highlands. This is not to say that Tenancingo had anything like a captive market in the central highlands. Far from it. Centers of rebozo production were scattered through central and southern Mexico, including towns in San Luis Potosí (Santa María del Río) and Guanajuato (Uriangato and Moroleón), as well as Oaxaca (Oaxaca City), Michoacán (San Mateo Ahuiran and Aranza), Mexico (Tenancingo), and Guerrero (Chilapa) (Ventura 2002). Of the major production centers, rebozos from Tenancingo, Oaxaca, and, especially, Santa María del Río were the most widely known and regarded. Merchants from these towns were successful in using creative branding strategies to help maintain a position in the highly competitive urban markets. Merchants from Chilapa did this also, though less successfully, something that is apparent in the names of the rebocerías in Toluca, cited above.

This brings me to a final point about the shift from manta to rebozo manufacturing. Recall that an outstanding characteristic of the manta industry was its strong organic connection to the local consumer market and its detachment from the import-export sector of the economy. With the shift to rebozo production, the wall of separation between these two spheres of commodity circulation was lowered somewhat. Rebozo producers depended on merchants not only to obtain exotic dyestuffs and machine-made thread but also to market many of the finished products. This dependence on merchants set up some of the conditions needed for the rebozo industry to develop the organizational characteristics of a classic put-out system, and at least one source indicates that the industry eventually did so (Ruiz et al. 1947). Weavers did not lose total control over production, however; one can hear echoes of the subdelegado's 1800 lament as recently as the mid-1940s, when weavers were again faulted for concentrating on locally consumed rebozos corrientes at the expense of higher-quality rebozos finos that were produced for export (Ruiz et al. 1947:24–25). Presumably there was sufficient competition among merchants selling thread and dyes to inhibit the sort of monopoly control needed for a put-out system to develop. Instead, well into the twentieth century, dyers and weavers obtained thread and dyes without surrendering production decisions or becoming otherwise beholden to elite merchants. If a merchant became intolerable, weavers were at liberty to avoid him by purchasing raw materials from another, by weaving rebozos corrientes, and by handling the marketing themselves or through the town's extensive network of petty retailers.

In the end, Chilapa's textile producers managed to make a living for the better part of a century by producing rebozos for local consumption and for export to urban markets in the central highlands and elsewhere. Rebozo production never supported the type of explosive demographic and economic expansion that the city had experienced with the initial rise of manta production; to the contrary, Chilapa's population, which is the best available proxy for the size of its economy, remained basically unchanged through the entire period when rebozo production constituted the town's principal industry. The rebozo industry did not support growth, but it did allow the city to sustain its urban economy, though on a scale much diminished from the boom years of the early nineteenth century.

In 2003, a store known as La Firmeza, on the southwest corner of Chilapa's zocalo, was shuttered for the last time. If only symbolically, this marked a definitive end to the city's preindustrial era, for this was the last of Chilapa's tiendas mestizas, a hybrid wholesale/retail operation that in its later years sold wheat flour, lard, yeast and other baking supplies, refined sugar, cooking oil, soap, matches, cigarettes, rubbing alcohol, kerosene, brooms and other cleaning supplies, exotic liquors, and a further diversity of goods whose association defies easy comprehension. They were the goods that remained after the proprietors (descendants of hacendados, elite merchants, and the owner of Chilapa's first car and cargo truck) had followed the path of other *comerciantes* and *tenderos* and gradually dropped from the store's inventory items such as metal tools, fine textiles and ceramics, glassware, and so forth that they had once exclusively controlled. After the 1950s, interregional transport costs had dropped to a point at which elite merchants lost their monopoly on access to distant suppliers. This allowed the town's army of petty merchants, a group who had previously trafficked in locally produced and consumed goods that circulated in the tianguis and the daily market, to gain access to imported goods and to thoroughly intertwine inter- and intraregional commerce. Although a few specialized retail stores have arisen and apparently prospered, mostly owned by newcomers to the region, most commerce has come to be dominated by petty merchants and generalized shopkeepers who survive by keeping both overhead and profit margins low. The days when profit could be made by the fortunate who possessed the resources needed to create and sustain commercial relationships with distant suppliers had passed. And the elite merchants mostly gathered up their resources and left.

In this, they followed a well-worn path. Even in its preindustrial heyday, Chilapa's urban economy offered few potentially profitable opportunities to aspiring elites. Recall that in 1791 the town's commercial, landowning, and administrative elites consisted of about twenty individuals. Adding the ten arrieros who owned at least an atajo of mules to this group brings the town's entire elite class to thirty households, roughly 5 percent of the total. Not many from this group stuck around to see the town through the transition from freighting to weaving. Indeed, a review of the surnames of elite families shows that new groups arose with every major economic transition in the region while the descendants of the previous elites either melted into the working class or, more commonly, took what fortune they possessed and moved to the central highlands. The urban economy simply provided too few hooks by which elites could wrest control over labor or commodities from the independent arrieros and artisans who populated the town and, in their own disorganized and inimical way, dominated its economy.

The prospects were different for the other 95 percent of the population. Here there was tremendous stability. Of the twenty most common surnames represented in the community in 1791, fourteen remained in the top twenty in 1840, and twelve remained in 1990.[23] From its beginnings as an urban center, Chilapa has always been friendlier to the working class than to elites. The town's occupational profile in 1900, or in 1940 for that matter, was strikingly similar to that recorded in 1791 (for details, see note 14), characterized by the same basic array of specialties in roughly equivalent proportions. There were two main differences. First, in the nineteenth century, there came to be a substantial increase in the absolute numbers of people who depended on markets for essential resources; this is reflected in an increase in the percentage of the workforce engaged in commerce as a principal occupation. The number of merchants rose from fewer than 10 in 1791, all elites, to 125 in 1900, a number that includes both elites and larger numbers of small-scale petty merchants. Neither the 1791 nor the 1900 count includes men who engaged in petty commerce as a secondary activity, nor does it include the still-larger numbers of women who had a virtual monopoly on petty retail trade in the weekly and daily markets. Had these historically invisible groups been enumerated, it is highly likely that the record would show them to have been a much more dominant presence in 1900 than in 1791.

The second major change in the city's occupational profile was the replacement of freight haulers by textile workers as the city's dominant occupational category. Where arrieros and sirvientes de arrieros together formed about half of the 1791 population, their numbers had receded to insignificance (to twenty individuals, or about 1 percent of the total workforce) by 1900. Textile production, which in 1791 occupied fifty-eight individuals (less than 10 percent of the workforce), provided a livelihood for over one-half of those citing an occupation in 1900 (DGE 1905a:180–99). Similar data from years between 1930 and 1947 show the same thing, an observation that leads me to suspect that at all times in Chilapa's preindustrial urban history (including the long-undocumented nineteenth century), roughly half the town's households derived most of their income from the day's dominant industry.

Other differences were minor in terms of their economic impact. For example, a printing press was imported in the early nineteenth century, and the town thereafter supported at least one household of printers (tipógrafos). Other additions to the economy included bookbinders, fireworks makers, photographers, and a telegraph operator, this last an introduction of the late nineteenth century. Perhaps the most incongruous arrivals were three watchmakers. Although the city was not exactly an environment hostile to their craft, it was certainly an indifferent one; given that meaningful temporal cues were announced by the sun, church bells, or skyrockets, one can only empathize with the lonely and underappreciated lives that Chilapa's watchmakers must have led.

In looking at the broad sweep of Chilapa's preindustrial urban history through the mid-twentieth century, one can readily identify three distinct phases. The first began sometime around 1750 and lasted until 1793. During this period, Chilapa underwent its initial transformation from an agrarian community to a small transportation depot and freighting service center. The rise of the cotton trade along a route that passed over the Sierra Madre del Sur through Chilapa drew Spanish, castizo, and mestizo merchants, arrieros, skilled craftsmen, and farmers into the community, displacing most of the earlier Indian population. Although the community took on certain trappings of an urban settlement, particularly an increase in the commercialization of most productive activities, including agriculture, its size remained unchanged and the town retained self-sufficiency in basic food production.

The second period spanned the years between 1793 and about 1850. It began when a textile industry erupted from amid the community's working class and swiftly grew to dwarf the earlier transportation sector of the economy. The growth of textile production supported a spectacular rise in population, a result in part from continued migration of Spaniards and mestizos from the central highlands and in part from the return of Indians who some decades earlier had been exiled to the surrounding countryside. During this second period, Chilapa outgrew the productive potential of the agricultural resources in the community's immediate surroundings and became a city whose residents relied on commercial networks to draw all or part of its food from farmers living in outlying communities. The reconfiguration of the countryside that this early phase of urban growth entailed forms the subject of the following chapter.

The third period began around 1850 and ended rather abruptly in 1947 (more on this in chapter 5). This was a period of accommodation to industrial development outside the Atempa basin, made necessary when competition from outside suppliers undermined Chilapa's earlier textile operations and prompted weavers to shift their attention to a new product that was comparatively safe from industrial competitors. After an initial period of sharp economic contraction between the second and third phases, the urban economy stabilized and thereafter exhibited no visible growth or development; in the Atempa basin, neither the Porfiriato nor the Mexican Revolution, two events generally thought to be watersheds in Mexican history, intruded one way or another upon a strikingly long stretch of economic stagnation. The configuration of the regional economy, particularly its political dimensions, during this third and longest period in Chilapa's preindustrial history is the subject of chapter 4.

THREE

RURAL GROWING PAINS

For Chilapa to have become the home of arrieros, mantaleros, reboceros, or practitioners of any of Chilapa's forty-odd other documented preindustrial occupations, there had to be a market through which flowed sufficient quantities of food to sustain the specialists and their households. The quantities involved were not insubstantial, certainly not by local standards. Chilapa's peak preindustrial population, estimated at 13,842 people in 1840 (Kyle 2003:106), would have required about 2,561 metric tons of maize for sustenance. Converted into burro loads of 100 kilograms each, this comes to 25,610 loads per year, or 70 loads per day. Spread over a year's worth of ten-hour working days, it works out to one burro every nine minutes. And this does not include allowances for consumption by poultry, swine, mules, and dogs, all of which also ate maize. Neither does it include the enormous amount of wood and charcoal needed as fuel to process maize, which by weight and volume exceeded the grain itself. A conservative estimate of the grain and fuel needed to support Chilapa in 1840 would be about 200 burro loads daily, or a load every three minutes, all day, every day. Although Chilapa did not always have this many mouths to feed, the broader point remains; provisioning the city was no easy feat.

It is not as though there had been a disciplined labor force waiting off in the countryside, ready to spring to life at the first sign of favorable market conditions or on orders from employers or overseers of some variety. Instead, there were only self-sustaining comuneros who lacked experience with anything like this. Placing the economy of a single community on a cash footing would have been tricky enough, even a community that fed itself and was populated by recently arrived gente de razón for whom a market-based existence was the only type they knew. Indians living in the Atempa basin had behind them the experience of centuries, probably millennia, of living on their own ingenuity, largely outside of a cash economy.

Regional overlords had long-before acclimated Indians to parting with a certain quantity of their time and effort to fulfill tribute obligations, but supporting a city on top of this was something else altogether. This change involved so many people and so much extra work, not to mention participation in novel types of social relationships, that, in retrospect, it is a wonder that it came off at all.

The Atempa basin's first regional economy — by which I mean an economy wherein residents of one or more communities relied on food produced in other communities — arose with the growth of Chilapa's textile industry in the late eighteenth century and ended in 1842. Through this fifty-year interval, the regional economy was bound together not so much by the force of the market as by the application of force. Regions that are tethered together by the operation of supply-and-demand relationships in a market have a definite spatial shape and structure, but this was wholly lacking in the Atempa basin until the mid-nineteenth century. The basic problem was that Chilapa's consumers found in the surrounding countryside not obliging rural producers but instead indifference that when pressured turned quickly into resentment. Efforts to put a stop to the dithering worked for a time, but the measures this entailed eventually provoked a violent backlash, the outcome of which, paradoxically, was the almost instantaneous appearance of the sort of internally differentiated region that had been so elusive before. Urbanism in Chilapa took only a generation or two to establish. In retrospect, this was the easy part of creating a regional economy. Restructuring the economy of the countryside was a much thornier proposition that took much longer to achieve.

Before examining the early, unsuccessful efforts to reorganize the countryside into a stable economic region, I need to pause briefly to consider certain features of the Atempa basin's preindustrial diet and agricultural systems and the general economic attributes of preindustrial regions. In so doing, I will show that the rural supply network that supported the initial growth of Chilapa's textile manufacturing economy was such an unlikely and costly arrangement that it was probably doomed from the outset. No matter what yardstick one chooses — be it weight, volume, labor investment, monetary expense, or some bio-energetic measure devised for the purpose — basic food production and distribution trumped other economic activities in importance to the region as a whole, constituting the most challenging productive effort to organize. However mundane food production and distribution may seem, these activities occupied the lives of a majority of the Atempa basin's inhabitants, and no account of the region's economy (or of the economy of any region, for that matter) can be complete without giving it due consideration.

FOOD AND AGRICULTURE IN THE ATEMPA BASIN

Preindustrial Mexicans did not live on maize alone, but they came close to it. Mexico was one of the world's great incubators of domesticated plants, contributing dozens of foods that were swiftly and thoroughly integrated into regional cuisines the world over. On any given Sunday in Chilapa's tianguis, there are scores, perhaps hundreds, of edible foodstuffs; markets in other regions of the country, ones that integrate different constellations of ecological zones, have different but comparably complex botanical assemblages. Yet in the actual diet of preindustrial Mexicans, all of this diversity recedes in significance next to the monotonous uniformity of the dominant foodstuff: maize. Take away any of the others and life would go on; take away maize and life would come to an abrupt halt. Maize was eaten in many forms — as tamales, in soups and stews, green straight from the cob, but mostly as tortillas. It sometimes seems that the chiles, the beans, the myriad of other fruits and vegetables eaten in Chilapa were kept around solely to lend a bit of variation to the maize that formed the core of the diet. Other foods certainly supplied nutrients that maize did not, such as amino acids, vitamins, minerals, and fats, but there were alternative sources for each of these nutrients and, for most, no great inconvenience involved in gaining access to them. Of the secondary foods, beans (a source of amino acids missing in maize) came nearest to maize in importance, but the key nutrients they supplied could be had from several other sources as well (notably, but not exclusively, from squash seed). Maize occupied a unique place in the diet not because of the proteins, vitamins, and minerals it contains, though it is rich in all of these things but because it was the only available crop that could serve as a caloric staple.

To this point, I have resisted the temptation to present a quantity of numerical data sufficient to warrant a table. However, numbers sometimes matter a great deal, as in this case, and thus I yield to practical necessity. At issue are the amounts of maize that were consumed in the Atempa basin. Maize produced in the basin was destined for any one of four distinct fates, only two of which involved direct consumption by humans: maize that was consumed in the households of producers and maize that producers directed into commercial networks and ultimately to urban consumers (see table 1).

TABLE I. Maize consumption (in tons) in the Atempa basin, 1791–2000

	Population		Consumption of maize[a]		
	Chilapa	Rural	Urban	Rural	Total human
1791	3,562	—	659	—	—
1800	10,730	—	1,985	—	—
1815	11,091	—	2,052	—	—
1840	13,842	—	2,561	—	—
1845	9,817	—	1,816	—	—
1849	8,533	—	1,579	—	—
1860	6,523	—	1,207	—	—
1900	7,399	15,289	1,369	2,828	4,197
1910	7,339	20,322	1,358	3,760	5,118
1921	7,510	18,667	1,389	3,454	4,843
1930	7,143	20,396	1,322	3,773	5,095
1940	6,094	23,152	1,127	4,283	5,410
1950	7,336	28,612	1,357	5,294	6,651
1960	7,368	31,731	1,363	5,870	7,233
1970	9,204	38,688	1,703	7,157	8,860
1980	13,326	48,052	2,465	8,890	11,355
1990	16,332	54,177	2,352	10,023	12,375
2000	22,511	58,009	2,746	10,732	13,478

Sources: Except for the years 1800 and 1860, population estimates for Chilapa in years prior to 1900 are from Kyle 2003:106. The 1800 estimate is derived from the count given by the subdelegado (in AGN-H, vol. 122, exp. 2, fols. 38–43). The 1860 count is from García y Cubas 1861:54. Demographic information for Chilapa and all other settlements in the Atempa basin for the years between 1900 and 2000 is given in appendix 1.

Note: Consumption figures are based on the assumption that the annual per capita rate of maize consumption equaled 185 kilograms per person. At 362 kilocalories per gram (Hernández et al. 1983), this would supply 85 percent of the caloric intake to individuals consuming 2,200 kilocalories per person per day (see Food and Agriculture Organization 2000). These numbers are in accord with nutritional surveys conducted in preindustrial settings in Mexico (e.g., Anderson et al. 1946; Beals and Hatcher 1943; Benedict and Steggarda 1936; Steggarda 1941). For a fuller survey of this literature, see Kyle 1995. To account for recent dietary changes, I have adjusted the estimate for the caloric contribution of maize to the diet of Chilapa's residents in 1990 and 2000 to 70 percent (144 kilograms per person per year) and 55 percent (122 kilograms per person per year), respectively.

In addition to the maize consumed directly by humans, a portion of the maize produced in the Atempa basin was fed to domesticated animals and another portion was consumed or destroyed by weevils, rodents, fungi, molds, and other pests. Among preindustrial farmers, postharvest losses to spoilage and pest damage are generally thought to be around 10–15 percent of an annual harvest (Haswell 1973:51; National Research Council 1978). Consumption by domesticated animals, including pigs, poultry, dogs, and (if present) mules, represents a still larger share of an annual crop. There has been very little research addressing maize consumption by animals in Mexico (Stuart 1990), and thus there is very little basis upon which to rest an estimate of the quantities involved. Of the domesticated animals just cited, pigs have the most voracious appetite; consumption of as much as four kilograms of maize per day has been reported for adult pigs being fattened for market (Kelly and Palerm 1952:88). This is an amount that is nearly eight times what an average human would consume. Pigs at other stages of their life cycle ate less, but how much less is not well known. Elsewhere, I have estimated that animal consumption approached 45 percent of the maize produced in the basin (Kyle 1995:123). In the present study, I have opted to sidestep these issues entirely (for reasons noted below).

As to the production of the region's maize supply, the environment of the Atempa basin is better suited to preindustrial farming than are most areas of the Sierra Madre del Sur. For example, there is more flat land in the Atempa basin than can be found nearly anywhere in the range outside of the Valley of Oaxaca. Roughly 35 percent of the relevant portion of the basin is potentially arable,[1] a higher percentage than can be found in most comparably sized areas of the Southern Highlands. The average annual rainfall in Chilapa is 830 millimeters, likewise an amount that exceeds that of most areas of comparable elevation in Mexico.[2]

The surface geology of the Atempa basin is a complex jumble of old igneous formations, sedimentary limestones, and very ancient metamorphics. This geological foundation, combined with the complex topography and the erosional and depositional processes that this creates, results in a bewildering diversity of arable soil types.[3] Elevations in the vicinity of Chilapa range from a low of 1,300 meters above sea level to a high of 2,350 meters. Most settlements in the Atempa basin are clustered between 1,350 and 1,600 meters. As is common in mountainous terrain, practically every field in the basin has a unique blend of features relevant to its use by farmers, including differences in soil texture, nutrient availability, and depth, in elevation, exposure, and slope, and in surface and subsurface drainage features. These differences shape the potential productivity of any given plot of land and condition the types of risk and uncertainty that anyone farming it must accept. They also shaped the alternative farming techniques that preindustrial farmers could use and the potential for shifting from one to another or otherwise intensifying production. I have reduced the diversity of agricultural systems found in the Atempa basin to three broad types, each conditioned mostly by attributes of the arable surface on which it was practiced. The three types are plow agriculture on the level plains of the basin's valleys and barrancas, plow agriculture on sloping upland surfaces, and agriculture on surfaces where the slope was too sharp to allow for the use of plows. Sharply sloping surfaces required that farmers practice a form of agriculture known as *tlacolol,* in which fields were prepared using hand tools (especially machetes and either digging sticks or palos). Each of the types has a certain measure of internal variability that affected productivity, but far more unity is evident within than between them. A fourth type — *tierra de riego,* or irrigated cropland, consisting of a small amount of land found in scattered locations — was not especially important in terms of maize production. Instead, the overwhelming majority of fields consisted of dry-farmed *temporal* (arable land with crops dependent on direct rainfall). The main determinant of the type of agriculture practiced in a particular field was its aspect and slope; the division of the arable land into three types is based on these two attributes.

The most consequential agricultural divide in the Atempa basin is between valley and upland surfaces. The floor of the valley system found at the basin's core was the region's most strategic agricultural resource; here, the maize that supported Chilapa's initial rise to urban standing (and sustained it thereafter) was produced. Chilapa is situated in the lower reaches of the Río Ajolotero valley, a landform that converges with the larger valley of the Río Atempa a few kilometers northeast of the town. The Río Atempa valley broadens into an expansive plain in three areas: an upper section, a middle section, and a lower section. Together, the middle section of the Atempa valley and the lower Ajolotero valley form the largest contiguous expanse of level surface in the basin. The lower Atempa valley has nearly as much level surface, followed by the upper portion. There are isolated pockets of comparable surfaces and soils scattered about the basin, especially in the middle Ajolotero valley, the middle and upper reaches of Barranca Coapala, and an internally drained area northeast of Chilapa near contemporary Pantitlán. The dominant soils in the Atempa basin's valleys

Figure 11. Farmers with a yunta and a scratch plow in Xochitempa in 1929. Photo by Leonhard Sigmund Schultze (1938).

are vertisols, dense clayey soils that contrast markedly with the much more coarsely textured soils of the uplands.

Vertisols in the Atempa basin have excellent water-retention properties and high fertility, but the heavy clay content (and the resulting density) made cultivation difficult given the technologies available in the Atempa basin prior to the second half of the twentieth century. Until steel mold-board plowshares were introduced in the 1950s, field preparation, weeding, and other agricultural tasks were done with either hand tools or ox-drawn scratch plows (fig. 11). The choice of technology depended on slope and soils, but plows were preferred everywhere and were used wherever conditions permitted because they saved labor in field preparation (Lewis 1949, 1951; Logan and Sanders 1976; Wilken 1987). A scratch plow was a simple device with three main parts: a yoke beam, a share beam, and a guide handle. The yoke beam was a hardwood shaft that attached to the yoke at one end and the share beam and handle at the other. The share was a smaller shaft with one end fashioned into a fire-hardened chisel (some-times sheathed with metal) that would cut (or "scratch," hence the name) a single furrow using the weight of the beams to keep the share in the soil. The plowman's main job was to guide the yunta and hold the plow handle in an effort to keep the furrows straight and appropriately spaced. In tight areas or small fields, a second person might be needed in the front to guide the yunta, but otherwise the contraption was managed by a single person.

Although generally an effective technology for the circumstances, scratch plows were less effective in the most densely textured vertisols. Because scratch plows were relatively light and had limited cutting ability, the share had difficulty in penetrating the surface and staying in the ground as the plow moved forward. This problem was resolved only with the introduction of the moldboard plowshare in the late twentieth century; not only were metal plowshares heavier, but also the share was shaped in a way that forced it to cut downward before turning soils, laying the displaced and upturned material in a neat pile beside the newly created furrow. The use of metal plowshares in vertisols required that farmers use larger and stronger oxen than elsewhere in the basin, but this was a minor concern when set against the greater difficulty of working these soils with scratch plows. In any case, although growing crops in the soils of the valleys was difficult for preindustrial farmers, the difficulties were offset by the fact that these soils offered the rare combination of high and reliable yields.

Surrounding the pockets of level plains are broad expanses of arable uplands. Here there is an immense amount of diversity, but the main divide for preindustrial farmers involved slope. Gradients in excess of about thirty degrees prohibited the introduction of scratch plows and mandated the use of hand tools. Scratch plows were comparatively easy to use on lesser slopes, but as the gradient increased and approached the thirty-degree cutoff point, a plowman would need to mount the plow, adding his weight to that of the yoke and share beams in an effort to keep the share from hopping out of the ground and jumping downslope (Kirkby 1973:53–54; see also Schjellerup 1986:183; Stadelman 1940:111). Steel plowshares eventually extended the range of plow agriculture onto slopes of up to forty degrees, but this did not occur until the 1960s and 1970s. Slopes of over thirty degrees were cultivated by preindustrial farmers in the Atempa basin only using hand tools. Breaking soil and planting fields in this way were difficult tasks. When compared to plow agriculture, tlacolol required substantially more labor to work a given area, and this limited the surface that a single farmer could effectively cultivate (Lewis 1949, 1951; Logan and Sanders 1976).[4]

In addition to differences in slope and soil texture, moisture and nutrient availability also varies among the three types of arable lands. The availability of soil nutrients varies widely in the uplands but is almost everywhere lower than in the valleys. Nitrogen replacement occurs more slowly in upland soils because both rainwater and organic materials (two sources of nitrogen) and leached nitrogen wash downslope and concentrate in the plains below. Another nutrient-related distinction stems from the parent materials from which soils derive. In a broad swath of territory west and north of Chilapa, soils are formed from the weathering of limestone or similar calcareous rock formations. Such soils have a high pH value (between 7.0 and 8.0) that causes phosphorus, a necessary plant nutrient, to convert into chemical forms that are unavailable to plants. In contrast, igneous rhyolitic parent materials, found south and southeast of Chilapa, are acidic; the soils found in these areas present less of a problem with phosphorus availability. Prior to the introduction of synthetic fertilizers in the late twentieth century, the universality of nitrogen deficiency in upland soils masked the more spotty distribution of phosphorus deficiency. This emerged as an issue when nitrogen fertilizers were introduced; in some areas, nitrogen fertilizers alone sufficed to greatly boost yields, while in other areas significant yield increases came only with the use of mixed formula fertilizers. In any case, nutrient depletion in upland soils required farmers to fallow fields to restore soil fertility much more often than was needed in the valleys.

An equally consequential distinction between the valleys and uplands involves water. Maize yields in the Atempa basin, or anywhere for that matter, respond to soil moisture conditions, especially in the days and weeks surrounding a critical period in late summer when plants enter the reproductive stages of their life cycle. Moisture-deficit stress during this period can sharply lower yields. Most upland soils are more coarsely textured and are much more porous than the vertisols of the valleys. Not only is water lost from sloping upland surfaces through direct overland runoff, but greater soil porosity also leads to water losses resulting from downward percolation through soils and from evaporation. The yield of crops sown in upland fields is thus far more directly affected by the amount and the precise sequencing of rainfall than is that of crops sown in the valleys. If rainfall was consistent during a growing season, particularly through the critical weeks immediately before and after maize plants enter the reproductive phase of their growth cycle, freshly fallowed upland fields can offer yields that approach those obtained in valley fields. But even a short rainless period can result in soil desiccation and cause yield reductions across wide expanses of the uplands if it occurs at the wrong time. The greater moisture-retention capacity of vertisols shields crops sown in valleys from this particular malady. As a result, farmers of upland areas had to adapt to rather more uncertainty and to much wider variations in grain output. Crops sown in the uplands run some danger from excessive rainfall as well. If rainfall is abundant soon after fields are sown, the plants do not root deeply. When this happens on sloping surfaces, plants can later be washed away in torrential downpours. Excessive rainfall can cause problems in a couple of locations in the basin's valleys, where fields are prone to inundation, but more commonly drainage is adequate to protect crops. Thus, farmers who planted their crops in upland fields were exposed to greater risk from excessive as well as deficient rainfall.

These differences in soil density, slope, nutrient availability, and moisture-retention capacity profoundly shaped the land use and settlement history of the Atempa basin. The combination of high nutrient content and excellent water-retention capacity made fields in the valleys the most desirable ones in the basin. Although these fields were not always easy to work, yields were comparatively high and they were reliable from one year to the next. Fields in gently sloping upland areas were easier to work than fields in the valleys, but the labor savings that might otherwise be realized were undone by the combination of lower soil fertility and greater susceptibility to water-deficit stress. For farmers of the uplands to ensure that a given quantity of food could be produced even in a bad year, they had to plant a larger overall area than farmers in the valleys, and thus the work was harder in the uplands. Farmers of the uplands also had to come up with some means of disposing of the surplus that was regularly produced as a hedge against drought. Finally, the highest labor costs and the most erratic yields converged in the more sharply sloping uplands that supported tlacolol agriculture; fields of this type were the least desirable in the basin for preindustrial farmers.

POPULATION, LOCATION, AND LAND USE

In addition to the physical properties of soils and the characteristics of preindustrial agricultural production techniques and technologies, three other factors — population, location relative to Chilapa, and patterns of landownership — conditioned the economics of food production in the Atempa basin. With regard to the first of these, as a general proposition, anthropologists and others assume that people will work only as hard as is needed to support their lifestyle and to provide a bit of a cushion to smooth over predictable economic ups and downs.[5] Adding to a population requires that more work be invested in obtaining needed foodstuffs. For subsistence farmers, this means planting more land. If no more land is available, or if the only available land is marginally productive, farmers must work harder in existing fields in an effort to boost production or must expand the arable surface into marginal areas and accept the lower productivity and increased risk that this entails. Working harder in existing fields, a process known as intensification, generally results in lower productivity per unit of invested labor in much the same way as expanding into a marginal portion of a landscape does. Lower labor productivity can result from intensification for a variety of reasons. For example, efforts to boost production from a field by shortening the length of a fallow period can lead to yield reductions due to nutrient depletion and increased weed competition. The overall amount of grain produced in the field might rise, at least if considered over several years, but the yield per unit of invested labor would decline. Or a farmer might try to boost and stabilize yields by digging drainage canals to divert runoff from adjacent hillsides and thereby increase soil moisture in his field. Although this would technically qualify as intensification only if the extra work yielded a lower rate of return than had work invested in the field before the canals were dug, even if the output increment matches or exceeds the added labor investment, the broader point remains; feeding more people takes more work, and in many cases it takes disproportionately more work.

The three classes of arable surfaces identified in the previous section presented farmers in the Atempa basin with different possibilities for intensifying production, but everywhere there were limits to the amount of labor that fields could absorb before a point was reached at which no further productivity gains could be achieved.[6] This point, the physical limit to intensification, was probably never actually hit anywhere in the Atempa basin, because the effort it would have required is so tremendous that none would bother. Long before the absolute productivity limit was reached, in other words, people likely gave up and either suffered the consequences by eating less or relocated to a less overtaxed area, to the city, or out of the region entirely. In the end, population growth could be, and was, accommodated in the Atempa basin, but with limits and at a cost.

Were the Atempa basin ever populated only by subsistence farmers who had free access to the basin's arable resources, the intensity of land use should have mirrored the size of the population, which should have been distributed across the landscape in a manner that perfectly reflected returns on labor investments. If we may judge from the distribution of communities in the early and middle colonial periods, the Spaniards made a fair effort to achieve something much like this in selecting sites for congregaciones, nearly all of which were situated either adjacent to or atop the basin's most productive arable surfaces. In the late colonial period, the circumstances found in the Atempa basin departed from this theoretical ideal in two ways. First, farmers did not have free access to land, which was instead titled and assigned variously to individuals or corporate entities, including Indian villages and religious corporations. Second, with the rise of Chilapa as an urban settlement, there emerged a great, gaping pocket of intense market demand for food, something that utterly deformed spatial aspects of land-use decision making in the basin. I will discuss land ownership patterns and the impact these had on the regional economy in just a moment. First I want to make a few general observations about the impact of a city on an agricultural landscape.

In the opening paragraph of this chapter, I mentioned the circumstances regarding transporting maize to Chilapa from the surrounding countryside, noting that burros could haul maize, wood, charcoal, and other locally produced goods one hundred kilograms at a time from production areas to the urban market in Chilapa. The situation was actually a bit worse than I depicted in that much of the maize, fuel, and whatnot was moved by human porters using tumplines, about twenty-five kilograms at a time, rather than by burro. Unlike the movement of cotton through the Atempa basin, maize, fuel, and other locally produced and consumed goods were transported not by professional arrieros but rather by producers. It was not an especially efficient means of hauling goods,[7] but it was all that the available technologies and the existing organization of society would allow. Profit margins on locally produced consumer items were too low to tempt Chilapa's entrepreneurial elites to get involved, and thus arrieros and their mules generally sat on the sidelines of this business. It fell instead to individual agricultural producers to arrange for transportation, and to do so at their own expense.

Like the urban working class, local farmers had a high tolerance threshold for participation in marginally profitable endeavors, if only because these were about all that the region offered. Still, there were limits beyond which they would not go unless forced to do so; where the force drawing grain to a market was the combination of consumer demand and the prospect of a profit, the high cost of transportation meant that maize and other agricultural commodities could be moved to the market from a certain distance and no farther. Like any staple foodstuff, maize commanded a low market price given its bulk and weight, attributes that sharply limited the distance over which it could be moved before the cost of moving it overtook its value. For a host of reasons, price cannot today be used as a guide in predicting the radius from which grain could be moved to Chilapa. Price information in eighteenth- and nineteenth-century Mexico was generally collected only where political authorities regulated a market, by maintaining a granary, for example (e.g., Van Young 1981:41–42). In Chilapa, there was no granary and few price data are found in the surviving records. Even if this information were available, we would still be left with the task of assigning a monetary value to labor, to burro upkeep and depreciation, and so on. Farmers surely had a keen sense of the value of their time and effort and of the utility versus the cost of keeping burros around to do odd jobs, but they neither recorded this information nor shared it with others who did. Elsewhere I have attempted to assign values to these things and to calculate the cost of human portage and burro haulage in the late twentieth century (Kyle 1996a). I can attest with some authority that it is an exceptionally tricky business even where the data are comparatively rich and the work observable firsthand; in a historical setting, as here, I am prepared to declare that the data that are needed to perform a direct calculation of transport costs are unrecoverable.

Fortunately, there is a way around the problem. Residual evidence in the form of settlement patterns and population dynamics allows us to see certain of the effects of transportation costs, if not to assign actual monetary values to them. In preindustrial settings, the friction of distance between producers and consumers regularly created concentric divisions within urban hinterlands wherein producers focused on the production of commodities that, because of their unique transport qualities, conferred a competitive advantage when produced in particular locations (Thünen 1966). All else being equal, commodities that had high value relative to their bulk were produced in distant locations; for high-value commodities, transportation costs constituted only a small portion of the final selling price. The exceptions here include truck crops, such as tomato, tomatillo, chile, lettuce, cabbage, cilantro, and so on, and fresh dairy products. These goods had a high market value relative to their weight and bulk but were too perishable to be produced in distant locations. Thus, an inner band of territory on the outskirts of a city was normally devoted to truck crop and dairy production; high-value goods that were less perishable were generally consigned to peripheral locations. Between the two fell a broad grain belt, where staple foodstuffs and other goods that have a low value relative to their bulk were produced.

These spatial considerations shaped the intensity of land use as well as decisions regarding commodity production strategies. Take two maize farmers, both with one hectare of land at a distance of two kilometers from Chilapa in the first case and ten kilometers from Chilapa in the second. Using a tumpline, moving one metric ton of maize from the field to the market requires forty hours of labor for the first farmer and two hundred hours for the second.[8] Divided into eight-hour days, this comes to five days of labor for one and twenty-five days for the other. If both farmers vow to work only one hundred days at producing and transporting maize, the first farmer would have ninety-five days to spend in his field, while the second would have only seventy-five days. For the farmers to realize an equal return, the labor invested in farming would have to allow the second farmer to produce in seventy-five days the amount that it took the first farmer ninety-five days to produce. All else being equal, in other words, commercial farming nearer to a market center will be more intensive, meaning that the return on labor invested in farming will be lower, than commercial farming at greater distances, where transportation constitutes a greater share of the overall production and marketing effort. This greater intensity of effort nearer to the market took a variety of forms, depending mostly on the class of soil in which maize was sown. The most common intensification techniques included fallowing fields less frequently or for shorter periods, increasing time spent weeding fields, and investing time and effort in digging ditches or canals to control runoff.

In considering the preindustrial economy of the Atempa basin, I have found it useful to divide the area around Chilapa into zones based on transportation costs. Measuring out over trails from the zocalo in Chilapa, I divide the basin into four zones, each four kilometers wide (map 5). These divisions are in some respects an artifact of my analysis, a heuristic device to facilitate analysis and discussion. The zones are not entirely arbitrary, however. For example, Zone 1, the area within four kilometers of the zocalo, was farmed by residents of Chilapa unless farmers engaged in specialized or labor-intensive forms of agriculture, in which case they were likely to move to and live at the site of production. Even comparatively extensive dry-farming of maize entailed relocation if the fields were more than four kilometers from Chilapa's zocalo. Perhaps the most arbitrary of my divisions is that between Zones 2 and 3. Although much unites these

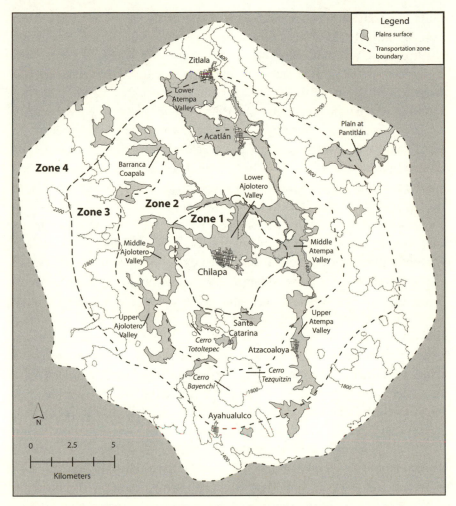

Map 5. Transportation zones and high-quality agricultural land in the Atempa basin.

areas, insofar as people's behavior was shaped by commercial considerations there should be some visible distinction between those located
nearer to the market and those at greater distances. I have thus divided the
area between four and twelve kilometers out from Chilapa into two zones
to create a division that is sensitive to commercial trends and tendencies.

The divide between Zones 3 and 4 is much less arbitrary. Somewhere
at or near a twelve-kilometer radius, people faced a significant spatial
barrier in that traveling to and from the urban center from these distances
required an overnight stay, generally in Chilapa. One could, in theory,
make a round-trip to Chilapa from a distance of sixteen kilometers in an

eight-hour day. In practice, eight hours of continuous travel is more than people routinely do, at least on market days, and even if they did attempt the trip, there would be very little time to conduct business in the market. The outer spatial limit of intensive participation in Chilapa's market was instead well shy of sixteen kilometers, nearer to the twelve-kilometer radius that I have used to mark the outer limit of Zone 3.[9] The outer boundary of Zone 4 is the most arbitrary, set at sixteen kilometers simply because it must be drawn somewhere and little of analytical usefulness is gained by extending it any farther. Certainly, households at greater distances participated in the market, which regularly drew buyers and sellers from villages as distant as Tlacoapa, some sixty kilometers as the crow flies and much farther on foot (see Oettinger 1974:96, 201, 209). But participation in the market from these distances, by anyone living beyond Zone 3, was much less intensive, measured either in frequency or in the volume of transactions, than it was for those living in Zones 1 through 3. Whereas households within a twelve-kilometer radius of Chilapa would normally venture to Chilapa weekly, or nearly so, this quickly dropped to monthly or even less often among households at greater distances. With regard to maize, the commodity of greatest interest here, the urban market seems never to have exerted sufficient pull to draw supplies from beyond Zone 3 without the use of modern transportation technologies. As we will see, only coercive pressure exerted by Chilapa's political and military institutions was ever able to achieve this.

In considering spatial divisions in Chilapa's hinterland, a couple of points should be kept in mind. First, although proximity to the urban market came to be an important force in shaping patterns of economic differentiation in the region, this was not the only factor conditioning economic decision making. Farmers centered much of their work lives around the production of goods that were consumed in their own households. The production of goods for the market was an important but decidedly secondary consideration. The impact of spatial proximity to the market thus recedes somewhat in importance and becomes thoroughly mixed with other considerations, including the physical character of the arable surface and the density of population relative to arable lands, in shaping land-use patterns. As a result, and contrary to all of the laws of economic geography, land use at substantial distances from Chilapa could be as intensive or even more intensive than it was much nearer to the urban center, though the motivation for intensive farming would have been a high population density in the first instance and the tug of market demand in the second. The presence of an urban market certainly deformed the economic landscape by creating opportunities that varied from one location to the next. Furthermore, location and transportation costs constituted important considerations in shaping economic decisions, even where the decision-making outcome was to forgo whatever opportunities the market offered; commercial opportunities, however limited, were in the background, if not in the forefront, of all decisions involving cropping strategies, production intensity levels, and balancing subsistence and commercial production. A final factor that sometimes proved decisive in shaping land-use decisions consists of patterns of landownership, and it is on this topic that I rejoin the historical narrative.

LAND TENURE AND LAND USE IN THE TIME OF COTTON AND SUGAR, 1603–1791

Since the dawn of recorded history, the landscape of the Atempa basin has been divided into a number of bounded territories that were titled or otherwise claimed by Indian communities, the descendants of the indigenous ruler, the Jesuit and Augustinian orders, and Spanish, castizo, and mestizo labradores and hacendados. The year 1603 is as good of a starting point for this discussion as any, for this is the year when Spanish colonial authorities completed their final congregación. As part of this program, corporate titles to the lands that had been vacated to form settlements were granted to the Indians. In this way, at least six communities were assigned titles to great tracts of land, the approximate locations of which are shown in map 6. The area surrounding Chilapa had a somewhat different history, and I consider it separately.

We generally think of Indian communities as internally organized in an approximation of the models outlined by Sol Tax (1937, 1941) and Eric Wolf (1957) in their comparative studies of Indian communities in Mexico and Guatemala. Birth in an Indian community conferred rights of membership that included access to various types of corporately held resources, hence their designation as comuneros (stakeholders in commonly held resources). The most important and universal of these resources included a residential lot, within the traza if the town ran to this physical design; arable land, generally held by households in usufruct; and use rights to common areas where animals were pastured and forest resources collected. Comuneros solidified their standing in their natal community through par-

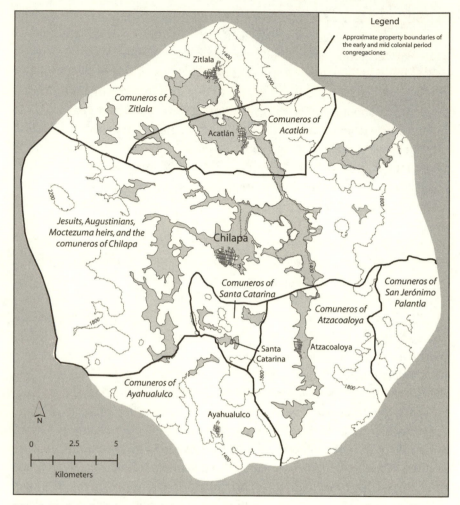

Legend

/ Approximate property boundaries of the early and mid colonial period *congregaciones*

Zitlala

Comuneros of Zitlala

Acatlán

Comuneros of Acatlán

Jesuits, Augustinians, Moctezuma heirs, and the comuneros of Chilapa

Chilapa

Comuneros of Santa Catarina

Comuneros of San Jerónimo Palantla

Comuneros of Atzacoaloya

Santa Catarina

Atzacoaloya

Comuneros of Ayahualulco

Ayahualulco

N

0   2.5   5

Kilometers

Map 6. Early colonial period territorial boundaries.

ticipation in a community assembly and in a network of civil and religious offices through which men cycled as they matured until graduating into the ranks of the *principales,* or elders. At various times in history, one or more of these offices might be recognized and sanctioned by outside authorities as community representatives. Most positions were sanctioned only by local custom, however, and were recognized by no one outside the community. Within communities, the principales generally constituted the ultimate decision-making body, though on matters of broad importance their decisions would typically reflect a consensus forged in an assembly of male townsmen and the guidance they received from the community's higher-ranking political officers, known variously as *alcaldes, goberna-dores,* or *comisarios,* who were on the brink of becoming principales themselves.

In this, Chilapa was different. In addition to the customary network of political officers typical of Indian communities, Chilapa was also home to the heir of the region's indigenous ruler, a status that passed from one generation to the next through primogeniture in a family that took the name Moctezuma in the early colonial period, and the seat of both an Augustinian doctrina and a provincial civil administration, the alcaldía mayor. The Moctezuma heir, the convent prior, and the alcalde mayor all held standing in the community that easily superseded the authority of the principales and the hierarchical political organization of which they were a part. This organizational difference set Chilapa apart from other communities formed through the congregaciones, and it created a unique historical experience in terms of land tenure, among other things.

The period between the final congregación in 1603 and the mid-eighteenth century was a comparatively uneventful one for the residents of the six Indian communities outside Chilapa. Comuneros participated in the colonial economy in the manner described in the previous chapter, performing occasional labor service and, more regularly, gathering together specie for tribute payments. Specie was collected by elected community officials and remitted to colonial officers in Chilapa for transfer to Mexico City. Comuneros probably participated in some manner in Chilapa's tianguis as well, supplying the early embryo of a regional market with readily transportable goods that were favored by the ecological circumstances of the lands they controlled. Most work done in Indian communities was aimed at supplying the immediate consumption needs of the producers' households and had nothing to do with colonial tax obligations or with market exchange. Comuneros spent the majority of their time growing maize, beans, squash, chiles, and other foodstuffs; collecting wood and water; gathering wild herbs and other useful items; pasturing goats and cattle; tending to poultry, pigs, and burros; spinning cotton and weaving clothing; and firing ceramics, distilling mescal, making candles, processing food, washing themselves and their laundry, and otherwise going about the business of everyday life. One thing they did not have to worry a great deal about was access to land. Territorial endowments varied from one community to the next, but all of the communities held sizable tracts of land given the population that then existed.[10] The holdings of the original congregaciones were so vast that when an opportunity arose they readily leased land to Spaniards as a means of accumulating specie to help defray their tribute obligations.

In considering the six Indian communities surrounding Chilapa, one should appreciate that the residents' outlook on the world was very provincial, something that was typical of preindustrial Indians in Mesoamerica (Tax 1937, 1941; Wolf 1957). While they spoke a common language (Nahuatl) and were all ostensibly Catholic, they did not, and in most cases do not, perceive themselves to be a united group. In fact, communities were typically at odds with their neighbors, often bitterly so, over territorial boundaries. Each community had its own patron saint and an entire corpus of religious and life-cycle rituals and festivities that were executed in ways that differed from their neighbors. Likewise, in the clothing worn by women and even in nuances in their speech, members of each community were set apart from others. The communities were almost wholly endogamous (i.e., they married only within the community), and the limited interactions with outsiders consisted mostly of anonymous interactions in Chilapa's tianguis. The glue that bound the members of a community together and set them apart from others was the shared interest they held in corporate property. The loss of a corporate holding would generally result in an equally swift loss of internal homogeneity and solidarity within a community. Such a circumstance would compel community members to look elsewhere for work, to sectors of the colonial or postcolonial economy and society in which the lingua franca was Spanish, and the customs typical of urban gente de razón.

The resulting loss of ethnic distinctiveness was a fate that eventually awaited Indians of several communities, the first being Chilapa. As with those of other congregaciones, Chilapa's Indians were granted a corporate title to land in the early colonial period — but ownership and control were clouded by the territorial claims of the Moctezuma heirs and other elite landowners. The territory that appears to have been depopulated in creating early colonial Chilapa included the middle Atempa valley, the entire Ajolotero drainage, the lower and middle reaches of Barranca Coapala, the uplands surrounding these drainages, and the mountainous ridges that formed the eastern and western boundaries of the basin. Of this area, a portion was granted to the Augustinian convent and other areas were deemed tierras baldíos, or vacant and unclaimed lands, and were awarded to wealthy petitioners to the Spanish Crown. This still left much of the land in the hands of Chilapa's Indians, but the Moctezuma heirs would later claim that this was an entailment and part of the larger set of rights that had been awarded to them in the immediate aftermath of the Spanish conquest. The tierras baldíos were granted to individuals in the years between 1615 and 1620, and most were thereafter sold by the original grantees to the Jesuit Colegio Máximo de San Pedro y San Pablo. The Jesuits also bought tracts of land located much nearer to Chilapa from the Moctezuma heir in 1620 (see Santos and Álvarez 1990:93–94). By the mid-seventeenth century, the Colegio Máximo had amassed titles to a tremendous amount of land in and around the Atempa basin.[11]

For Chilapa's comuneros, these transactions were little more than paper-shuffling exercises that aroused no particular concern at the time they occurred; the comuneros might not have even been aware of the transactions. The Jesuits used their holdings as dry-season pasturage for cattle and sheep herds that were moved into the region after the maize harvest. This use did not conflict with farming, and Indians continued using the land in the customary manner without interference from the Mexico City–based Jesuit property managers (Santos and Álvarez 1990:80). The same seems to have been the case with the land held by the Augustinians and on land that the Moctezuma heirs would eventually transfigure into private property.

Such was the state of affairs leading into the early eighteenth century, when the Jesuits began divesting themselves of their holdings, something they had accomplished well before their expulsion from New Spain in 1767. The 1771 withdrawal of the Augustinians merely confused matters further in that comuneros, the Crown, and private landowners all laid claim to portions of the Augustinian holdings.[12] Through the middle decades of the eighteenth century, there was much buying and selling of land placed on the market by the Jesuits, Augustinians, and Moctezumas, variously consolidating smaller holdings into larger ones and splitting larger holdings into smaller ones. Whether the titles being bought and sold were legitimate was not always clear, but with the proper political connections in Chilapa (or, better still, in Mexico City), a buyer could, at a minimum, tie the matter up in court, often for generations. Once a dispute got to this point, the legitimacy of a claim became secondary to the question of which party had better political connections and, most important, actually held and could maintain a physical presence on the land in question.

In the long run, these conditions were not favorable to Chilapa's comuneros. Although colonial courts often supported the territorial claims of Indians (Borah 1983), the colonial system of governance did not include provisions for a strict separation of powers as has come to characterize (at least in principle) governments formed since the European Enlightenment. The colonial government instead offered would-be litigants a multitude of venues to plead a cause, including the same cause that had earlier been heard elsewhere. In this way, and for this reason, land disputes were never really resolved until one party conceded defeat. This is what happened in the case of Chilapa's comuneros. The forces arrayed against them — the Moctezuma heir, the Jesuits, the Augustinians, and the individuals who bought property titles from these groups — were too well connected and had pockets too deep for the comuneros to successfully oppose.

Chilapa's comuneros first filed suit against the Moctezumas in 1716 in a dispute that remained alive through 1766, by which time relations between comuneros and the Moctezumas had sunk to a point at which colonial administrators feared that violence might erupt (Álvarez 1845:42–43). By the mid-eighteenth century, it had become clear that the Moctezumas were actively attempting to clear comuneros from the immediate environs of Chilapa, asserting that the comuneros were illegal squatters (Álvarez 1845:110). Most were eventually displaced and the land sold to small farmers, the labradores, who were among the gente de razón migrating into the region. The last known suit filed by Chilapa's comuneros involved the 1771 sale of land by the Augustinians to don Antonio Navarro, who had bought a tract of land near Chilapa that he apparently intended to subdivide and resell to labradores. Although the suit was initially decided in favor of don Antonio, the comuneros won on appeal in 1776 (see AGN-T, vol. 1514, exp. 6, fols. 3–5). Victory in court did not translate into control on the ground, however: Chilapa's Indians had nearly disappeared by 1791, their land having fallen into the hands of labradores. Though the history of Chilapa's comuneros is quite poorly represented in the archival records, the sharp decline in Chilapa's Indian population that was recorded in the 1791 census makes clear that, by one means or another, the Moctezumas, don Antonio Navarro, and probably other wealthy land speculators had by that time wrested effective control over the land that had once been held by Chilapa's comuneros.

The distinction between labradores and hacendados was an important one that went beyond the size of the associated landholdings. Labradores were farmers who either bought or rented comparatively small tracts of land, mostly in the immediate vicinity of Chilapa. Like Indian comuneros, the labradores blended subsistence and commercial production, differing mostly in putting more emphasis on the latter over the former. The market for basic foodstuffs in Chilapa was too small and insufficiently profitable to warrant significant capital investments by hacendados, however, so most of the temporal around Chilapa came into the possession of labradores. The hacendados were prominent representatives of the region's class of idle elites, a group for whom work consisted of managing investment portfolios. The land they acquired was placed under the day-to-day control of hired hacienda administrators and labor bosses (*mayordomos*) who, in turn, directed the efforts of peones or arrendatarios.

Hacendados found profit by engaging their capital in one or both of two activities: pasturing animals and growing sugarcane. Pasturage, preferably situated near the trails over which cotton was moved, was sought partly to raise cattle but mostly because arrieros could be charged fees for pasturing mules. The most highly prized class of land was not pasture but instead consisted of small, sometimes tiny, patches of potentially irrigated farmland that would support the production of sugarcane and the manufacture of panela and aguardiente. Although sugarcane had been grown in the basin for decades before the rise of the cotton trade,[13] Chilapa's transformation into a transportation depot and financing center had substantially increased sugar's appeal, giving panela the sort of allure that Spaniards elsewhere in New Spain more typically reserved for silver; as a perfectly acceptable currency in coastal cotton markets, panela performed a role in the local economy that was not unlike silver coinage. Unlike maize, which grows to full maturity during the summer rainy season, sugarcane cultivation requires water year-round. During the height of the dry season, surface water is exceptionally rare in the Atempa basin, and water that can be diverted onto fields is rarer still. On land associated with Chilapa (attributed to the Jesuits, Augustinians, Moctezumas, and comuneros of Chilapa in map 6), the requirements for sugarcane cultivation could be met on small tracts of land in four locations: Tecoyutla, La Ciénega, Trigomila, and Chautla. Tracts of land acquired as pasturage were found at Pantitlán, Mimistla, and Ahuihuiyuco. Each of these locations came to form the core of a small hacienda in the late eighteenth century.

Unfortunately for the Indians in the congregaciones surrounding Chilapa, there was at least as much land of the desired types on the territories they controlled as there was on land held by residents of Chilapa. Most of this was found on the slopes of Cerros Tezquitzin and Bayenchi, the remnants of an extinct cinder cone south of Chilapa. The impervious igneous rock of which the mountain is composed gives rise to numerous seeps and springs, particularly on the windward southern slope. Maquiscoatlán, Tula (probably today's Zizicazapa), El Jagüey (occasionally known as Nancintla), Xiloxuchicán, San Angel, Acalco, Tlaxinga, and Zoquitipa were all locations with sufficient land suited to sugarcane production to justify the construction of rudimentary *trapiches* (mills). Likewise, Ocituco and Topiltepec offered pasturage that was conveniently located relative to both Chilapa and to the trails leading north and south. Of these locations, one was originally held by Atzacoaloya (Tula), one by Acatlán and Zitlala (Topiltepec), two by Santa Catarina (Maquiscoatlán and Ocituco), and the remaining six by Ayahualulco. By the late eighteenth century, all of them had fallen into the hands of Chilapa's landed elites.

Map 7 shows the approximate location of landholdings in the vicinity of Chilapa in the late eighteenth century, including those that were the subject of contested ownership claims. Much of the land attributed to the labradores of Chilapa might have been represented as contested as well; I have not done so because the conflicts were resolved after the early 1770s, the labradores and the Moctezumas having established, by right of use and occupancy, control over a sufficiently large portion of the area to undermine the integrity of Chilapa's Indian community, which never again filed a lawsuit or otherwise acted as a collective social unit. For comuneros in other communities, the conflicts persisted in 1791. Perhaps the most bitter dispute pitted the Meza family against the comuneros of Ayahualulco, a community whose control over land suited for sugarcane production combined with its location near the main trail leading south had attracted the attention of elites. By one account, the problem began when the community's original property title was entrusted to a Moctezuma for safekeeping. The title subsequently disappeared; some years later, probably in the 1730s, a different Moctezuma claimed ownership of Ayahualulco's lands on behalf of the *cacicazgo* (the hereditary entailment of the Moctezumas) just before selling portions of the property to don Bartolomé de Meza (Santos and Álvarez 1990:67–68). Don Bartolomé's widow and sons created additional controversy in the late 1740s by claiming that rent payments don Bartolomé had made for land that he leased from Atzacoaloya were instead installments on a purchase agreement that was paid in full upon his death (Álvarez 1845:46–47, 141–42). In the late eighteenth century, don Bartolomé's principal heir, don Juan de Meza, held the sites of Maquiscoatlán, Ocituco, Zoquitipa, Tlaxinga, and Acalco.[14] Similarly, don Antonio Navarro's 1771 purchase from the Augustinians involved Topiltepec, claimed by the comuneros of Acatlán and Zitlala, as well as by Chilapa's beleaguered comuneros. This too was litigated (Álvarez 1845:43–44, 140–41), first by don Antonio and later by his son, don Juan

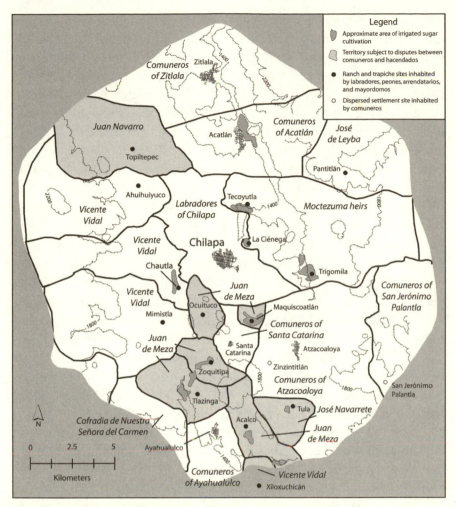

Map 7. Late colonial period territorial boundaries and settlement distribution.

Navarro. Despite decisions in favor of Zitlala's comuneros, the Navarros maintained their claims and were eventually able to establish control over the disputed territory. Only San Jerónimo, located in a mountain redoubt that lacked the type of land that appealed to hacendados, escaped the depredations.

To secure control over land, what was more important than property titles and successful lawsuits was physical occupancy. For this, the hacendados needed people willing to live and work on the land that they claimed to own. Most of the Indians whose land hacendados had expropriated had been left with enough arable land for their own support; thus, they felt no urge of a pecuniary nature that might overcome the political revulsion they must have felt toward the hacendados. Such a circumstance would shortly develop in the Río Azul drainage to the south, but in the Atempa basin, only the comuneros of Chilapa had lost a sufficient amount of arable land to make subsistence production impossible. In this way, Chilapa's Indians, some 2,200 persons in all, were made available for recruitment by hacendados. As far as can be known today, the villages that arose on hacienda lands in the late eighteenth century were populated by Chilapa's disenfranchised comuneros and by a much smaller number of Spanish, castizo, and mestizo mayordomos, labradores, and *vaqueros* (ranchers).[15] Given the hacendados' singular lack of interest in anything other than grazing land and sugarcane, settlers in the new villages are likely to have been granted favorable terms of access to as much surrounding arable temporal and forest land as they desired and as the hacendados could offer. In this way, the ranching communities of Pantitlán, Mimistla, Ocuituco, Ahuihuiyuco, and Topiltepec, and the trapiche sites of Tecoyutla, La Ciénega, Chautla, Trigomila, Tula, El Jagüey, Acalco, Tlaxinga, and Zoquitipa came to be surrounded by tracts of dry-farmed lands and forested uplands that were used for subsistence production (and probably petty commercial production) by workers who were allowed unrestricted use-rights to the dry-farmed lands and woodlands in exchange for labor tending livestock and working in the irrigated sugarcane fields and trapiches.

Back in Chilapa, it fell to the labradores to supply the beginnings of Chilapa's urban market with basic foodstuffs. Through the early 1790s, the labradores would not have had a particularly difficult time producing the needed supplies. The town's 1791 population of 3,562 people required an amount of maize that could be produced without looking far beyond the high-quality land in the immediate vicinity of the settlement; relatively small amounts of grain were probably produced in the uplands south of the town, but there would have been no call to draw supplies from residents of other settlements. A larger problem than land was probably labor; if each farmer worked two hectares of land, some three to four hundred farmers would have been needed to amass sufficient maize to support Chilapa. This is a number larger than can be identified in the 1791 census, in which (adding labradores and the Indians who remained) evidence of fewer than two hundred can be found. Presumably the balance of the agricultural labor force consisted of part-time arrendatarios and peones, people who cited other pursuits as their principal occupation.[16]

By 1791, the rural economy of the Atempa basin had been nicely

tailored to meet the needs of the cotton trade. Achieving this configuration
had taken much effort and, as we know from the abundance of litigation
records, had caused no small amount of animosity. The Spaniards and
mestizos who arrived in the mid-eighteenth century first secured control
over the land used by Chilapa's comuneros. They then changed the terms
of access to these lands, flatly excluding comuneros from some areas and
imposing new conditions on their use of others. For most Indians, these
conditions included relocation and the obligation to work under the direction of a Spanish or mestizo mayordomo. Landowners simultaneously
orchestrated successful efforts to establish control over locations owned by
other Indian communities, where their ownership claims were still more
dubious. These areas too were colonized by Chilapa's Indians and smaller
numbers of gente de razón at the behest of hacendados. Residents of the
communities whose lands had been taken objected, but they generally
expressed these objections through proper legal channels. The worst-hit
community was Ayahualulco, but even there, the hacendados actively
pressed claims only to isolated pockets of irrigable land and enough surrounding dry-farmed land to support the subsistence needs of their employees. To the comuneros of Ayahualulco, Santa Catarina, Atzacoaloya,
Acatlán, and Zitlala, the hacendados and their peones, arrendatarios, vaqueros, and mayordomos were an alien and irksome presence but not an
immediate threat to the communities. In the end, and despite these rough
spots, the countryside in 1791 was suitably configured to support both the
needs of the basin's residents and the then-booming cotton trade.

Urban Growth and the Problem of Food, 1791–1842

This economic configuration of the countryside was suited to supporting the cotton trade well enough, but it was not at all up to the task of
weathering the turn-of-the-century decline in this trade, and it was still less
capable of supporting the 1790s growth of Chilapa's textile industry. Thousands of people streamed into Chilapa in the 1790s as textile production
expanded; among the immigrants were many of the Indians who in earlier
decades had been forced out of Chilapa and into the newly formed villages.
Sugarcane's commercial appeal had gradually diminished as labor became
more difficult to retain and as the cotton trade to which it was linked
contracted. One after another, the hacendados involved in sugar operations
pulled up stakes and sold their properties. Two of the three major land-

holders, don Juan de Meza and don Vicente Vidal, were gone by 1800. Their properties were sold piecemeal, mostly to persons unknown, but some of the more productive portions went to the Moctezuma heirs. The Moctezumas, who moved to Mexico City sometime after independence (1821), held their properties until 1838, when the estate was sold in its entirety in the largest and most audacious land transaction ever attempted in the region. The buyer was one don Manuel Herrera, a man whose infamy is considered further below. Of the late-eighteenth-century hacendados, only don Juan Navarro (heir to don Antonio and the ostensible owner of Topiltepec) attempted to weather the economic transition in the regional economy. The others sold their properties or otherwise withdrew from active involvement in the region while the villages that had grown up on their ranches and around their trapiches declined or disappeared altogether. Indeed, the countryside came close to reverting to the settlement arrangement that had existed a century earlier, with nearly all of the basin's inhabitants distributed among a very small number of settlements. For anyone in Chilapa who felt an urge to eat, this was a big problem.

To appreciate just how big a problem it was, we need to look more closely at the agricultural resources near Chilapa. Zone 1 has a total of 1,419 hectares of arable land (table 2). This was Chilapa's primary agricultural production and supply zone; in 1791, it was owned and farmed, with the exception of the irrigated areas at Tecoyutla and La Ciénega, by labradores living in Chilapa. The highest and most reliable maize yields could be obtained in the valleys, especially on the broad plain of the lower Ajolotero valley. There were 578 hectares of such land, some 70 hectares of which (at Tecoyutla and La Ciénega) were likely irrigated and sown in sugarcane. Another 771 hectares of arable land were found in the surrounding uplands. Most of the fields in the uplands in Zone 1 could be plowed (the balance worked with hand tools), but in most cases, yields would have been neither high nor reliable. I have relegated a technical discussion of the productivity of preindustrial agriculture in the Atempa basin to Appendix B, where I estimate that farmers living in Chilapa could have reliably supplied the city with something under 750 tons of maize annually. This is less than half the 1,985 tons that must have been supplied in 1800 for the observed urban population to have existed. The land within Zone 1 could sustain no more than 4,000 people, a threshold surpassed in the mid-1790s; by one means or another, farmers residing outside Chilapa have supplied grain to the urban market ever since.

Market forces alone were inadequate to the task of inducing farmers in

TABLE 2. Arable land in the Atempa basin

Zone	Total area (ha)	Arable area (ha)	Arable area (%)	Tierra de riego	Valley temporal	Upland temporal	Tlacolol
1	3,152	1,419	45	70	578	501	270
2	9,949	4,606	46	76	1,864	1,552	1,114
3	15,008	5,391	36	53	1,774	1,639	1,925
4	18,934	5,500	29	0	998	2,890	1,612
Total	47,043	16,916	36	199	5,214	6,582	4,921

Note: The methods used to calculate the basin's arable surface are described in appendix 2.

outlying communities to produce and deliver maize to Chilapa in the early years of its urban history. The textile industry had certainly exerted a magnetic force in attracting labor into the city, but no corresponding magnetism drew labor into the region's agricultural sector. We know this because had agriculture attracted workers it would have left a footprint in the settlement pattern in the form of new villages arising somewhere near Chilapa. With ranches and sugar estates, the location of production relative to consumption centers was a relatively unimportant consideration. Livestock moved themselves and panela and aguardiente were low-bulk, high-value commodities and could be moved profitably over great distances. The determinants of production sites, and thus the associated settlements, had more to do with the distribution of pasturage and irrigated tracts of land than with either the productivity of dry-farmed land or the location of land relative to the urban market. With the rise of a city and the corresponding increase in demand for maize, circumstances changed. As a high-bulk, low-value commodity, maize was best grown as near as possible to the site of consumption. Given that Zone 1 could be farmed by residents of Chilapa, Zone 2 (the belt of land from four to eight kilometers out from the zocalo) is where we could reasonably anticipate seeing evidence of the changes that occurred in Chilapa's economy in the 1790s. What we see instead is a practically empty countryside and a tremendous amount of idle land.

Within Zone 2, land was held by Indian villages, hacendados, and small numbers of labradores. It includes 4,606 hectares of arable surface, some 1,864 hectares of which are prime valley temporal and another 76 hectares of tierra de riego (table 2). To the north and south were Acatlán and Santa Catarina, respectively, both congregaciones populated by comuneros. Those of Santa Catarina must have watched with relief as Maquiscoatlán and Ocuituco fell into disuse and were abandoned. As in earlier years, comuneros in Acatlán and Santa Catarina continued producing maize and other goods for themselves, paying their tribute, and buying small amounts of merchandise in Chilapa's markets; with this, they must have considered their lives complete. They might have produced and marketed a certain amount of extra maize to allow them to replace homespun with thread and manta manufactured in Chilapa, but otherwise they had no particular needs that could be satisfied by selling additional grain in the Chilapa market. Indeed, if the market price of maize rose in lockstep with the growth in market demand, something that the lack of price information prevents me from demonstrating but that seems safe to assume, then comuneros might actually have delivered less grain to Chilapa simply because the higher rate of return allowed them to fulfill their limited needs with a lower overall investment of time and effort.

Atzacoaloya, itself in Zone 3 but holding land in the southeast corner of Zone 2, warrants special mention. Although demographic information on Atempa basin communities in the nineteenth century is scanty, both tax records (which list only adult males) and parish burial records can be used to derive rough estimates of the population of Chilapa, Santa Catarina, Ayahualulco, and Atzacoaloya in several years between 1790 and 1855.[17] These numbers, though none too exact, show general trends with reasonable clarity. Whereas Santa Catarina and Ayahualulco held steady or lost population between 1800 and 1842, Atzacoaloya's population rose sharply early in this interval and stayed high thereafter. Indeed, Atzacoaloya's population through these years hovered somewhere between three thousand and four thousand, higher than it had ever been before or than it would ever be again. Elsewhere I have suggested that at least a portion of this growth was fed by an influx of refugees from surrounding communities (Kyle 2003:117). Why there should be refugees in these years and in this area will shortly become clear. For now I simply note that Atzacoaloya had swollen to a point at which its residents would have been doing well to provision themselves; at least in this one Indian community, located just beyond the boundary between Zones 2 and 3, people were in no position to supply food to Chilapa.

Other land within Zone 2 was controlled by hacendados. In terms of potential maize productivity, the most significant hacienda lands were the valleys east and west of Chilapa, the middle Atempa and middle Ajolotero valleys, respectively. Villages in these areas declined in number and probably in population as well. In Zone 2, there were six villages on hacienda lands in 1791, three in 1825, and two in 1840.[18] This is an exceptionally puzzling occurrence. The problem here was not a want of pecuniary drive, something with which the landowners were amply, perhaps excessively, endowed. Instead, the problem was labor. Hacendados could not compete with Chilapa's textile industry for the available labor supply, and they had no means to compel Chilapa's Indians or anyone else to work as arrendatarios. It had been possible in earlier years to recruit disenfranchised Indians from Chilapa to work in sugarcane fields and trapiches because the Indians could be granted unimpeded access to dry-farmed land as part of the arrangement and because they had been left with no other choice. Most of the work in sugarcane fields and all of the processing in the trapiches occurred in the dry season, in January through April, when maize fields sat idle in anticipation of the summer rainy season and, as a result, farmers were otherwise unoccupied. Converting these farmers into arrendatarios was another matter. Like all the other farmers in the region, arrendatarios would have had to produce maize for consumption within their households. In addition, they would have been compelled to pay rent in maize — under the typical arrangement, an amount roughly equal to what they produced for themselves. This would have entailed a sharp increase in the amount of land they had to farm during the summer rainy season. Had there been no alternative, perhaps farmers might have yielded to these terms. But for Chilapa's Indians there was an alternative in the form of work in the textile industry. Thus, land that hacendados might have used for commercial maize production instead sat unused for want of labor.

Chilapa's Indians could not, of course, have abandoned the trapiche sites and other hacienda lands and taken up work in Chilapa's textile industry if they and others did not find in the Chilapa market food that could be bought with earnings from textile production. Somewhere outside of Chilapa, there were those who responded, or were forced to respond, to the initial rise in urban demand for basic foodstuffs. Those who most clearly did so were hacendados who owned land in the adjacent Río Azul drainage to the south. This area had a historical background that was in some ways similar to the Atempa basin's. The largest town in the Río Azul valley was Quecholtenango, about thirty kilometers south of Chilapa. Though smaller, Quecholtenango was not unlike Chilapa in that it too was on the coastal cotton route and had become a freighting center that attracted labradores and hacendados in the late eighteenth century. As in Chilapa, Indians in the Azul basin were pushed off their land and onto nearby sugar estates by the combined pressure of labradores and hacendados. Here the similarity to Chilapa ends, however; no textile or any other industry arose in Quecholtenango. When trade along the cotton route contracted, sugar-cane production declined, and the demand for maize in Chilapa rose, estate workers had no means of escape, and they accordingly found themselves forced to work as arrendatarios for hacendados, who shifted their opera-tions from commercial sugarcane production to the commercial production of maize.

In the Azul drainage, the ownership claims of hacendados were no less controversial than in the Atempa basin. In fact, most of the hacendados who claimed land in the Azul valley lived in Chilapa and were drawn from the same pool of families who owned estates in the Atempa basin, financed the cotton trade in the late eighteenth century, and drifted in and out of government offices in the colonial administration in Chilapa. For example, don Pedro Uria, who was cited in the 1791 census as the "capitán de militias" (AGN-P, vol. 16, fols. 107–221) and is elsewhere said to have been the *compadre* of subdelegado don Pascual José Portillo (i.e., god-father of don Pascual's son) (Álvarez 1845:45), held a tract of irrigated land on the outskirts of Quecholtenango, a site known as San Sebastian Buenavista (Reina 1980:85). Challenges to don Pedro's ownership of San Sebastian by Indian claimants were rejected by his compadre, don Pascual, whose decision was upheld on appeal. As was typical of landowners of his generation, don Pedro sold the estate in the early nineteenth century, and by the early 1840s it had come into the possession of the ill-fated don Rafael Gutiérrez Martinez. We will meet up again with don Rafael in just a moment.

In the years between the early 1790s and 1842, Chilapa's elites adopted a variety of strategies (none salutary from the point of view of farmers) to draw maize into Chilapa. Most members of the older, more-genteel moneyed class had by this time left the region. They ceded political offices, commercial niches, and property titles to a still-more-adventurous group, one willing to tolerate lower profit margins and to take higher risks. Given that the cotton trade had faded to insignificance and the textile industry evolved in a manner that placed it beyond their control, the new generation of elites directed much of their pecuniary attention to the problem of urban supply. In addition to their property titles (many of questionable legiti-macy) and courts staffed by their friends, the primary tool at their disposal was Chilapa's militia. This was a poorly trained force of a couple hundred weavers, smiths, shoemakers, labradores, and others of the urban working class, all gente de razón, led by a few trained officers who doubled as merchants, landowners, and civil officials. The militia was used when needed to ensure public tranquility, something that in this setting required that comuneros and others be timely and obliging in making tax payments and that rental agreements be honored by arrendatarios.

Regarding taxes, colonial authorities in Mexico (prior to independence in 1821) commonly restrained local officials in their efforts to forcibly collect tribute in the face of resistance, something that arose with crop failures or disease outbreaks.[19] These restraints evaporated in the early Republican period. Worse, tribute obligations that had been levied on communities in the colonial period were converted into a head tax after independence. This was a deeply unpopular move. Whereas the earlier tribute obligations allowed for a variety of exemptions for particular classes of individuals and households and had made Indian communities as whole responsible for payment, the new tax system eliminated the exemptions and placed responsibility for payment on individuals. Comuneros could no longer (or at least not as easily) discharge their obligations using revenue earned collectively, from land rental or communal labor on a portion of the community's land that had been earmarked for this purpose. The overall tax burden thus rose, and it became more difficult to pay (Guardino 1995a, 1996). This, of course, suited merchants and consumers in Chilapa because it forced villagers to generate the needed income by producing and selling additional commodities, including maize, in the urban market. In this way, the early-nineteenth-century changes in Mexico's system of taxation served to boost Chilapa's grain supply. The head tax was first collected in the 1820s. Initially the tax amounted to six reales annually, but this was doubled in 1841. A final attempt to increase the tax was made in 1843 (Guardino 1996:152), but by then control over the region had been lost, and the tax was never collected.

With regard to property titles, there could be no better illustration of the intrepid character of the elites of the early nineteenth century than don Manuel Herrera.[20] In 1838, don Manuel (emboldened by an established network of cronies in key political and judicial offices in Chilapa) bought the Moctezuma entailment in its entirety for a consideration of $21,473.[21] The purchase involved a breathtaking amount of territory, including portions of the earlier Meza and Vidal holdings as well as land that the Moctezumas had long claimed (map 8). It also included land held by Indians who to that point had never confronted a territorial challenge. Specifically, the purchase covered all lands, houses, and even agricultural equipment

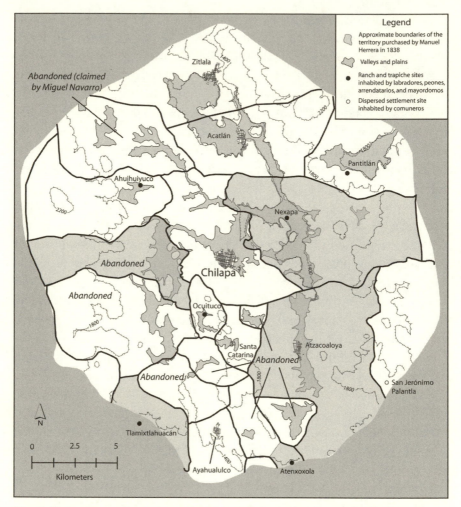

Map 8. Early-nineteenth-century territorial boundaries and settlement distribution.

used by the comuneros of Atzacoaloya and a handful of Indian communities in the Río Azul drainage.[22] Properties covered by the purchase were scattered over a wide area, but the portions that most concern me are those nearest to the urban center.

There are many statistics that I could cite to emphasize the dramatic scope of don Manuel's ambitions, but the most direct are these: don Manuel used this purchase to assert a claim over about 38 percent of the arable valley land (1,704 of the 4,440 hectares) and 33 percent of the arable uplands (2,618 of 8,025 hectares) in Zones 1 through 3. Objections were anticipated in the bill of sale, which allowed don Manuel to deduct any associated litigation expenses from the purchase price. On this score, don Manuel had little cause for concern. Staffed by his allies, the local court in Chilapa refused to hear the comuneros' complaints. Without a decision from the lower court, comuneros were unable to move the case to the appellate level. It remained only to mobilize the militia and to use this to instruct thousands of comuneros that they were now arrendatarios and that rent was due.

And mobilize the militia for this purpose is exactly what don Manuel did. Juan Álvarez, a national power broker with strong ties in the region, chronicled the use of threats, beatings, intimidation, and assassination by a group of Chilapa's elites in their efforts to keep opponents, including state-level judicial officials, at bay. He also chronicled the activities of a militia run amuck in the countryside, making daily excursions from the city to extract livestock, maize, and money from rural households while beating, jailing, or executing those who objected. In this way, don Manuel was said to have amassed some $10,000, nearly half of the purchase price of the Moctezuma cacicazgo, in addition to livestock and maize. Other land-owners reportedly collected sums ranging from $300 to $1,000 (Álvarez 1845:108–14). At least for a few years, don Manuel became the region's largest landowner and principal supplier of food to the urban market. Consistent control over such a large share of the region's food supply would have enabled him to manipulate urban grain prices and in this way exert leverage over the entire regional economy. Even the urban textile industry, which had to that point ranked alongside the rural congregaciones as a great bastion of relative freedom from elites, could have been brought to heel. It was an audacious gambit, one that for four years following the 1838 purchase apparently paid dividends. And then, in the spring of 1842, it abruptly ceased to do so.

THE 1840S

The regional hinterland that had supported Chilapa's initial urban growth was summarily destroyed on March 20, 1842.[23] Early in the morning on that day, arrendatarios from San Sebastian Buenavista descended on Quecholtenango, where they attacked and killed the hacendado don Rafael Gutiérrez Martinez, his estate manager (don Gabriel de la Torre), and the manager's brother (don José María de la Torre). The trouble began when don Gabriel, acting on behalf of don Rafael, made an attempt to collect rent

of eight *cargas* of maize (just under one metric ton) from two tenants, Juan
Santiago and Juan Blas. The Juans were delinquent in paying their rent,
something they attributed to a poor harvest that had left them unable to pay
the specified amounts. Don Gabriel, who served both as the administrator
of the estate and as the justice of the peace in Quecholtenango, summoned
Juan Blas to his presence, where Juan Blas was beaten. Receiving a similar
invitation, Juan Santiago wisely disappeared. This prompted don Gabriel
to muster the town's militia for the purpose of burning Juan Santiago's
home down and forcibly collecting the maize owed by Juan Blas. Fifteen
men and eight mules were dispatched to execute the deeds. They managed
to burn the home of Juan Santiago, but they found the home of Juan Blas
empty and deserted and were thus unable to collect rent. According to
surviving reports (especially Álvarez 1845:32–38), the militia then turned
to harassing and assaulting other arrendatarios living in the vicinity. This
prompted the men from San Sebastian to kill the hacendado, his administrator, and the brother.

Quecholtenango's Spaniards and mestizos, a group that numbered 114
men and their families in 1825 (AGN-TC, vol. 24, exp. 8, fols. 392–94)
and probably about the same in 1842, collected the bodies and made a
hasty flight to Chilapa. Urgent appeals for military assistance were dispatched to Chilpancingo while villagers from nearly all of the communities
between Chilapa and Quecholtenango, including Ayahualulco, Santa Catarina, and Atzacoaloya, joined together in revolt. Chilapa's militia, which
counted something under two hundred in 1791 but might have been somewhat larger (though not necessarily better equipped) in 1842, was probably
enough to defend the city but would not have been effective in conducting
offensive operations against massed Indian opponents. They thus awaited
reinforcement by regular troops, who arrived in Chilapa in early April. The
combined forces marched south toward Quecholtenango on April 17 but
made it no farther than the base of Cerro Matlala, just south of Ayahualulco. There they were ambushed and scattered by a force of Indians reportedly numbering in the thousands. Despite this initial defeat, forays into
rural areas continued through the following weeks. Ayahualulco, which
can count among its many misfortunes a location along a corridor linking
Chilapa to Quecholtenango and points south, was sacked in May; residents
of other communities, among them Santa Catarina and Atzacoaloya, were
harassed (and some probably killed).

Although a truce was negotiated in the summer of 1842, it did not long
hold. Tension in the region was palpable, and villagers had instituted a

devastating boycott, if not a blockade, of the Chilapa market. The negotiations had left Chilapa's consumers in an impossible bind. In a move that has the look of an act of utter desperation, in early 1843 the town's political authorities attempted to enforce a further increase in the federal head tax.[24] Not surprisingly, violence erupted again, this time spread over a much larger area. Efforts to collect the tax had spread discontent more uniformly across the countryside, to villages that were not locked in disputes with hacendados and had earlier sat on the sidelines of the rebellion. Indeed, don Manuel Herrera and his territorial claims joined don Rafael and the de la Torres brothers in the cemetery in Chilapa on February 19, 1843 (LDS, Reel 603363, libro 4, fol. 30), his death the result of an unrecorded cause. Still the rebellion continued. By this time, it had gone beyond the issues of land and rent to become a response to the full range of coercive measures that had served to leverage food from the countryside and into the urban center. The rebellious communities of the Atempa and Azul basins were joined by others in the Río Petatlán drainage to the east. The revolt gathered steam through the summer of 1844, when a large force of villagers — many from the Ahuacuotzingo area (in the Río Petatlán drainage) — laid siege to Chilapa. In September, Chilapa's defenders negotiated a surrender that granted them and their supporters, several thousand in all (including a substantial number of Chilapa's gente de razón), safe passage out of the region, most to Mexico City. Although refugees began returning to Chilapa as early as 1845, the city would never fully recover.[25]

After 1844, most appeals issued from Chilapa for outside military assistance fell on deaf ears, and Chilapa's beleaguered militia was forced to face the upstart villagers on its own. Outside authorities simply wanted the mess brought to a close and thus encouraged the parties to negotiate a resolution to the underlying conflicts, which they saw to be land tenure and taxes (see Álvarez 1845). Chilapa's leaders, perhaps aware that the real problem involved the urban food supply and not land tenure or taxes per se, thwarted negotiations whenever an opportunity arose. What finally ended the violence was neither a decisive military victory nor a negotiated resolution. Rather, in the summer of 1850, a devastating cholera epidemic swept through the region, leaving thousands dead, many more than had been killed in the rebellion. The epidemic knocked the wind out of both sides. By the time the dying ended, in the fall of 1850, most leaders among the villagers had been killed in combat or by cholera. Chilapa's hacendados had likewise died or otherwise disappeared, taking their territorial ambitions with them.[26]

The spark that triggered the 1842 rebellion was a dispute over maize in San Sebastian Buenavista. Although the conflict was often portrayed as a dispute over property or taxes, food in fact lay at the core of the region's difficulties throughout the first half of the nineteenth century. Population growth in Chilapa, fed by the swift rise of its textile industry in the 1790s, had dramatically increased urban demand for food, especially for maize. Labradores in Chilapa answered the market's call; comuneros did not. Into the breach stepped hacendados and Chilapa's political authorities. Backed by a ragtag militia drawn from the urban working class, they attempted to accomplish by force what the force of market demand could not. Together Chilapa's hacendados, political authorities, and the militia attempted to reorganize the countryside into an urban hinterland. The result of these efforts was such a misshapen arrangement that I hesitate to call it a "region" at all. Beyond the immediate vicinity of Chilapa, there existed a fertile but vacant landscape, one whose emptiness was interrupted here and there by comuneros who neither sought nor appreciated the attention that the city's rise had directed at them. Only beyond the first ring of villages and the associated communal landholdings did one begin to encounter significant amounts of commercial maize production. There farmers were hemmed in by neighboring villages and squeezed from within by predatory haciendas and the militias that acted on the hacendados' behalf. Delivering maize to Chilapa from these distances could not have been especially profitable without dealing in substantial quantities, something that induced hacendados to deal harshly with arrendatarios. It was only a matter of time until these dealings became too harsh. When don Rafael pressed his claims to maize produced by Juan Santiago and Juan Blas, therefore, he set in motion a regional collapse that was long in the making — a collapse, but not an end.

FOUR

HERE BE DRAGONS

History is not always written by the winners, Mr. Churchill's dictum to the contrary notwithstanding. Sometimes victors are illiterate. Some victories are so decisive and the position of those left standing so secure that no purpose is served by a follow-up propaganda campaign aimed at lending legitimacy to the outcome. And then there are cases where victors only stand to lose by drawing outside attention to the fact of their victory. Some aspects of all of these possibilities might have been at play in the Atempa basin in the aftermath of the 1842 rebellion. Although their heads did not end up on stakes in the center of Chilapa, the region's hacendados were nevertheless dealt a decisive defeat. In the context of late-nineteenth-century Mexico, especially the period dominated by Porfirio Díaz, when (or so a later historiographic tradition would have it) hacendados reached the apogee of their power, arrendatarios and comuneros would have been foolish to speak too loudly of the bloody means they used to cleanse the Atempa basin of its hacendados. No mythology grew up around the 1842 rebellion as one later would around the Mexican Revolution. Yet this in no way diminishes the fact that it was the rebellion of 1842, and not the Mexican Revolution, that proved pivotal in shaping the economic contours of the balance of the Atempa basin's preindustrial history.

The economic region that developed in the rebellion's aftermath was one shaped not by the power of private property and the institutionalized coercive force, the political offices in Chilapa and the associated militia, that sustained it but instead by the responses of independent smallholders and comuneros, of weavers, craftsmen, petty traders, and others of the rural and urban working classes to supply-and-demand relationships as these were manifest in their households and in Chilapa's daily and weekly markets. In the countryside, farmers held the ground they had gained by instituting forms of political organization that gave them the capacity, when aroused, to thwart the best efforts of absentee landowners to reestablish territorial control. These political institutions were effective as well at limiting the size of landholdings and the concentration of wealth even among the victorious farmers themselves. In the end, from the perspective of affluent Mexicans in search of investment opportunities the Atempa basin might as well have been erased from Mexican maps, perhaps with a notation to the effect of "Here Be Dragons" scrawled into the space once occupied by Chilapa and its surroundings.[1] Attempts to maintain notary and court records became exercises in futility, and tax collectors were nowhere to be found. Even commerce and communication with the outside world became exceptionally risky. In short, farmers in the countryside had finally caught up with the independent weavers, craftsmen, and petty merchants in Chilapa who had managed to elude the shackles of elite merchants and financiers at least since the 1790s. A handful of elite merchants notwithstanding, moneyed interests would cause no great amount of mischief in the Atempa basin again until the middle of the twentieth century, when the federal government moved in and took control of the regional economy. This carries me into the industrial age and to the subject of a later chapter. Here my concern is with the political institutions that emerged in the region following the 1842 rebellion. Coupled with summer rain and labor in their maize fields, these political institutions enabled humble farmers and craftsmen to exercise their initiative in creating a regional economy that proved remarkably resilient through an exceptionally tumultuous century of Mexican history.

THE 1850S

We have the Catholic church to thank for preserving about the only documentary records that exist bearing on the region's political economy in the years immediately following the rebellion.[2] Priests in Chilapa and *tenientes de curas* (a sort of deputy priest) in the outlying congregaciones paused briefly during the height of the violence but soon resumed the normal business of presiding over baptisms, confirmations, marriages, and burials, all of which they meticulously chronicled and in so doing left to posterity a record of comings and goings that can be used today to reconstruct the outlines of the early years of the second phase of preindustrial regional development in the Atempa basin.[3]

The rebellion brought about three broad changes that were to shape the region's subsequent preindustrial economic history. I have already mentioned the sharp decline in the number of people living in Chilapa and the probable shift in the urban textile industry from thread and manta to rebozo production. The third change, probably a leading cause of the first and a contributing force driving the second, occurred in the countryside following the collapse of the institutions of government that had protected and sustained the haciendas of earlier years. The collapse opened vast areas of land to colonization by the region's farmers. And colonize vast areas they did. People poured forth from overcrowded settlements into the empty spaces that had been created and sustained by propertied interests and the militia of earlier decades.

The land rush of the late 1840s and 1850s was not a random scramble for just any land but was instead a patterned migration that reflected the spatial distribution of economic resources and opportunities (map 9). In all cases, one sees the centrality of subsistence maize production to the economic sensibilities of the population and of the times. For some, mostly from Atzacoaloya, this seems to have been the principal aim; there were those who opted to move to distant locations, to areas outside the Atempa basin that offered arable land, isolation, and the promise of being left alone. A larger number moved to the abandoned trapiche sites, where they resumed the earlier pattern of combining subsistence and small-scale panela and aguardiente production, though this time on their own account rather than at the behest of hacendados and their mayordomos.[4] But the largest numbers fanned out into Zones 2 and 3, especially Zone 2, where they established themselves in locations and on lands where they could combine subsistence farming with the production of commodities for the Chilapa market. After fifty years, the market finally triumphed, molding the countryside into a coherent urban hinterland.

Most of the migrants originated in Chilapa and Atzacoaloya, two communities where notable demographic and economic imbalances had evolved in the early nineteenth century. In Chilapa, the 1842 boycott of the market imposed by comuneros in outlying communities and the simultaneous destruction of the hacienda economy led to an immediate and devastating disruption in the flow of food into the city. The gravity of the problem was so great that the evacuation of gente de razón from the city in the late summer of 1844 probably owed as much to the lack of provisions as to the military threat posed by the besieging farmers. Long before 1842, labradores in Chilapa had probably intensified production throughout Zone 1, but no matter how hard they tried, the productive potential of land within

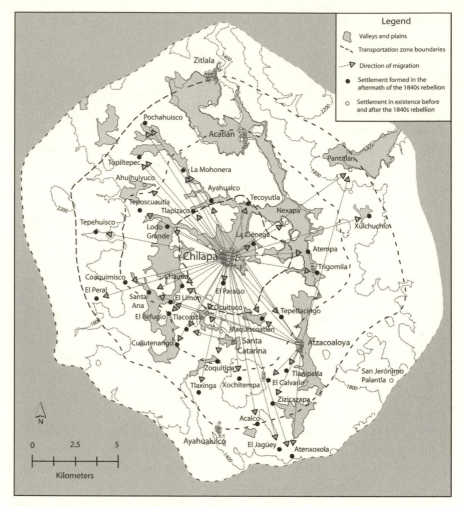

Map 9. Mid-nineteenth-century population movements and settlement distribution.

their reach simply was not enough to support the population that existed in Chilapa after the 1790s. When the combined efforts of hacendados, arrendatarios, and the urban militia failed to satisfy the unmet demand, urban residents were forced to create a new system of urban supply. The result was a wave of urban-to-rural migration. Indians, who at the turn of the nineteenth century had found work in the textile industry preferable to life as arrendatarios, responded in the greatest numbers, though they were joined by plenty of gente de razón. In fact, with regard to residents of Chilapa, this distinction between gente de razón and Indians had steadily less meaning through the early decades of the nineteenth century. When the midcentury migration began, few urban residents spoke Nahuatl or retained other distinctive Indian features. The migrants were instead members of an ethnically undifferentiated urban, then rural, working class.

In Atzacoaloya, the circumstances were different. This community likewise had experienced a dramatic increase in population in the early nineteenth century, but this was not a result of the growth of an urban industry as in Chilapa. Even at its peak, when the town's population flirted with and perhaps surpassed four thousand (see Kyle 2003:106), Atzacoaloya remained an agrarian community with no market and no means to obtain food from external suppliers. As in Chilapa, Atzacoaloya had outgrown the numbers that could be supported from its fertile valley lands alone (about 330 hectares), in this case the lands of the upper Atempa valley; its farmers were thus compelled to expand maize production into marginally productive areas on the slopes of the hills east and west of town. This entailed accepting lower yields, greater risk, and more travel to and from fields (owing to the high frequency of fallowing and the resulting expanses of idle land). Cumulatively, the result was a considerable amount of added work associated with subsistence production. Indeed, in looking at the population numbers relative to the amount of arable surface near the town, one cannot help wondering how much of its early-nineteenth-century population growth came at the expense of per capita consumption. In any case, the pressure that had built up within Atzacoaloya was immense and, as far as I can see, is explicable only as an outgrowth of the violence and intimidation to which comuneros were subjected in the years leading into the 1840s. Comuneros who would otherwise have moved to small outlying hamlets situated nearer to their fields, a settlement arrangement that developed around Atzacoaloya after the 1840s, were simply too exposed to depredations by Chilapa's militia. People instead sought safety in numbers in the nucleated center, despite the very real inconveniences this created.[5]

All of this pent-up demographic pressure in both Chilapa and Atzacoaloya found release in the late 1840s and 1850s. Farmers spilled forth from both communities to the destinations shown in map 9. Regarding the numbers of people involved, the best that can be done with the surviving data is a rough estimate. From Chilapa, several thousand of the city's nearly 14,000 residents evacuated in 1844; many of these, perhaps as many as 2,000, never returned. At least 1,058 perished in the 1850 cholera epidemic. This leaves about 11,000 of the original 1840 population. My estimate of the population of Chilapa in 1849 is roughly 8,500 (Kyle

2003:106), a number that would leave 3,500 unaccounted for and a fair, if crude, approximation of the number who moved out of the urban center and into the new agricultural communities prior to the 1850 epidemic. Chilapa's population continued to trend downward after 1850, partly a result of a second visitation of cholera in 1854 (166 dead) and small-pox outbreaks in 1852 (152 dead) and 1856 (120 dead) and partly from continued movement to outlying villages. In 1860, Chilapa's population stood at just over 6,500. In the end, of Chilapa's 1840 population, roughly 2,000 migrated out of the region, just over 1,500 died in epidemics, and some 4,000 spread out among the growing number of outlying agricultural settlements.

From Atzacoaloya, the numbers were fewer but still substantial. Unfortunately, I have no reliable basis for estimating the town's population for the years between the late 1840s, when it held roughly 3,500 people, and 1900, when 1,059 were counted in the first national census (DGE 1905b). However, parish records of the late 1840s and 1850s and a smaller sample of records from later years suggest that the pattern of movement from Atzacoaloya was similar to that from Chilapa. Both communities contributed to an initial wave of heavy urban-to-rural migration that began in the late 1840s, slowed to a trickle by the late 1850s, and ended by the turn of the twentieth century. Together, the number of people leaving both Chilapa and Atzacoaloya for outlying settlements through these decades probably approached 6,000. As something of an eddy in the general flow of people from city to country, there were small numbers of people from Santa Catarina and somewhat larger numbers from elsewhere in Mexico who migrated into Chilapa during these decades. Still, a preponderance of residential movements evident in the second half of the nineteenth century involved people leaving Chilapa and Atzacoaloya for small farming settlements.

By 1855, the basic settlement configuration that would persist for the next century had been established. And because settlement patterns so manifestly reflect underlying economic activity, there must have been tremendous continuity in the regional economy through these years as well. Excluding Chilapa, the number of settlements in Zones 1 through 3 rose from seven in 1840 to thirty-seven in 1855. Forty-five years later, in 1900, there remained thirty-seven settlements in this same area. Most of the new communities were concentrated around the expanses of fertile plains that had sat unused in the years before 1842. The most important group of communities materialized in the valleys west and east of Chilapa (the middle Ajolotero and Atempa valleys, respectively) and in the lower and mid-

dle reaches of Barranca Coapala. Together with the comuneros of Acatlán, those who colonized these locations (including residents of Chautla
and Lodo Grande in the middle Ajolotero valley; Trigomila, Atempa, and
Nexapa in the middle Atempa valley; and Ayahualco in Barranca Coapala)
were those best positioned to address Chilapa's mid-nineteenth-century
supply problems. Evidence that they did so is presented in the following
chapter.

POLITICAL RELATIONS IN THE ATEMPA BASIN AFTER 1842

The people who left Chilapa and Atzacoaloya and spread across the
countryside did not trouble themselves to any great extent with property
titles or ownership claims. In a word, they were squatters. However, they
did organize themselves into communities and institute forms of governance modeled on the political institutions of the earlier congregaciones.
As described in the previous chapter, there were three basic elements to
these institutions: a broad assembly of adult male community members, a
hierarchical organization of political officials, and a council of principales
composed of individuals who had previously served as community officials. Collectively, these institutions served to protect the territorial interests of community members against outside threats and to regulate the
allocation of resources among community members. From without, the
main threats came from absentee landowners in Chilapa and from residents
of adjacent communities. From within, political institutions operated to
prevent community members from exercising outsized territorial claims.
The result was a landscape populated by farmers, almost all of whom had
access to enough land to support their households and to participate in
various forms of commodity production.

The evidence in support of these assertions is, admittedly, somewhat
thinner than I would prefer. Repositories of both state and local government records, including notary and litigation records, were destroyed by
marauding armies, militias, or rural rebels on several occasions in the
nineteenth and early twentieth centuries, and this precludes a direct examination of any property deeds or litigation records that were produced in
these years. For a first line of supporting evidence, I would point to the
suddenness of the dispersal of migrants from Chilapa and Atzacoaloya and
to the destinations they chose to colonize. Nothing about the land rush of
the late 1840s and 1850s suggests that landowners in Chilapa were direct-

ing the process through the selective sale or rental of parcels of land. Geographically, it instead has the look of a near-random scramble for the best available land. A second line of evidence is a bit more direct. In the aftermath of the Mexican Revolution (1911–17), a land redistribution program initiated by the federal government brought surveyors into the region to attempt to disentangle property relationships and apply new laws governing the distribution of land. The reports issued by these surveyors are among the most powerful lines of evidence available on the political and economic circumstances that existed in the region. A final line of evidence includes a collection of miscellaneous observations by travelers and anthropologists (including me) that bear on the character and functioning of the region's various political institutions.

AGRARIAN REFORM AND THE POPULAR IMAGINATION

I need to preface my consideration of property relations and the early-twentieth-century agrarian reform with some background information, as many readers will recognize disparities between the experience I describe in the Atempa basin and that which conventional scholarly wisdom would lead one to anticipate. There has been much attention of late directed at changes in Mexico's Agrarian Code, a part of the broader set of neoliberal reforms instituted by the Mexican government over the past couple of decades. There is, I think, a widespread assumption among scholars and others that these reforms have been epochal and will be seen as such by future historians. Few of these policy changes have inspired more conversation, speculation, and research among my anthropological colleagues than those set forth in the Agrarian Code of 1994 (e.g., Cornelius and Myhre 1997; DeWalt and Rees 1994). I have long felt like something of an outsider in these conversations, almost as though I worked in a different country or culture area. While I recognized certain commonly identified manifestations of neoliberal reform in the Atempa basin (see chapter 6), in other respects it seemed to me that my colleagues were either capable of great exaggeration in assessing the impact of government policies or that social life in the Atempa basin was simply different from life elsewhere in Mexico. This sense of alienation was never more acute than when the topic of conversation centered on recent changes in Mexico's Agrarian Code.

Social scientists have typically marked the beginning of modern Mexico with the Mexican Revolution and its institutional aftermath, institutions enshrined in the 1917 Constitution. The Revolution is generally seen as a collision of a multitude of often-conflicting class interests, but all historical treatments of the subject accord prominence to the role of impoverished farmers. Likewise, considerations of the country's subsequent history routinely make reference to the inclusion in the 1917 Constitution of the concerns of the rural poor in the form of provisions for land redistribution. Even where the provisions regarding land ownership and distribution, outlined in Article 27 of the Constitution, were not faithfully or fully instituted, this failure is seen as a fact of cardinal importance, as a sort of betrayal of the country's revolutionary ideals and heritage. Between these and similar provisions addressing urban laborers (Article 123), the 1917 Constitution was once hailed as perhaps the most progressive such document ever written (e.g., Chase 1931). That federal officials of the early postrevolutionary years had no real stomach for implementing these provisions was a problem, but the document itself held the promise that someday things would be different. Modern historians generally agree that this someday arrived in 1934 with the presidency of Lázaro Cárdenas.

Cárdenas spent his six-year term (1934–40) giving practical effect to the unfulfilled promises of the 1917 Constitution. He implemented, among other things, almost all of its labor provisions and distributed more land to farmers than all of his predecessors combined had done. He also nationalized key industries, including Mexico's petroleum industry. So bold were his actions that they might well have earned him a hearty rebuke in the form of armed intervention from Mexico's more temperate neighbor to the north had the United States not been preoccupied by the nagging effects of the Great Depression and the brewing trouble in Europe. The programs and policies implemented by Cárdenas swiftly came to be seen as the defining elements of Mexico's twentieth-century political economy. Journalists and scholars had found nothing amiss in Cárdenas's commitment, motives, or personal habits, and he emerged in history as the veritable embodiment of the Mexican Revolution and its most high-minded ideals.[6] Unsurprisingly, subsequent politicians regularly sought what refracted legitimacy they could garner by invoking Cárdenas's image.

That politicians would pledge fealty to the programs and priorities of their more popular predecessors is neither unusual nor even slightly surprising. Where the case took an interesting turn was when scholars, an oftentimes skeptical and cantankerous breed, generally agreed with the broad outlines of the government's rhetoric. A decidedly Manichaean historical narrative thus emerged as an odd collaborative effort between politicians and academics (the distance between the two being somewhat narrower in postrevolutionary Mexico than is typical) wherein the Mexican Revolution, the 1917 Constitution, and Cárdenas's implementation of Articles 27 and 123 were merged into a single pivot point in Mexican history. It marked the end of a long string of precipitating outrages, not least the passage and implementation of the 1856 Reform Laws, known as La Reforma. These were legal measures intended to outlaw corporate landholdings. Although the Reform Laws were initially aimed at the Catholic church, the laws were also suited to assaults on the corporate holdings of Indian communities. The exploitative possibilities came to full flower during the Porfiriato, a long period (1876–1910) dominated by Porfirio Díaz. Díaz has gone down in history as a first-rate dictator who governed with ruthless disregard for the interests of the toiling classes. To landholding villagers, perhaps his most infamous deed was to open the countryside to foreign investors while providing both foreign investors and the country's homegrown elites with a safe and lucrative investment environment. The pendulum then swung, and there came the bloodletting of the Revolution, the 1917 Constitution, and the Cárdenas administration. From this, the Mexican government emerged with a new image. No longer the blunt repressive instrument of the few, the state took on a new mantle, that of guarantor of the security and well-being of the poor.

Subsequent policies and actions by the Mexican state have been interpreted in terms of these contrasting images. For example, the state's image took a significant hit in 1968, when hundreds, perhaps thousands, of protesting students were slaughtered by the military in Mexico City, and then again in 1985, when the government responded to a devastating earthquake by mounting a heroic effort to unearth bank vaults and similar strategic resources while survivors lay trapped and unattended beneath the rubble. Episodes such as these were seen as object lessons on the imperfection of Mexico's system of presidential succession. It was a system that kept both politicians with unbridled ambition and the Mexican military out of the presidency but otherwise did little to intrude upon any authoritarian disposition that might become manifest in an incumbent.

What these episodes did not affect were the populist economic and social policies inherited from the Revolution and from Cárdenas that were seen as central pillars of the Mexican state. Even the most cynical observers were thus unprepared for the 1992 amendment of Article 27 of the Constitution and the related Agrarian Code of 1994. Together, these put an end to the program of land redistribution to agrarian communities, and they provide mechanisms through which land that had been redistributed could be transferred from communities to individuals and converted into what amounts to private property. To many of my academic colleagues, it looked like a reprise of the 1856 Reforma. While not many did so in print, in private conversations anthropologists routinely spoke of these changes in almost apocalyptic terms, as though the pendulum had reversed course and the country poised on the cusp of a second Porfiriato. Academics were not alone in holding this view. The 1994 Zapatista uprising in Chiapas and the 1996 emergence of the shadowy Ejercito Popular Revolucionario in Guerrero and Oaxaca, both militant movements whose propagandists cited a betrayal of Mexico's revolutionary heritage as justification for their actions, vividly demonstrated that the imagery of the Mexican state as the protector of the poor had thoroughly permeated the public consciousness as well. These are images with deep roots in Mexico, roots that extend through its political culture and popular consciousness as much as through the relevant scholarly discourse.

While I will refrain from declaring the story line to be pure mythology, I must emphatically state that it does virtually nothing to advance, and does much to obfuscate, an understanding of the political economy of the Atempa basin. The problem goes beyond the simple fact that in the Atempa basin the Porfiriato was not so hard on the poor, nor the Revolution so hard on the rich, as the standard narrative would lead one to predict. In fact, the Reforma, the Porfiriato, the Revolution, and everything associated with these came and went without having more than a superficial impact on life in the Atempa basin. Armies certainly came and went from Chilapa during the Revolution, but this had been a routine feature of life since José María Morelos called in 1811. Nor can it be said that the opportunities afforded by Article 27 of the Constitution found no takers in the region. Far from it. Land grants to communities in the Atempa basin were among the earliest in the nation. Most rural Mexicans had to await Cárdenas's presidency before their petitions for land were acted on, but in the Atempa basin, more petitions were submitted and grants awarded before Cárdenas came to power than during or after his tenure in office. Of twenty-four land grants for which I have information, nineteen were concluded by Cárdenas's predecessors and five by Cárdenas. In terms of overall area, 11,558 hectares were distributed before Cárdenas came to power and 3,992 hectares were distributed by Cárdenas.[7] Where I find cause to object to much recent work done by my academic colleagues is in their tendency to take as a starting point for analysis the assumption that the implementation (or,

conversely, the lack of implementation) of government policies and programs had everywhere been decisive in shaping social life. In fixating
attention on the impact of shifting policies and programs, researchers often
skip over the more basic question of whether the policies and programs
actually had behavioral, as opposed to mere rhetorical, substance. The
history of land reform in the Atempa basin is a case in point.

"Agrarian Reform" in the Atempa Basin

Almost before the dust of the Revolution had settled, newly minted
bureaucrats arrived in the Atempa basin bearing their new Constitution and
possessed with what I do not doubt was a sincere conviction that its pages
held the key to earthly salvation for the rural masses. In more recent years,
information about government programs and procedures has been dissemi-
nated in village assemblies; I assume this was the case in the past as well.
In general terms, the Constitution guaranteed to Mexican farmers the right
to land in amounts sufficient for their needs. Eligibility requirements and
the procedural hurdles that exercising the new right entailed were outlined
in the frequently revised Agrarian Code.

Mexico's postrevolutionary government issued three forms of grants
to communities in the Atempa basin under Article 27: *dotaciones, confirmaciones*, and *ampliaciones*. Dotaciones originated with a petition submitted by a group of landless or near-landless farmers. Typically the petitioning groups consisted of all the adult males of a community, though in
some cases there were individuals in petitioning communities who opted
not to join in the petition and in other cases there were petitioners who were
found to be ineligible and were thus excluded from the eventual award.
Eligibility rested on a finding by agrarian reform officials that individual
petitioners possessed less land than was deemed necessary to sustain a
household, an amount that varied depending on the quality of the land
(generally 6–10 hectares). The land awarded through dotación was to be
expropriated from individual landowners. To be eligible for expropriation,
a landholding had to be privately owned, to encompass at least 125 hectares of dry-farmed land, and to lie within seven kilometers of a petitioning
community. Landowners were permitted to hold or retain up to 125 hectares of land and were to be compensated for any losses they suffered with
government bonds. Confirmaciones, as the word implies, were intended
merely to confirm the legitimacy of an existing ownership claim. In effect,

the law provided communities with an opportunity to exchange an existing corporate title for a new one or to otherwise renew official recognition of claims that were subject to no more than niggling border disputes. The general intent of the law enabling grants of confirmación was simply to preserve the status quo with regard to the administration and distribution of land. Finally, population growth, dissatisfaction with an initial award, or any of a host of other circumstances could induce communities to apply for more land in the form of grant known as an ampliación. Most land in the Atempa basin that was eligible for expropriation was distributed to petitioners in the first round of awards; as a consequence, there have been few ampliaciones. Once a petition (of whatever type) was submitted, investigative commissions descended on the area to confirm the eligibility of the petitioners, survey relevant land, and identify any conflicting ownership claims that might complicate an award. If petitioners requested a dotación or ampliación, the surveyors also identified any private holdings that were eligible for expropriation and redistribution.

The agrarian reform officials who received the petitions from villages in the Atempa basin quickly confronted circumstances that had not been anticipated in the Constitution or in the related procedural codes. Again, the 1842 rebellion had ended with the regional government and militia eviscerated and don Manuel Herrera, the most ambitious of Chilapa's hacendados, dead (and apparently without an heir). The countryside had been thrown open, and squatters had poured out of Chilapa and Atzacoaloya into newly created settlements. Four distinct patterns of territorial occupancy emerged in the ensuing land rush, all vaguely recognizable in the reports issued by the agrarian reform commissions that waded into the confusion. The agrarian reform officials ended up awkwardly consolidating two of the four into a common category, creating, on paper, three legally and administratively distinct classes of landholdings. These include *bienes comunales* (communal holding), *ejidos* (a second form of communal holding), and *pequeñas propiedades* (smallholdings).

La Reforma notwithstanding, broad swaths of the Atempa basin remained under the undisputed control of five of the seven early-seventeenth-century congregaciones.[8] Two, Chilapa and Ayahualulco, had been dismantled beyond repair through the combined actions of earlier hacendados and later squatters from Chilapa and Atzacoaloya. The five that survived include Zitlala, Acatlán, Santa Catarina, Atzacoaloya, and San Jerónimo Palantla. Residents of at least two of these, Atzacoaloya and San Jerónimo Palantla, were able to produce documents attesting to their territorial

claims,[9] but none of the five met significant challenges from rival claimants.[10] Perhaps for this reason, residents of the region's surviving congregaciones were slow to submit petitions or to otherwise deal with the agrarian
reform officials.[11] When they finally did, mostly in the 1940s and 1950s, it
was generally a defensive maneuver to prevent encroachment by neighboring communities or to inhibit surveyors from including contested border
areas in grants awarded to others. The swarms of surveyors who had arrived
in the region and the flurry of claims and counterclaims that erupted along
their borders created enough anxiety to induce even those with seemingly
unquestioned control of their land to seek the added security that came with
a grant of confirmación. The resulting properties were known as bienes
comunales (communal resources), held by communities known as *comunidades agrarias* (agrarian communities). These terms of technical jargon
refer, respectively, to an inalienable tract of land held corporately by a
community and to a community that retained the legal right to handle its
internal affairs, particularly regarding land use and land tenure, in accordance with local custom and without outside interference.

A second circumstance was unveiled by the agrarian reform commissions in areas where, for one reason or another, hacendados simply abandoned territorial claims after the 1842 rebellion. The most important of
these areas was the territory (minus Atzacoaloya) covered in the Herrera
purchase. Chilapa's Indians would have had a valid claim to much of this
land had they survived as a cohesive group and not already melted into an
ethnically mestizo working class. Instead, the agrarian reform commissions were confronted with petitions issued by well-organized squatters,
people who had arranged themselves into tight-knit communities. The
commissions eventually dispensed with the petitions submitted by these
groups by granting confirmaciones based on the inaccurate but convenient
assertion that the descendants of the petitioners had held the land "since
time immemorial." In this way, a handful of relatively new villages —
including Xulchuchio, Lodo Grande, La Providencia, Cuadrilla Nueva,
Coaquimisco, Tepehuisco, Pochahuisco, and Topiltepec — joined the older
congregaciones as comunidades agrarias.[12]

A third circumstance, one that proved considerably messier than the
first two, arose in territories where hacendados' territorial claims survived
the 1840s rebellion. Here, too, most land was occupied by squatters who
were generally left alone by the would-be hacendados. Investigators dealt
with the claims of at least ten landowners with holdings in excess of 125
hectares, but petitioners who told investigators that they paid rent were

found in only four villages: Pantitlán (owned by Modesto Acevedo and Isabel Bello), Chautla (Camilio Miranda), Tlacoaxtla (Camilio Miranda), and Zoquitipa (Emilio and Ignacio Silva). Even in these cases, it is not entirely clear that the petitioners' claims were accurate.[13] Circumstances such as those found in Axopilco seem to have been more common. Axopilco was a small village on land ostensibly owned by Ignacio and Emilio Silva, brothers who stood alone among Chilapa's landowners in mounting a legal challenge to the expropriation. When it became clear that their cause was lost, the Silvas requested that the developed portions of their Axopilco holdings, including a trapiche, irrigation works, and small tracts of irrigated sugarcane fields, be left in their possession, as allowed by law. Investigators who surveyed the land reported that they found only the ancient ruins of a trapiche, no developed irrigation systems, and sugarcane grown only on tiny parcels in farmers' house lots (*Diario Oficial,* January 22, 1929).

The earliest petitions for land grants (submitted as early as 1919) were issued by villagers living on land claimed by absentee landowners who lived in Chilapa. Many came from the Ayahualulco area, where squatters who originated in Chilapa and Atzacoaloya had to contend with the claims of Ayahualulco's comuneros as well as the claims of absentee landowners. Because only the would-be landowners were able to produce documents demonstrating ownership, grants to these villages took the form of dotaciones, not the simple confirmaciones that were issued to the intact congregaciones and to the squatters living on the Herrera purchase. The result was the award of an ejido grant. Ejidos and bienes comunales were similar in that both were inalienable awards of large tracts of land. Likewise, recipients of both types of grants were obligated to form similar administrative institutions, known as *comisariados de ejidos* and *comisariados de bienes comunales.* The difference centered on the manner in which land was distributed among petitioners and the authority granted to the comisariados. Recipients of ejido grants were obligated to adhere to methods of land distribution outlined in the applicable agrarian code, a process overseen by the comisariados and federal agrarian reform officials. In the comunidades agrarias, these strictures did not apply; the comisariados were free to handle internal administration and land distribution as they saw fit.

A fourth and final form of land occupancy found by agrarian reform commissions was the messiest of all, and it made the implementation of Article 27 downright ugly as a practical cadastral matter. Within and be-

tween many of the tracts of land awarded to villages through confirmaciones and dotaciones, there were pequeñas propiedades. Some of these
were the core areas of haciendas that remained after the holding had been
reduced to the allowable 125-hectare limit. Others were properties held by
farmers who either opted not to join those from their communities who
submitted a petition or by those who signed petitions but were found by the
investigators to be ineligible on grounds that they already held an amount
of land sufficient for their needs. Practically none of the pequeñas propiedades were precisely delineated by surveyors. They were simply preserved as private property through the insertion of clauses in the award
decrees stating that the embedded or surrounding pequeñas propiedades
were unaffected by the dotación or confirmación. In this way, many ejidos
and bienes comunales had unsurveyed but privately owned enclaves within
them (e.g., *Diario Oficial,* October 8, 1949, and July 2, 1956; Illsley et
al. 2003:12–13; Matías 1997:109–14).[14] Finally, in addition to enclaves
within ejidos and bienes comunales, there were contiguous expanses of
land where farmers did nothing pursuant to Article 27. These were areas
where no threat that could be ameliorated through the agrarian reform
process existed either from absentee landowners in Chilapa or from farmers living in neighboring villages. Most of the area farmed by Chilapa's
labradores, for example, and substantial portions of the middle Ajolotero
and Atempa valleys were held by *pequeños propietarios* (small holders)
who managed their affairs without known incident.

Unlike the inalienable bienes comunales and ejidos, pequeñas propiedades were small parcels of land that could be bought, sold, rented,
used, or left idle as the owner saw fit, at least as a matter of formal law.
There is relatively little in the historical record bearing on the origins
of pequeños propietarios, only indications that they emerged at different
times in different places. Each of the region's major economic transitions
had been accompanied by a fragmentation of some haciendas and the
formation or consolidation of others. For example, pequeñas propiedades
in Acalco, one of the small towns near Ayahualulco, seem to have originated with the partitioning of don Juan de Meza's haciendas at the turn of
the nineteenth century. Likewise, Ahuihuiyuco appears to have been split
into small fragments when don Vicente Vidal sold his properties at about
the same time. Pequeños propietarios found in the immediate environs of
Chilapa were descendants of the late-eighteenth-century labradores. Perhaps the largest numbers, and the most geographically dispersed group,
emerged from among the ranks of the squatters who had spread across the

countryside after the 1842 rebellion. Squatting could be made somewhat less irregular by buying and selling parcels and creating a paper trail that could later be produced to demonstrate the legitimacy of the occupants' territorial claims.[15] Although "laundering" property in this way may seem like a transparent ruse that would fool no one, this technique had been perfected by the Moctezumas, whose original early colonial period prerogatives had involved rights over tribute but should never have included ownership of the vast tracts of land that they nevertheless sold.[16]

Wherever their claims originated, pequeños propietarios had rights as a matter of formal law that were fundamentally different from those accorded to comuneros and *ejidatarios*. Squatters, by definition, had no legal right to their land. As a matter of practical reality, however, the line separating these four groups was much finer than the formal laws governing land tenure would have it. In fact, more than a few rural neighborhoods were populated by villages of pequeños propietarios or squatters (the line here being exceptionally blurry) living in apparent peace until those within one village — overcome by a fit of anxiety or frustration induced by a border dispute — organized themselves and submitted a petition to agrarian reform officials requesting that their inventory of properties be deemed a single tract of bienes comunales by means of a confirmación. The resulting influx of surveyors then induced comparable anxiety among their neighbors, who would repeat the process by requesting a confirmación of their own. In this way, several chain reactions began and swept through portions of the Atempa basin, summarily converting thousands of pequeños propietarios and squatters into comuneros with a few strokes of a pen.

In practice, if not in formal law, the only difference between villages of pequeños propietarios (and squatters) and villages of comuneros, and between either of these and communities of ejidatarios, involved a territory's settlement history and the nature of any perceived territorial threat. Farmers situated on or near land that emerged from the Revolution with an absentee landowner clinging to an ownership claim petitioned for and generally received dotaciones and in this way ended up as ejidatarios. Farmers occupying land not claimed by hacendados became either comuneros with use rights on their village's bienes comunales or pequeños propietarios with a parcel of land amid a larger contiguous block of parcels that were all held by the residents of the same community. It would be a mistake of the highest order to infer from these legal categories that there existed some fundamental difference in the internal political and economic organization of the communities, however. Residents of all the newly founded settlements instituted forms of political organization and governance that were essentially identical to those found in the earlier congregaciones. This was as true of the Spaniards and mestizos who left Chilapa for rural destinations as it was of the Indians from Atzacoaloya who joined them.

REGIONAL POLITICAL INTEGRATION AFTER 1842

That there was a change in the political organization of people living outside Chilapa following the 1842 rebellion is clear by contrasting the findings of tax collectors of the mid-1820s with the institutional arrangements that existed in the years following 1842.[17] In 1825, tax collectors spread through the countryside to collect a newly established head tax. They found households living in three types of political settings. First, the largest group lived in the established congregaciones (organized as described in the preceding chapter). Whereas tribute had previously been collected as a lump sum from town political authorities, the new tax collectors bypassed the established political organization and instead went directly to adult males and heads of households, all of whom were carefully named in the tax rolls along with the amounts collected. A second group consisted of a far smaller number of peones and arrendatarios who lived on hacienda land under the supervision of mayordomos. Like the entries from the congregaciones, the records for taxpayers living in ranch and trapiche sites appear under the heading of a named community, as in Hacienda de Tlaxinga or Laborio de Chautla. There was also a third group, all gente de razón and presumably labradores and forerunners to the pequeños propietarios of the twentieth century. Though small in number, what is most striking and historically unusual about this group is that its members lived in dispersed homesteads rather than in named communities. They were cited in the tax rolls under headings such as Rumbo de Maquiscoatlán (Direction of Maquiscoatlán) or Rumbo de Atempa, all in locations along the boundary separating Zones 1 and 2. Of the 1,916 taxpayers outside of Chilapa, 1,728 lived in the original congregaciones, 117 at ranch or trapiche sites, and 71 in dispersed homesteads.

Scattered homesteads such those documented in 1825, households with no affiliation to a hacienda or an organized and named community, do not appear in any known records postdating the 1842 rebellion. In the previous chapter, I argue that the political climate of the early nineteenth century generally prevented farmers from living in small villages, much less in isolated homesteads. The exception proving the rule lies in the small numbers of labradores, all gente de razón with strong social ties to Chilapa. This group would have had little to fear from the local militia and may themselves have been well represented in the militia's ranks. As taxpayers and commercial farmers, they were doing their part to support the urban center. The militia's attention had instead been directed at the far larger numbers of Indians living in the congregaciones and at the ranch and trapiche sites.

Isolated homesteads of gente de razón living under the protection of Chilapa's militia disappeared after the 1842 rebellion. Any from this group who survived the rebellion either moved to Chilapa or joined with the newly arriving squatters and filled the organizational void that existed in the rebellion's aftermath by organizing community political institutions of their own. Households in rural neighborhoods, some of which were tightly compact clusters of households and others homesteads scattered widely across the landscape, all developed political institutions modeled on those found in the preexisting congregaciones. While capable of mounting lim- ited offensive territorial actions, these institutions were best suited to de- fense. Once control over land was established through occupancy, it was preserved primarily by means of a prohibition on the sale of land to anyone other than a member of the village. Renting land to outsiders was likewise prohibited, though village authorities could and occasionally did allow exceptions when residents could demonstrate economic necessity and offer assurances that the rental agreement was a temporary expedient that posed no threat of permanent alienation of the rented land.

These basic ground rules applied both before and after the agrarian reform laws were implemented after the Mexican Revolution. Further- more, they were enforced equally in villages populated by people who would become comuneros, ejidatarios, and pequeños propietarios, despite the formal rules applying to each of the various classes of landholders. Notably, ejidatarios, who as a matter of formal law were enjoined from selling or renting land under any circumstances, arranged sales and rental agreements among themselves as readily as did anyone else. Conversely, although formal law allowed pequeños propietarios to sell or rent land to whomsoever they pleased, village authorities and assemblies routinely intervened to restrict sale and rental agreements to community members. The formal rules governing land tenure long had the weight of federal law behind them, but this weight proved to be feather-light; the real force shaping tenure patterns consisted of village political institutions and local customs, not deeds, bills of sale, or the pertinent agrarian code.

At this juncture, I must confess that in demonstrating this argument I am severely handicapped by a dearth of firsthand accounts bearing on political relationships between and within communities in the Atempa basin in the years between 1842 and agrarian reform surveys of the 1920s and 1930s. One small exception of an anecdotal nature was written by Adolfo Dollero, an Italian traveler, writer, and amateur geologist and economist who passed through the basin with a companion late in 1909 (Dollero 1911:602–607). The Dollero party must have telegraphed ahead from Chilpancingo, because upon arriving in Chilapa from the west, they were greeted by no less a figure than the district prefect (successor to the late colonial subdelegado). Although the following year another group of visiting notables reported that the city had one respectable hotel and numerous inns for the poor (Andrade 1911:84), Dollero, in the finest tradition of the pampered traveler, and much as would the NHK film director many years later, lumped the hotel together with the inns and dismissed them all as inadequate. He was instead quartered in the prefect's home. For present purposes, we can skip over his stay in Chilapa and cut straight to his departure. With his companion and a Nahuatl-speaking guide recommended by the prefect, Dollero traveled north in the direction of Tepecuacuilco and Iguala. Departing just before sunrise, the party came first to Acatlán, where they intended to have breakfast. They were met by "Indios poco civiles" (uncivilized Indians). Their entry into the town was blocked by a party led by the gobernador (the highest-ranking community political official), who informed them that they were not welcome, that they would not be fed, and that they should continue on their way. Expecting the same or worse in Zitlala, the travelers bypassed that community altogether and did not stop (or find food) until they made it to Totolcintla, on the Río Balsas well north of the Atempa basin. Dollero and his party almost certainly arrived in Acatlán with the strongest of recommendations from the district prefect, and they were accompanied by a guide and translator who would have ensured that the travelers' references and intentions were fully understood. That Acatlán's gobernador, speaking for the broader community, would disregard the prefect's solicitations vividly demonstrates that as of 1909 the prefect's influence did not extend beyond Chilapa itself.

In this, not much had changed between Dollero's visit and my first experiences in the Atempa basin in the late 1980s and early 1990s. I too moved about the basin under the protection of a talisman in the form of a written solicitation for cooperation addressed to community officials by Chilapa's *presidente municipal* (successor to the district prefect). By this time, roads and vehicles had been built, and travelers passing through rural communities, though not common, were not the novelty that they had been in 1909. I was met only once, in Teposcuautla, by a reception committee akin to the one the people of Acatlán had rolled out for Dollero and his party.[18] More often, I had one of two experiences upon first entering a rural community. If I was simply passing through, people would surround me in an odd cordon that formed at a distance of about fifty meters in all directions. It moved with me, mysteriously retaining its shape and structure no matter how unpredictable my movements. Cordons of this sort were staffed mostly by women and children, who stood and gazed apprehensively from their distant posts. The work of ensuring that I not slacken my pace was left to their noisy, if not quite vicious, dogs. If I planned to stop in a community to conduct some sort of detailed inquiry, I went to the church, clinic, school, a tienda, or anyplace where I could get near enough to someone to inquire as to the probable whereabouts of the community's comisario (successor to the earlier gobernador). My goal was to locate the comisario, present him with my letter, offer an oral explanation of my purpose, and humbly request cooperation. Often these gestures sufficed to collapse the cordon described above; most often, they were met with a shrug of indifference and some polite conversation, first with the comisario and later with newly reassured residents.

On several occasions, I was told by a comisario that he lacked the authority to respond to my request and that I should return at a later date, usually the evening of my appearance, to present my request to an assembly of the community's principales, political officeholders, and adult males. Bearing packages of unfiltered cigarettes and a bottle of mescal in the customary manner of a supplicant, I attended about a dozen such meetings. The first couple of times I felt positively awful. After all, my "request" was really more of an announcement that in the coming weeks and months I might be found in or around the town and that I might have questions, which could be answered or not as seemed fitting, about people's efforts to make a living. Indeed, I first feared that setting in motion a community's political machinery and inconveniencing its entire adult male population over an issue this trivial would put me at some risk of creating, not averting, reticence among would-be informants. As it turned out, my requests for permission to conduct inquiries were always granted quickly and expeditiously. Most often the presiding principales dispensed with my request in a matter of minutes and then turned the assembly's attention to much more weighty community matters.

Before considering samples of these weighty matters, let me turn back to Chilapa for just a moment to offer a few incidental observations about the business end of the higher-level administrative and judicial institutions that, at least on paper, had authority over the comisarios of rural villages. When I first arrived in the Atempa basin, formal law, if not order, was enforced among a regional population of more than 75,000 by a contingent of something over a dozen uniformed municipal police officers. Armed with ancient and, one suspects, unloaded small-caliber weapons, a group of six to eight could be seen coming and going from Chilapa and traveling about on rural roads while mounted in the bed of a rickety pickup truck. As one branch of the force conducted these rural patrols, the point of which I never discovered, a second group, usually two in number, stayed behind and held the city's centrifugal social forces in check from an emplacement (a chair) strategically positioned in front of the municipal jail and the palacio municipal. This was no Swiss Guard. Between 1987 and 1991, I spent some twenty months living on or within a couple of blocks of the zocalo; through it all, I never saw the police do anything beyond conducting their ineffectual patrols and holding their position (often while napping) at the palacio municipal. On occasion, the local paper and the town crier (papers were sold by criers who plied the city streets) would conspire to ensure that all in the city were made aware of the latest display of depravity by the region's criminal element, but even the most exaggerated accounts of crime cast the municipal police in little more than a ceremonial role.

In truly exceptional circumstances, a category that includes the more colorful of the criers' subjects, the municipal police drew reinforcements from state and federal police or military forces stationed in Chilpancingo. In the late 1980s, reinforcements of this sort could be mobilized and on hand in Chilapa in a matter of a few hours; before the road that linked Chilapa to Chilpancingo was built, the municipal police had to hold their positions for at least two to three days before they could be reinforced. Although a fairly common presence in the late 1980s, until the 1950s these more lethal organizations were drawn into the Atempa basin in only the most exceptional circumstances, usually when there emerged some direct threat to the city government in Chilapa. When state or federal troops did enter the region, they remained under separate command and did not involve themselves in the everyday business of local administration.[19] This was a charge that after the 1842 rebellion fell to the local police, a force whose composition was, as far as I can tell, very similar to the one I observed in the late 1980s.

Where these admittedly impressionistic observations bear directly on our subject is in regard to the imposition of judicial decrees, the enforcement of property rights, or any similar exercise of authority or control by district or municipal officials in the social and economic affairs of those living in the countryside. The broader issue can be stated as a general proposition: when concentrated in the hands of a few, property or wealth is vulnerable and must be preserved by means of a standing coercive force, either by police or by a militia of some sort. In a nutshell, this fairly describes the circumstances of the Atempa basin prior to 1842. The successful extraction of tribute or tax payments from households and the territorial control enjoyed by hacendados were made possible only because behind both existed the threat that Chilapa's militia would rain violence down upon the uncooperative. The vulnerability of wealth and property diminishes as it becomes more widely dispersed through a population, as it came to be after 1842; under these circumstances, a large standing police force or militia had no meaningful role to play in sustaining the structure of the regional economy. Although Chilapa often hosted garrisons of one or another military force in the years after 1842, these were not under the direction and control of local officials and practically never became involved in local affairs. The presence of troops in Chilapa did little more than drain the city of resources and expose it to attack.[20]

Outside Chilapa, the institutions that did the daily work of managing property and preserving the peace were hierarchies of unsalaried civil officeholders, assemblies of male townsmen, and councils of principales, not the formal institutions of the Mexican state.[21] Villages that received dotaciones and confirmaciones after the Revolution created at least the shell of an administrative structure, the comisariados, as a polite acknowledgment of the applicable laws, but otherwise only one official, the comisario, had standing recognized by outside authorities. As with other officeholders within village political hierarchies, the comisarios were elected by the male assemblymen and served one-year terms of office before graduating into the ranks of the principales. Through the period of his tenure in office, a comisario served as the focal point of interaction between villagers and municipal (or district) officials. In theory, this was the point of administrative articulation between the local community and Chilapa's district or *municipio* administration. In practice, comisarios held political standing in their villages that was somewhat below that of the principales. This subordination of comisarios to both municipal authorities in Chilapa and the councils of principales commonly left comisarios to deal with conflicting mandates, which were routinely decided in favor of the principales.

For example, in early January 1991, I walked in on a village assembly in Xochitempa, where ongoing elections were taking place in defiance of a new push within the state to enforce a law that would have comisarios serve a three-year term rather than the customary one-year term. Although the law applied only to the office of the comisario, because this office was embedded in the village's hierarchy of political positions the change would have upended the regular pattern of succession through which men cycled through the course of their lives. Those in Xochitempa, as in every other village in the Atempa basin, wanted nothing to do with it. Along with others, Xochitempa's comisario merely tendered his resignation to the presidente municipal, and the town convened an election in accordance with long-standing custom. Now readers familiar with Mexico will appreciate that in 1991 there could hardly have been a more grotesque manner of assault on the dignity of a midlevel Mexican politician than the spectacle of democracy erupting unbidden among his subordinates. Just the same, the mass resignation of comisarios went far beyond anything the presidente municipal had the power to prevent, a fact that he was forced to acknowledge to the state governor, the local press, and Chilapa's indomitable criers.

The exact composition of village governments varied from one to the next, depending on a village's size and the particulars of its economy. There were differences as well in the titles attached to the offices, with many left untranslated from Nahuatl (Gutiérrez 1988:115–18). To use the terms most familiar to anthropologists, the most common positions included the comisario (or, in earlier times, the gobernador), a number of *juezes* (judges), *alguaciles* (police), *regidores* (councilmen), *alférezes* (deputies to higher-ranked officials), and *topiles* (messengers). Incumbents to these positions handled the routine business of life in a small community; they adjudicated minor disputes, jailed annoying drunks, mediated domestic disturbances, cleaned or otherwise maintained the comisaría, and organized public works projects. Any issue that went beyond the routine or affected all or most of a town's residents, as, for example, the unexpected appearance of a foreign anthropologist wanting answers to questions, could be referred to a general assembly of the town's adult males. These met in the comisaría, a public meeting hall that doubled as an office for the comisario and a courthouse for the juezes. In a fashion, the comisario and the principales presided at community assemblies. In those assemblies that I attended, debate was robust and freewheeling; decisions were made not by majority vote but by simply arguing until one side grew exhausted from the effort and yielded to the other. If passions ran high and no consensus was reached, the item was shelved. Where internal dissension had territorial dimensions, it not infrequently led to a fissioning of the village. Thus, if sentiment within a localized faction of a village held that the broader assembly was insufficiently supportive of their particular needs, they could organize a set of parallel institutions, coin a town name, petition for recognition from the ayuntamiento, and in this way create a new community.

Beyond the minimal components of a village government, many of the larger towns had particular problems around which committees were formed. Among the best documented was the constellation of government institutions found in Acatlán in the early 1990s and described by Marcos Matías Alonso, a native of the community and a trained anthropologist (Matías 1997:98–125).[22] Acatlán had at least seven hierarchically organized branches of civil government. There was the ubiquitous *comisariado municipal,* structured as described above. Following the community's successful petition for a confirmación (received in 1956), a parallel administrative structure, the comisariado de bienes comunales, was formed to handle interactions with agrarian reform officials. Next, there was a *consejo de vigilancia* (oversight council) charged, among other things, with conducting periodic patrols of the town's territorial borders to verify the proper placement of boundary markers (typically stone cairns) and to prevent encroachment by farmers, cattlemen, goat herders, or wood gatherers from neighboring villages. The *comité guarda campo* (crop protection committee) oversaw the pasturing of livestock with an eye toward preventing animals from damaging standing crops or overgrazing particular portions of the common pasture lands. Finally, there were three *comités de huerteros* (truck crop production committees), each overseeing the maintenance and allocation of water from one of the town's three small canal irrigation systems.

Matías's description of the functioning of these various councils and committees is rich in details pertinent to my purpose, but a couple of items are so directly on point that I cannot pass them over without comment. One of these involves the comité guarda campo (see Matías 1997:101–105). The daily work of the comité involved ensuring that horses, burros, cattle, and goats were pastured in rotation and were moved by their owners from forested hills in the rainy season onto harvested fields in the dry season.

During critical times of the year, the comité members conducted thrice-daily patrols to ensure that no animals had invaded fields with standing crops. Repeated violations of the rules could result in a comunero's being stripped of the right to pasture animals on the town's commons. Comuneros were permitted to have no more than five animals grazing on common lands, no more than two of which could be oxen used as draft animals. Two oxen formed a yunta, and thus comuneros were allowed to own only a single yunta. During the planting and growing season, draft animals were given privileged access to the limited supply of high-quality pasturage because the animals needed to be well nourished to pull plows through the town's extensive tracts of dense vertisols. In explaining the underlying rationale for these restrictions, Matías cited Acatlán's limited pasturage and the danger that overgrazing posed to forests and fields. But he also noted that the rules were aimed at preventing individual comuneros from accumulating too large a share of the community's resources. This threat came to a head with respect to yuntas, a vital item of capital equipment that substantial numbers of farmers (how substantial is unclear) did not possess. Farmers without yuntas had to rent them from yunta owners. In prohibiting individuals from owning more than a single yunta, the comité accomplished two related ends. First, it ensured that no comunero developed anything like a monopoly on the community's limited supply of yuntas. Second, it prevented an individual farmer from working or otherwise exercising control over more than a few hectares of arable land. The restriction on yunta ownership was thus part of a broader effort to limit the concentration of land in the hands of individual comuneros.

This brings me to a point featured in anthropological discussions of the 1950s and 1960s, when there arose a lively debate about the extent to which the political institutions of Mexican communities served to level wealth differences among community members. Most of the ensuing argument centered on the costs associated with serving in particular offices within the civil and the parallel religious hierarchy of offices. This line of research and argumentation stemmed from suggestions put forth by some (e.g., Wolf 1956) that higher-level offices were so costly that only members of an embryonic upper class could afford the expense. The assignment of these offices to rich individuals drained them of resources and thereby nipped emerging class differences in the bud. Other anthropologists were less impressed with the efficacy of this mechanism and adduced evidence to show that comparatively rich individuals remained comparatively rich even after serving terms in the supposedly taxing offices (e.g., Cancian 1965). The debate preoccupied anthropologists well into the 1970s, when it finally faded without a clear resolution. I have no particular desire to see it rekindled, but I would point out that relevant avenues of inquiry were left unexplored in the original debate. Much attention was directed at wealth transfers that resulted from the performance of duties associated with political (and religious) offices, but little attention was directed at much more blatant means used to flatten wealth differences. The actions of Acatlán's guarda campos is one example. Another, which in the Atempa basin was perhaps the most effective of all, was to replicate internally the technique used to great effect against absentee landowners: the organized land invasion.[23]

The most consequential land invasions in the Atempa basin centered on the great expanses of land claimed by Chilapa's hacendados and occurred behind the poorly documented fog of the middle to late nineteenth century. Land invasions did not end with this, however, and enough examples were recorded or witnessed in the twentieth century to permit a reconstruction of the general outlines of the process. These more recent examples involved much smaller tracts of land only because earlier episodes had so effectively disposed of the claims of those with more grandiose territorial ambitions. Indeed, the more recent episodes are especially interesting precisely because they were as likely to involve the holdings of local pequeños propietarios and comuneros as the holdings of absentee landowners living in Chilapa. If a consensus could be reached among neighbors, particularly if the consensus was reached in a formal village assembly, then any property determined to be unreasonably large was vulnerable. The customary understanding of "unreasonable" in this connection evolved through time and from one village to the next, evolving alongside the size of the village's population and the perceived degree of land scarcity. By the late twentieth century, any farmer in the Atempa basin who claimed to own (or hold in usufruct) more land than could be worked by his household would most likely have run the risk of expropriation. The risk would have increased exponentially once this size threshold was exceeded.

I witnessed an example of a village's political institutions asserting control over arable land early in the summer of 1990. The setting was a formal assembly in Lodo Grande that had convened to hear my appeal for cooperation. This village had long been populated by pequeños propietarios, descendants of squatters who took the opportunity occasioned by don Manuel Herrera's death to make themselves at home on a portion of his former estate. Seized by a localized outbreak of territorial paranoia that swept through the vicinity in the late 1960s, the community applied for, and in 1981 received, a confirmación that changed the legal classification of the village's lands from pequeñas propiedades to bienes comunales. As a purely practical matter, this change left unaffected the town's governing institutions, and the drama that I saw unfold could thus have played out in the same fashion no matter what legal classifications attached to the land and to the protagonists. At the assembly, my request was handled in a matter of moments, and the group's attention promptly shifted to the case of a comunero who had committed the incendiary act of renting a parcel of land to someone from neighboring Teposcuautla. The comunero and his family had held the land "since time immemorial." He had argued that a recent decline in his health and changes in the demographic composition of his household had left him unable to work the parcel but in need of the income that renting it would generate. The only person he could find who was willing to enter into a rental agreement was a farmer from the neighboring town. The debate over the propriety of the arrangement was passionate and interminable, and it ended without an apparent consensus; in the end, the rental relationship was left intact (the field had already been planted) but the landowner was given a clear understanding that the rental agreement was to be terminated once the crop was harvested. Many, perhaps all, present at the assembly felt sympathy for the landowner, but this was offset by a stronger sense that any form of alienation of land to an outsider was improper. The assembly came but a small step from organizing an effort to prevent the arrendatario from resuming work in the field. This circumstance was averted, and the rental arrangement was allowed to continue, because there were those in the village, mostly younger men, who felt that the changing nature of the local economy and the declining profitability of farming had already rendered the blanket prohibition on alienating land to outsiders an impractical relic of an earlier era. This argument was echoed at the national level a few years later with the amendment of Article 27 and the publication of the Agrarian Code of 1994. As of 1990, Lodo Grande's customary prohibition on alienating land to outsiders, even under transitory rental agreements, was showing signs of strain but nevertheless remained in force.

That said, had the rented parcel of land in Lodo Grande been held not by a poor and aging farmer but instead by a farmer who held more land than he regularly planted, then the scene that I witnessed might well have ended differently. Matías provides an example that illustrates the mechanics of a land invasion (1997:109–11). This was a case involving an eighteen-hectare tract of irrigated land claimed by an absentee landowner from Chilapa. The community first attempted to gain control of the land through proper legal channels, but the effort badly backfired when the agrarian reform investigators responded by confirming the legitimacy of the land-owner's claim and formally verifying that the tract of land fell below the legal size limit. Frustrated, a group of twenty comuneros from Acatlán took matters into their own hands and, in 1982, liberated the tract by sowing it in crops and working it as their own. Agrarian reform officials intervened on behalf of the landowner, at which point the community assembly went into conclave and emerged with a collective plan of action. It was decided that the twenty squatters could not hold the land alone and that the safest course of action would be for the community as a whole to assume control. For the next six years, great teams of men, women, and children collec-tively plowed, planted, weeded, and harvested crops on the contested land as a joint enterprise. In 1990, the comisariado determined that the immedi-ate threat from the landowner and agrarian reform officials had passed and that it was time for a more lasting arrangement. The eighteen hectares were divided into thirty parcels (some of one-quarter hectare, others of one-half hectare), each rented for three-year periods before passing to someone else. Landless or near-landless comuneros had priority when determining who would be allowed to rent parcels. The rent payments were held in a legal defense fund that was overseen by a newly created committee.

This case attracted more attention and involved more legal maneuver-ing than most land invasions because one party to the incident was an absentee landowner in Chilapa, because agrarian reform officials became involved, and because the land was rich, irrigated bottomland. Most pe-queñas propiedades were held by rural villagers and consisted of dry-farmed land or pasture. Even so, if ownership claims were asserted over more land than could be actively worked by a single household, there existed a risk of takeover. This was a threat that plagued agrarian reform officials beginning with the initial surveys of the 1920s, when numbers of pequeños propietarios opted not to join with others in their community in petitioning for dotaciones but instead requested that agrarian reform offi-cials recognize and protect their territorial claims (e.g., *Diario Oficial*, December 21, 1936). By midcentury, pequeños propietarios who feared squatters, not dotaciones, had become those most likely to turn to agrarian reform officials for protection.

In the end, the cases of land invasion that have come to the attention of outsiders, either to anthropologists or to agrarian reform officials, are merely the tip of the iceberg. Pequeños propietarios exhibited tremendous reluctance to solicit assistance from agrarian reform officials in resolving these sorts of issues, in part because a powerful stigma attached to any who would willingly invite municipio, state, or federal political authorities to meddle in a village's internal affairs but also because it has long been appreciated that when set against community sentiment these authorities stood little chance of imposing an outcome. In the end, pequeños pro-piedades, whether owned by absentee landowners in Chilapa or by fellow villagers, were steadily whittled down to dimensions that were sanctioned by evolving and progressively less tolerant community standards.

The result can be seen, if somewhat vaguely, in figures collected in the decennial agricultural censuses of the late twentieth century. Before 1970, these censuses were administered in too small a portion of the region to be useful in the present connection; in addition, unfortunate changes were made in the content of questionnaires used by census takers and in the classes and aggregations of published data. After 1970, these problems became less acute, and it is in these data that one can find the following genuine pearl of a comparison: in 1970, the municipio of Chilapa was home to eighty-eight individuals who reportedly each owned tracts of land in excess of 5 hectares. Taken together, this group claimed 1,649 hectares of land, an average of nearly 19 hectares per landowner (DGE 1975:7). Twenty years later, the municipio had only fifty-one individuals who fell into this class. Collectively, the 1990 group claimed to own only 419 hectares, an average of just over 8 hectares each (INEGI 1994:84–85). What accounts for the discrepancy? And where were agrarian reform offi-cials in all of this?

The magnitude of this change is greater than anything that can be attributed to a predictable cycle of fragmentation resulting from the death of landowners and the subdivision of estates among heirs. Twenty years is too short a period for this to occur; in any case, it would not be likely to have resulted in a simultaneous decline in both the number of large landholdings and their overall area. Rather, if a fragmentation of holdings were occurring as part of a generational land transfer, the number of such landholdings might reasonably be expected to rise rather than fall. Nor have I ever heard that there was any sort of rush by landowners to sell land through this period. To the contrary, throughout the years that I have worked in the Atempa basin, land has been highly valued and would be eagerly acquired by Chilapa's elites, among others, given the opportunity. As for the involvement of agrarian reform officials, these stood squarely, if ineffectually, in defense of the rights of landowners, having long since expropriated and redistributed all land in the municipio that met the legal criteria of affectability. The fragmentation of land evident in these censuses instead occurred despite the occasional involvement of agrarian reform officials, as we saw above in the case of Acatlán.

Most of the territorial claims that were reported to census takers involved pasture and wooded uplands that were marginal for agricultural purposes. They were assertions of ownership rights only and had little or no practical effect on the ground. Population growth and increasingly acute pressure on land through the interval between 1970 and 1990 led farmers to expand into ever-more-marginal areas, and in so doing, they steadily exposed the hollowness of the landowners' claims. What these censuses capture, in other words, is a continuation of a pattern that took shape in 1842, one in which farmers routinely banded together and simply appropriated the land they needed. Landowners were free to proffer ownership claims, but to actually exercise the prerogatives of private ownership required more coercive might than landowners commanded.

WEALTH AND POWER IN THE PREINDUSTRIAL ATEMPA BASIN

In the absence of a standing militia or police capable of projecting force outside of Chilapa, the only institutions that retained the power to prevent individuals from simply rooting themselves on a piece of land were the raucous public assemblies, the hierarchies of political officials, and the councils of principales found in rural villages. Through discussion and debate at assembly meetings and the consent, either overt or implied, of the principales, a village could organize a group — which those with no sense of diplomacy might call a mob — that was equally capable of protecting or overriding a claim to village resources. The result was a striking measure of equality among households in rural communities. Households controlling tracts of arable land in excess of five hectares were exceedingly rare. So too were landless households. With a limited number of apparent exceptions, rental arrangements were uncommon, and those that existed were more likely to involve younger sons awaiting an inheritance or others in some comparable stage of sociological transition than members of an entrenched class of arrendatarios. Economic inequality was held to a tolerable minimum by community political institutions not so much through the compulsory redistribution of wealth, as had been suggested by an earlier generation of anthropologists, as through a more direct, if inchoate, process of allocating rights of access to land (and livestock) among community members.

With the 1842 rebellion, both in the city and in the countryside, there came to be a striking absence of concentrated wealth in the Atempa basin. Certainly a measure of concentration and the resulting scourge of economic inequality was not completely erased after the rebellion, particularly in the urban center. Valuable real estate (urban if not rural) and much moveable wealth remained in the hands of Chilapa's elites. Skilled craftsmen, trained professionals, and, above all, the city's wealthier merchants were in positions to accumulate compact and portable wealth in the form of silver pesos. This created a vulnerability that left this the segment of the society that would have benefited the most from organized protection. In the absence of such protection, elites were forced to handle security on their own. The problem was compounded by the absence of banking institutions prior to the mid-twentieth century. These security concerns gave rise to the custom of burying hoards of currency in house lots to protect the money from plundering armies or would-be thieves.[24] Another form of moveable wealth was embodied in the merchandise of comerciantes. This was safe enough once it arrived in Chilapa. After all, what would a plundering army or a would-be thief do with a trove of Spaulding boxing gloves, Hinds Honey and Almond Cream, or Pebeco toothpaste?[25] Once the countryside had been cleansed of haciendas, the region's most vulnerable manifestation of wealth became this sort of merchandise as it was being transported to Chilapa and rebozos as they were being transported away. Through most of the period between 1842 and the Mexican Revolution, there was very little security along Mexico's commercial thoroughfares, and bandits made regular sport of capturing the cargo of arrieros and ransoming it back to Chilapa's merchants (e.g., Arce 1872:5–6, 21–22; Salazar 1998:221). But if the risks of long-distance commerce were high, so too were the merchants' profits, at least by the standards of the Atempa basin.

Of capital equipment there was very little; what did exist presented no particular concerns in terms of either access or security. The city's major industry used looms and spinning wheels that were technologically simple devices made by local carpenters at minimal cost (see Muñoz 1963:94; Sayer 1988). Some households drew upon incidental labor (Muñoz 1963:94) supplied by young apprentices, widows, orphans, or others living on the fringes of the social order. Among these were probably fair

numbers of younger sons and (especially) daughters from rural households, sent to the city seasonally to earn wages and to remit currency back
to their natal households. Yet most textile manufacturing was done using
labor available within producers' households and not with hired labor
at all. In the early twentieth century, one or two elite merchants established rebozo workshops, the largest on record with twenty looms (Muñoz
1963:94), and there were other "factories" devoted to the production of
soap, cooking oil, and aguardiente (Andrade 1911:83). These were exceptions and not the rule, however, and even in these cases the proprietors
were forced to compete for labor with independent weavers and against the
allure of squatting in the countryside. In the end, the city never developed
an entrenched urban proletariat, nor did it have a bourgeoisie worthy of the
name; labor unrest, accordingly, was unknown.

Chilapa's political institutions suffered a grievous blow in the 1842
rebellion and thereafter played only a minor role in protecting property.
District or municipio officials lost any clout they once held in the surrounding hinterland, leaving the city as a small island with a local government
loosely articulated with the state and federal governments. It existed amid a
vast sea of self-governing agricultural communities. These were populated
by farmers whose relationship to municipio, district, state, and federal
political institutions varied along a continuum that began with indifference
and ended with overt hostility. One of the most pressing problems faced by
Chilapa's political authorities was revenue. Tax collection in the countryside had ceased following 1842 (e.g., Arce 1872:11). The city government had to make do with amounts that could be collected from small
taxes, fees, and surcharges levied on various types of activities in the urban
center. Fees were charged for the right to conduct commerce, for example,
including commerce in the daily and weekly markets. There were taxes on
the consumption of paper and fees for notary services and for the entry of
vital statistics in the civil registry. Individually the taxes, fees, and surcharges amounted to relatively little, but collectively they sufficed to support a collection of salaried officials and minions who attended to the basic
organizational tasks that life in a city required.

I conclude this chapter by returning to a question raised in the discussion of the ideological underpinnings of the postrevolutionary Mexican
government. To sustain the argument that the Mexican Revolution, the
1917 Constitution, and the implementation of agrarian reform were decisive forces in shaping political and economic relationships in the Atempa
basin, one would have to answer the following question in the affirmative:

did the implementation of the reforms result in significant changes in the region's political economy? The weight of the evidence compels one to respond unhesitatingly in the negative. Even the earliest and most enthusiastic petitioners sought dotaciones simply to preserve a status quo that had them already in possession of land. This was true, as well, among those who later submitted petitions for confirmaciones. Through the decades separating the 1842 rebellion and the Mexican Revolution, ownership claims by would-be hacendados in Chilapa abounded, but the actual exercise of ownership rights was a very different matter in that possession and occupancy trumped formal property titles and bills of sale. In this, nothing changed after the Revolution. Far from being protectors of the rural masses, agrarian reform officials bought out Chilapa's hacendados and made themselves the outside agents who would impose rules and restrictions on the Atempa basin's farmers. In this, the officials made no bigger dent in local custom than had their predecessors. Farmers had opportunistically invoked elements of Article 27 for strategic purposes, but they proceeded to treat the formal rules of the Agrarian Code with an indifference that was every bit as superb as had been their earlier posture with respect to Chilapa's hacendados. Agrarian communities in the Atempa basin had their own means of dealing with land that neither Chilapa's hacendados nor twentieth-century agrarian reform officials significantly altered.

It was not through these overt political means that the Mexican government finally gained the ability to exercise its will, if a government could be said to have a will, over those living in the Atempa basin. The region's preindustrial economy, the material underpinning of the political institutions discussed in this chapter, was structured in a way that left households impervious to these sorts of outside influences. As long as rain continued to fall, those in the countryside faced no threats that they could not overcome with a bit of organization and a dash of collective resolve. Farmers benefited from healthy market demand in the city, but nothing the government did before the late twentieth century caused much of a change in this respect. Indeed, the region's only essential point of interaction with the outside was that provided by the city's merchants and arrieros, and here the allure of profit sufficed to sustain the required contacts. Yet there were underlying weaknesses in the Atempa basin's preindustrial economy, weaknesses that would have been familiar throughout much of the preindustrial world. Political liberty is all well and good, but those who enjoy it unfortunately must eat. And it was on this rather major point that things in the Atempa basin went awry.

FIVE

MATURATION AND DECLINE

The 1842 rebellion brought an ignominious end to any meaningful political integration at the regional level, but it had exactly the opposite result with respect to the economy. Farmers operating behind the protective curtains formed by their local communities' political institutions became free to adjust their household production strategies in response to opportunities that varied by location within the basin. The result was an urban hinterland with recognizable patterns of internal economic differentiation. This hinterland had sprung into being in the rebellion's immediate aftermath following only a brief period of adjustment, during which the market calibrated a suitable deployment of producers among rural and urban sectors of the economy. Among those in the region whose livelihood rested on artisanal or agricultural production, the years that followed must have been positively glorious. Land was effectively free for the taking, requiring only that farmers participate in and submit to the local town assemblies, committees, and councils. Urban politicians were forced to adjust to a domain of sharply reduced dimensions and had to learn to ignore the piteous entreaties of would-be landowners, but elsewhere in the city, weavers, craftsmen, merchants, and shoppers busily went about their business. Demand in the city's daily and weekly markets remained robust, yet supplies were more forthcoming than ever before and at a newly affordable prices.[1]

Both 1793 and 1842 are convenient years to mark transitions in the political economy of the Atempa basin, even though both transitions were really processes that played out over several years rather than events with a definite and recognizable beginning and end. It is more difficult to achieve similar chronological exactitude with respect to the next great historical transition, namely, the transformation of the regional economy from a preindustrial to an industrial footing. Glimpses of the future could be seen, though perhaps not always recognized, as early as the mid-nineteenth century, when, for example, Chilapa's textile producers shifted from the use of locally spun thread to a machine-made product. A similar harbinger arrived early in the twentieth century when reboceros found their supply of natural dyes replaced by lower-quality synthetics (Muñoz 1963:96–97). A still more jolting apparition appeared on January 10, 1926. With a show of pageantry and jubilation befitting a royal coronation, practically all of Chilapa turned out on that day to witness the spectacle of an automobile lumbering across a bridge over the Río Ajolotero and into the city (Casarrubias 1989:147–48). It was a machine that had been pushed, prodded, pulled, lifted, rolled, and otherwise conveyed through the mountains and barrancas between Chilapa and Chilpancingo, for what purpose I would not venture to guess. Eleven years later, the approximate path taken by those who engaged in this heroic effort had been expanded into what passed as a road over which one could, at a price few in the region could afford, catch a bus to the state capital and from there to the world at large. The twentieth century was full of small milestones like these. When experienced singly, or even if one took a moment to reflect on those that accumulated over a period of several years, they would hardly have been recognized as epochal.

That said, the industrial transformation of this or any preindustrial economy has an attribute that earlier historical transitions did not, one that allows, given the appropriate information, a reasonably precise temporal demarcation. Whereas these other transitions involved a mere change in the organizational structure of the regional economy (specifically, the regional economy's first appearance in 1793 and its internal reorganization and adjustment in 1842), industrialization was a different order of event altogether. Industrialization likewise witnessed a wholesale restructuring of political and economic relationships but went well beyond these things in that it involved a fundamental change in the production system itself. No longer was the economy built around a set of technologies and social institutions that collectively transformed sunlight, rainfall, and seeds into food and distributed this among consuming households. With industrialization, there was instead a fundamental change in production technologies and in the underlying energy sources that powered them. Sunlight, rainfall, and seeds continued to play a role, but this was greatly overshadowed by the use of technologies powered primarily by the controlled combustion of fossil fuels. In marking the onset of industrialization in the Atempa basin, we shall be looking for a key moment when there emerged demonstrable and direct physical dependence on fossil fuel–based technologies.

This moment did not arrive for all households in the Atempa basin at exactly the same time or in exactly the same way. For example, re-bozo producers had piggybacked atop industrialized producers with the mid-nineteenth-century adoption of machine-made thread. As the indus-trialized world expanded and inched its way toward the Atempa basin, many similar adaptations emerged. What this selective exploitation by the Atempa basin's preindustrial producers of opportunities created by indus-trialization elsewhere lacked, and what developed within the basin only much more recently, was direct physical dependence on industrial produc-tion and distribution technologies. This arose in the Atempa basin only in the 1960s; even then, the beginnings were tentative. At first, it involved only farmers in portions of the countryside, urban consumers in Chilapa, and newly introduced vehicular transportation systems that linked the two groups. It was a fragile beginning, one that could have been reversed or forestalled insofar as the vehicles, at least during the earliest years, did not so much lift a physical impediment to the movement of goods as they did lighten the associated burden. The depth of dependence on in-dustrial technologies changed by several orders of magnitude in the late 1970s: this is when industrialization took root and became irreversible, as the Atempa basin's population rocketed past numbers that could be sus-tained by the use of preindustrial production techniques and the resources available within the basin. With this change, the industrial revolution in the Atempa basin was complete.

I must admit to some temptation at this juncture to take a moment to wax nostalgic at all that has been lost and perhaps to issue a cynical broadside at industrialization's tremendous social toll. Yet to do this would be a disservice to the many in the Atempa basin for whom the industrial revolution came not as an unwelcome imposition but as a godsend that could not have arrived quickly enough. We will have occasion to see at least some aspects of the economic and political toll it has exacted, but I must point out that when industrialization finally transformed the political economy of the Atempa basin, it swept away a preindustrial system that had already outlived its useful life. The year 1947 stands out in this regard. This year witnessed a monumental collapse of Chilapa's rebozo industry, which cast into stark relief deep flaws in the preindustrial regional econ-omy, flaws that had, in the approach to 1947, left the economy increas-ingly unstable and made an eventual collapse inevitable. The problem was rooted in the balancing act required to keep inter- and intraregional trade in passable harmony. The problem was not simply one of delivering food to the city in adequate amounts, though this was part of it. The regional economy arrived at a point of collapse through an insidious process of slowly rising and increasingly volatile urban food prices. As the cost of living in the city progressed along an inexorable rise, it gradually eroded the profit margins accruing to the city's reboceros and the merchants on whom they relied. The point arrived, in 1947, when these margins fell too low and the rebozo industry abruptly contracted. This triggered a cascade of economic effects that swept up city and country alike, forcing practically all of the region's inhabitants to reevaluate their economic options. What this reevaluation revealed was that they had very few options indeed, and none that was especially attractive.

We will never know whether, given time, people in the Atempa basin could have overcome the midcentury economic crisis and re-created a coherent and tolerably stable regional economy without outside assistance. This is because the Mexican government moved into the breach that was created with the rebozo industry's collapse by introducing programs and instituting policies that proved too tempting to ignore. The government's movements were initially tentative and halting but gathered steam as improvements in transportation and communication offered broader scope. Setting aside infrastructural investments and the temporary employment opportunities these created, the government's initial interventions involved subsidy programs aimed first at artisanal producers and later at farmers. Particularly after construction on Highway 93 was completed in the early 1970s, government agencies intervened directly in the market, manipulating prices for basic goods and services in ways that attracted ever-greater numbers of people into sectors of the economy that relied on industrial inputs.

Given the grim desperation that pervaded the region, one could hardly find fault with the actions of the responsible government officials. Yet government officials came and went, and those who came did not always share the knowledge and priorities of their predecessors. From the perspective of those who have lived in the Atempa basin in the past fifty years, the government as a whole has seemed possessed of the attention span of a proverbial mayfly, barely seeing one initiative beyond the planning stage before flitting on to the next. The result has been a string of wild economic gyrations as people have tumbled into and out of momentarily favored branches of the economy. Something over a decade ago, there came some recognition that things had gone crazy and that the government had taken on more regulatory functions than it could sustain. This was perhaps a sensible read, but what could be done about it? To the architects of Mexico's contemporary economy, the answer has been to effect a controlled withdrawal of the government from direct intervention in markets while instituting or, better still, contracting out to nongovernmental organizations (NGOs) palliative programs to ease the inevitable suffering.

In this and the following chapter, I outline the specific steps through which the industrial transformation of the Atempa basin was effected, its preindustrial economy dismantled, and the political and economic consequences therein. This chapter opens with a survey of the Atempa basin's mature preindustrial economy. I then narrow the focus to the region's commercial maize supply and the relationship between this and the urban rebozo industry. The chapter concludes with the rebozo industry's midcentury collapse. This is followed, in the next chapter, by an examination of the cascade of economic effects set in motion by the rebozo industry's decline, of the growing role of the Mexican state in the regional economy, and of the industrial transformation that drew the region's preindustrial history to a close.

The Regional Economy at the Beginning of Its End

The regional economy that took shape after 1842 was configured to meet the patterns of market demand that evolved at the time of its creation. The problems that arose in the twentieth century can be traced back to this earlier configuration and to the limited room to maneuver that it enabled. Specifically, population growth in communities that had originally taken on the task of producing the region's commercial grain supply led to a reduction in the amounts of grain that households could release into commercial exchange networks, which is to say, into the city. In itself, this would not have been particularly problematic, except that households in the other communities that controlled high-quality land, to whom urban consumers might otherwise have turned for additional maize, had long since settled into an existence that rested on other commercial specialties and had allowed their own populations to grow to a point where they lacked the productive capacity to take up the slack. Urban consumers were instead compelled to look farther afield and, more ominously, to increasingly marginal arable surfaces. The result was a steady rise in urban grain prices as the overall cost of transporting the commercial supply increased and as the productivity of the land from which it derived decreased. A steady increase in price volatility also resulted as more maize was drawn into the city from upland fields where yields were highly responsive to the vagaries of the weather.

It is important to appreciate that the farmers who originally took upon themselves the solemn duty of producing grain for the urban market did so without regard for the unique importance this commodity held for urban consumers. In sorting among their various pecuniary opportunities, these farmers had opted to produce maize commercially because of the relative convenience of doing so. Farmers in most areas of the Atempa basin had found that commercial maize production was not convenient at all and instead opted to participate in the regional economy in some other manner. They grew maize for consumption in their households but were deterred from doing so as a commercial endeavor by high transportation costs, erratic maize yields, or both. Maize production as a commercial venture held the most appeal to those who controlled tracts of fertile plains near Chilapa, areas from which transport costs were comparatively low and where maize yields were comparatively high and reliable. Yet even among those who controlled fertile land near Chilapa, what mattered was that they engage in some form of remunerative activity, not that they engage in any form in particular. So when the population of households and communities of commercial maize farmers increased, there was hardly a sense that in making small accommodating adjustments in commercial production strategies they were tinkering with the health and stability of the regional economy upon which their livelihoods depended. That is just what they were doing, however. From a regional standpoint, maize was more than just another commercial alternative; it was the regional economy's lifeblood.

RURAL COMMERCIAL SPECIALIZATIONS

Before delving into the details of commercial maize production and distribution, I want to take a brief survey of the economic landscape outside the grain belt. These are areas of the Atempa basin where farmers combined subsistence agriculture with other commercial pursuits, ones that in some cases represented viable possibilities within the grain belt as well. An extensive menu of commercial alternatives was open to households in the Atempa basin, though for households in any particular location the menu was often fairly restricted. Some of these restrictions were a consequence of transportation constraints, others a result of environmental

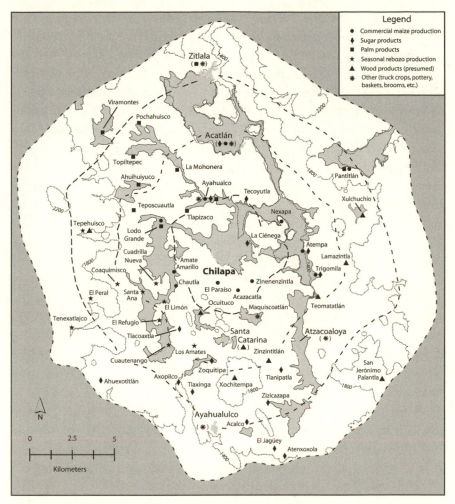

Map 10. Early-twentieth-century patterns of economic specialization.

possibilities and potentialities. There were four major rural industries that occupied households in multiple communities and crosscut transportation zones; a larger number of minor specializations could also be found, some concentrated in single communities and others distributed among communities throughout the basin. The four major industries include the production of sugarcane and sugar products, the harvesting of palm and the production of woven palm products, work as seasonal reboceros and empuntadoras, and the harvesting and sale of wood and wood products (see map 10). I consider each of these as well as specializations of more limited geographic distribution in the following paragraphs.

Through the first half of the twentieth century, most irrigated land in the Atempa basin was used to produce sugarcane. As I have indicated in previous chapters, patches of irrigated land were found scattered about the basin. Relatively large expanses occurred in a handful of locations, including La Ciénega and Tecoyutla in the lower Ajolotero valley, Trigomila and Atempa in the middle Atempa valley, Acatlán in the lower Atempa valley, as well as in small pockets in a swath of territory that runs along the south slope of Cerros Tezquitzin and Bayenchi, spanning land associated with the communities of Tlacoaxtla, Zoquitipa, Axopilco, Tlaxinga, Ahuexotitlán, Acalco, El Jagüey, Atenxoxola, Zizicazapa, and Tlanipatla. Some sense of the earlier scale and importance of sugar to the regional economy can be gained by comparing the circumstances that I found in 1990 to those documented by Maurilio Muñoz in the late 1950s and early 1960s. In 1990, there were three trapiches in the lower Ajolotero and middle Atempa valleys: at Ayahualco, Atempa, and Trigomila. I was able to identify the location of at least twelve trapiches that existed in this same area in the 1950s. In 1990, about ten hectares of land were sown in sugarcane within this area, as compared to an unknown but clearly much larger amount before the 1960s. A sense of how much larger can be seen from the fact that through midcentury, the work of harvesting sugarcane and processing sugar products in the trapiches was sufficiently demanding of labor to draw small numbers of migrants from the surrounding countryside through the four-month period of January through April (Muñoz 1963:62–63). In 1990, the sugarcane harvest and the processing work (fig. 12) done in the three surviving trapiches involved no migrant labor and was completed in a single month (March), both indicators that the three remaining trapiches were operated well below their capacity.

Although the amount of land used for sugarcane production in most areas of the basin is not of pressing concern for my purposes, the disposition of land in the immediate environs of Chilapa is an exception. From the observations just presented, my sense is that more than a hundred hectares of prime valley land in the lower Ajolotero and middle Atempa valleys were devoted to sugarcane through 1950. The industry thereafter underwent a precipitous decline that concluded by 2000, when all three of the trapiches that I had found in 1990 were gone. Three factors seem responsible for the decline: first, the midcentury economic turmoil in the city had reduced local demand for luxury items, including sugar products; second, the same turmoil created heightened urban demand for maize and thus elevated the opportunity costs associated with planting sugarcane in fields

Figure 12. Workers processing panela at a trapiche in Atempa in 1991.

near Chilapa; and finally, further tipping the balance in favor of maize was a technological change that led to a modest reduction in labor costs associated with growing maize in the dense vertisols around Chilapa. The technology in question was the steel moldboard plowshare, introduced to the region in the 1950s and 1960s. Of these three forces operating against sugarcane production, I am the least impressed with the first. Although the strength of urban demand for sugar products would clearly have been important to the industry, the quantities of sugar products that were produced indicate that many of the relevant consumers were actually located elsewhere. Panela and aguardiente were in all likelihood exported from Chilapa by itinerant merchants and arrieros who traveled circuits through adjacent drainages and beyond. Although Mexico's major urban centers were awash in sugar products, Chilapa's producers would nevertheless have had easy and preferred access to panela and aguardiente consumers in central Guerrero, among whom demand presumably remained constant even as production in Chilapa declined.

The second great industry found in the Atempa basin in the early twentieth century was likewise shaped more by local environmental possibilities than by spatial proximity to the urban market. Calcareous soils in the hills through virtually all of the northern half of the basin support extensive forests of *zoyate* palm (*Brahea dulcis*). The leaves of this plant formed the raw material used to make sombreros, bags and baskets, petates, items of apparel (including sandals and soyates), *coaxtlis* (saddle blankets for burros), and roof thatching, to name only the most important items. Communities that in the 1920s and early 1930s had concentrations of producers of palm goods include Tlapizaco, Ayahualco, La Mohonera, Teposcuautla, Ahuihuiyuco, Topiltepec, Pochahuisco, Zitlala, and Pantitlán. There are few indications of much specialization among these villages before the 1940s. As I discuss in the following chapter, in the 1940s a new export industry grew up around the production of palm goods. This corresponded with the collapse of rebozo manufacturing in Chilapa, which for a time the production of palm goods replaced as the region's dominant export industry.

A third form of participation in the region's commercial economy that spanned multiple communities and different transportation zones was directly linked to Chilapa's textile industry. West and southwest of Chilapa (beyond Chautla, Amate Amarillo, and Lodo Grande), there was a cluster of villages — including Tenexatlajco, El Peral, Coaquimisco, Santa Ana, Cuadrilla Nueva, Cuautenango, El Refugio, El Limón, and Los Amates — with households that sent labor to Chilapa, especially in the textile industry. Participation in the labor market by households in these villages took two forms. First, many migrants were dispatched to Chilapa in the dry season to work for wages, either in sugarcane fields or in household textile workshops, where they assisted in dyeing and processing the thread used to weave rebozos. Second, in their home villages, women worked year-round as empuntadoras, knotting the loose fringe on rebozos once the woven portion was removed from the loom (Muñoz 1963:93–97). Although the migrants who left Chilapa went in all directions after the 1842 rebellion, those who ventured west and southwest found fewer commercial opportunities than those moving in other directions; consequently, they maintained closer social and economic links with the urban neighborhoods from whence they came. These households became fertile ground for the spread of palm production after the midcentury decline of Chilapa's rebozo industry. That said, small numbers of empuntadoras remain in a few of these villages even today, knotting the fringe of the few rebozos that are still woven in Chilapa and others brought unfinished to the Atempa basin from Tenancingo (in the state of Mexico).

A fourth and final specialization that engaged households in multiple villages involved wood and wood products, including firewood, charcoal, furniture, kitchen utensils, plow beams, masks, construction materials, and many more. Most villages had sufficient forest reserves to provide for domestic needs, but this was not so for Chilapa, which had a voracious appetite for all sorts of wood products. Here I must admit to having only recently recognized the importance of a topic about which I regrettably know too little beyond the now-obvious observation that it warrants additional research. Martin Biskowski (2000) deserves credit for jolting me into an appreciation of the problem. Compared with rice or other grains, maize requires an enormous amount of fuel to process, and beans require even more. Tortillas, for example, require eight to sixteen times more fuel to cook than does rice; beans require forty to seventy times more fuel than rice.[2] These are stunning figures with important implications for our understanding of economic adaptations throughout Mexico. The introduction of gas stoves, in the 1970s in Chilapa and the 1990s in villages along paved roads, has relieved some pressure on the Atempa basin's forests, but by the time these new technologies arrived (and for many this day has not yet come), the region's population was nearly four times what it had been at the turn of the twentieth century. The intensification of land use that accompanied this population growth took a harsh toll on local forests, which have been depleted at a rate much faster than they can regenerate. These changes in the basin's floral communities, combined with a relative absence of historical records containing references to wood and wood products, make it difficult to reconstruct the history of commercial wood harvesting. Charcoal and *ocote* (pitch-pine) production were noted by agrarian reform surveyors who investigated a petition submitted by comuneros of San Jerónimo Palantla (*Diario Oficial,* January 9, 1947), a community that continues to supply these products to Chilapa. Beyond this, the records are silent.

For as long as I have worked in the Atempa basin, great numbers of porters, burros, and horses loaded with firewood have descended daily upon the city from the extensive tracts of oak and mixed pine-oak forests that are found on the ridges lining the eastern and western borders of the Atempa drainage (fig. 13). Most of the wood is destined for Chilapa's many bakeries, though most households in the city keep supplies of wood and charcoal on hand for the interval between when one gas bottle runs dry and a new bottle is delivered. In the late twentieth century, the people selling wood have mostly been from Tepehuisco to the west and Lamazintla and San Jerónimo Palantla to the east. I suspect that additional villages supplied Chilapa with wood in earlier times. Farming, pasturing livestock, and harvesting wood have resulted in severe deforestation in the vicinity of

Figure 13. A load of wood arriving in Chilapa from the hills east of the city.

most settlements in the basin. In Zones 1 and 2, even areas removed from
settlements have generally been stripped of forest cover. The woodlands
that occur in these areas are either stands of palm or low tropical deciduous
forest (composed mostly of thorny leguminous species). These floral communities can survive in thin soils, on sharply sloping surfaces, or in areas
that are today badly eroded from overgrazing or ill-advised agricultural
practices. Portions of the palm forest found today through the northern half
of the Atempa basin is secondary growth on land that supported more-
diverse oak and mixed deciduous forest as recently as the mid-twentieth
century (GEA 2003:37; Illsley et al. 2001:276–80). The southern half of
the basin is less hospitable to palm, which thrives in calcareous soils, but
here too deforestation has greatly modified floral communities and reduced
formerly forested areas to grassland or thorny deciduous forest.

The region's premier fuel and construction woods are oaks, especially
yellow oak (*Quercus magnoliifolia*), and pine (*Pinus pringlie*). Practically
no oak or pine can today be found anywhere near Chilapa. Stands of yellow
oak occur on the upper slopes of the basin's eastern and western ridges and
on Cerros Tezquitzin and Bayenchi in the south, areas in Zones 3 and 4.
Pine occurs only on the eastern ridge, mostly in Zone 4. Oak stands were
once more extensive, and much commercial wood harvesting was likely
done in several areas, especially by households on the northern slope of the

igneous ridge south of Chilapa. Cerro Totoltepec and the twin peaks of Cerros Tezquitzin and Bayenchi (shown in map 5) are part of this formation, along the crest or northern slopes of which are found the villages of Ocuituco, Santa Catarina, Xochitempa, and Zinzantitlán. These are among the few settlements that date to years prior to the twentieth century that are set in uplands amid comparatively marginal agricultural land. They are also among the few villages for which I have no information regarding early-twentieth-century commercial production activities. My hunch is that a good part of the commercial economy of these villages once involved fuel and construction wood and possibly charcoal. Today Ocuituco and Santa Catarina have practically no forest and, aside from subsistence agriculture and the production of palm goods, depend mostly on wage-labor opportunities in Chilapa and elsewhere. In Xochitempa and Zinzantitlán, the existing oak forest is secondary growth that gives every indication of having been nearly clearcut in the recent past. In contrast, patches of Cerros Tezquitzin and Bayenchi that are controlled by communities on its southern slopes are less ravished, and some lush stands of old-growth forest remain. Finally, Teomatatlán and Xulchuchio, both in Zones 2 and 3 east of Chilapa, are beside or amid extensive areas that once supported dense oak forest; wood products likely figured prominently in the commercial strategies of households in these villages as well.

In addition to these four activities, there were others of more limited geographic distribution. From Chilapa, among the more visible was the production of truck crops. Like sugarcane, truck crops required irrigated land, but they differed in that commercial quantities of most crops could be grown on small, often minute, tracts of land and thus competed less for arable land with maize, sugarcane, or anything else. Only tomato and tomatillo were sown in the manner of field crops, but neither was sown in areas so large that they need to concern us here. A larger list of crops — including lettuce, cabbage, cilantro, radishes, carrots, beets, and chiles — were grown on tiny, carefully manicured plots known as *tablones* (see Mathewson 1984; Wilken 1987:120–24). Some of these were carved into the sides of the ravines south of Chilapa, where tablones formed terraces that were irrigated by water moved from the barrancas by means of small diversion dams and canal networks. Others were situated in areas of the lower Ajolotero valley where the water table is particularly high, as it is in Chilapa and in adjacent fields to the east and northeast of the city. Within this area, tablones could be found in or adjacent to house lots or in portions of larger maize fields that were set aside for the purpose. Irrigation water was drawn from wells using buckets or, more recently, gas pumps. Nearly all production of highly perishable truck crops occurred in Zone 1, with the only exception just over the border in Zone 2 at Maquiscoatlán. Less-perishable crops were grown in a couple of more distant locations; examples include garlic, onion, and jicama, all produced in copious quantities in Atzacoaloya, and *camote* (sweet potato) and chile, produced in Acatlán.

Another commodity sold by residents of a handful of rural communities near Chilapa was labor. In addition to the seasonal migration of villagers from west of Chilapa to rebozo workshops in Chilapa and to sugarcane fields and trapiches north and east of the city, there was a third pattern that I observed in 1990–91 and that I suspect has fairly deep historical roots. It mostly involved residents of Santa Catarina, as well as smaller numbers from Ocuituco, Ayahualco, Lodo Grande, Atempa, and Nexapa, communities from which households regularly dispatched members on foot or on bicycles into Chilapa to engage in one or another form of wage labor, including day labor. Men from Santa Catarina today have a well-earned reputation in Chilapa for being champion workers, a reputation that I am confident derives from long experience. In addition to incidental day laborers, I knew men from Santa Catarina who commuted (on foot) and worked regular hours in lumberyards and in the construction trades. At six kilometers from Chilapa, Santa Catarina is a long commute — an hour at a brisk pace and one and a half hours at a more typical gait — but this commute was made regularly in the late twentieth century and most probably in earlier years as well.

The inventory of remaining rural specializations is now reduced to an array of miscellaneous products for which there was limited market demand. The exceptions include pottery and lime. Pottery was produced as a full-time occupation by members of at least thirty households in Chilapa as recently as the early 1960s and as a secondary activity for households in Ayahualco and, especially, Atzacoaloya (fig. 14), where it continues to be produced today (Muñoz 1963:98–99). Lime, used to prepare maize for consumption, was produced in a handful of communities in areas of calcareous soils, roughly paralleling the distribution of palm-goods production. Although some nonceramic storage containers were probably fashioned from palm leaves, the preeminent basket makers in the region were found in Ayahualulco, where household members wove baskets from *carrizo* and *otate,* both bamboos. Households in Zitlala manufactured the region's supply of brooms, using otate for the handle and *alelón,* a variety of sorghum, for the bristles. Finally, in addition to producing wood and clay

Figure 14. A potter in Atzacoaloya making a *comal,* a flat griddle used to cook tortillas.

Figure 15. Participants in a fiesta in Zitlala wearing masks. This fiesta features ritual fighting between representatives of rival barrios.

for Chilapa's potters (Muñoz 1963:98), residents of Tepehuisco manufactured an additional product that gave them a particularly exalted status among the region's fiesta lovers — a group that in my experience includes the entire population. Through the mid-twentieth century, the most common inebriant consumed in the region was the aguardiente produced in Chilapa, Acatlán, and probably elsewhere. To convert an occasion from common to something truly special required Tepehuisco's mescal.

In addition to localized specializations, there were other commercial pursuits open to the inhabitants of all rural communities. Makers of masks used in theatrical dances performed at saint's day fiestas were found scattered through villages throughout the basin (e.g., Cordry 1980:124). Masks were made of wood, leather, or (in recent years) papier-mâché, depending on material availability (fig. 15). Domesticated animals including chickens, turkeys, goats, pigs, cattle, burros, and horses were raised almost everywhere, and these and animal products were regularly sold in the urban market. There was a degree of spatial differentiation in this, with milk production restricted to Zone 1, cheese to distant areas, and pig husbandry scattered widely but particularly common in distant and upland areas. Beyond Zone 3, maize could not be profitably sold owing to high transport costs, but it could be converted into pigs, which obligingly, if reluctantly, would convey themselves to market. Chickens, eggs, turkeys, and goats seem to have been produced everywhere without much regard for location. There was also a seemingly limitless diversity of domesticated or semi-domesticated plants and plant products that were variously cultivated or gathered and offered for sale in Chilapa.[3] Some were consumed as foodstuffs, while others were valued for their medicinal attributes, and still others for their aesthetic properties. A comprehensive list would be virtually impossible to compile, though prominent on it would be various fruits (including all varieties of citrus, mango, papaya, banana, avocado, plum, guava, mamey, etc.), diverse field greens (weeds, to the uninitiated), flowers, and many more. Edible insects (*jumiles*) and insect products (honey and wax) were gathered for domestic and commercial purposes as well.

The point on which I would like to end this section is this: rural households in the Atempa basin aimed their productive efforts first at subsistence and secondarily at generating small amounts of currency through market transactions of one sort or another. Although rural producers had no one means of engaging in pursuits that would end in the accumulation of substantial wealth, a wide range of opportunities did exist for generating small amounts of currency. And small amounts of currency were all that

Figure 16. Farmers from San Jerónimo Palantla considering agricultural tools at a store in Chilapa.

households needed to cover the limited range of purchases, of salt, cloth-ing, cooking vessels, tools (fig. 16), and other incidental commodities.

COMMERCIAL MAIZE PRODUCTION

I preface my remarks on commercial maize production with an ex-panded note on the issue of risk management. Earlier, I indicated that maize yields from fields in upland areas respond much more directly to variations in summer rainfall than do yields from fields in the basin's valleys. Nearly 70 percent of the Atempa basin's arable surface consists of fields in the uplands. Whereas the yield of maize sown on the plains might vary slightly depending on the characteristics of summer rainfall (includ-ing the overall quantity of rainfall and its exact timing relative to the growth of maize plants) by perhaps 20 percent around a long-term average, yields in the uplands ranged much more widely, perhaps as much as 50 percent around the long-term average. In this way, a growing season with average rainfall would leave farmers with a certain quantity of maize that they could not have counted on having produced, a quantity that would be considerably greater for farmers working in the uplands than for those working on the plains.

Farmers took this feature of agriculture into account in devising both subsistence and commercial production strategies. For the vital subsistence component of their overall work effort, farmers calibrated their production strategies as best they could to ensure that the amounts needed for home consumption were forthcoming no matter what the rainy season brought. The result during a year of average rainfall was the production of a surplus, in amounts that were larger where land was of low quality and smaller where land was of high quality. As population growth led farmers to inten-sify their use of upland areas, this surplus grew steadily larger. Releasing the unneeded amount into the urban market might seem as though it would have been a reasonable and profitable means of disposal, but imagine the consequences if everyone did this at once. In a year with average rainfall, the sort of year when this surplus amount would exist, the market would be swiftly inundated, prices would fall, and the incentive to sell the grain would be lost. Aside from the greater effort that farming the uplands re-quired, this economic dynamic served as a strong deterrent against par-ticipation in the region's commercial grain market by farmers of the basin's uplands. All else being equal, farmers of the uplands, like those of the

valleys where the distance from Chilapa was great, relied on other commercial specialties and sank their surplus grain into livestock, especially
chickens and pigs, two species that depended on maize as thoroughly as did
humans.

This observation about the relationship between maize production and
chicken and pig husbandry explains a seemingly paradoxical situation recorded in the decennial agricultural censuses. The previously issued pro-
visos regarding the reliability of these numbers notwithstanding, the censuses record an apparent increase in the population of maize-consuming
animals after the mid-twentieth century (DGE 1957, 1975) at precisely the
time when feeding the basin's human population had become problematic.
On its face, this is an unexpected trend. It makes sense only if one appreci-
ates that these animals were not draining maize away from humans but
were instead serving as a sort of sponge, sopping up quantities of maize that
farmers routinely produced but could not sell at a reasonable price and
dared not become too dependent upon for their own sustenance. When bad
years arrived (as occurred every few years) and maize yields dropped, the
animals were sold or slaughtered, giving households a bit of a financial or
nutritional cushion while simultaneously reducing household maize demand to a sustainable amount (Kyle 1995:111–12).

Turning now to commercial maize production, I begin by reviewing
the issue of urban demand. Table 3 shows my estimates of the quantity of
maize that residents of Chilapa needed to obtain through commercial networks. Consumers in Chilapa entered the twentieth century requiring the
annual delivery of about 905 tons of maize from farmers living in outlying
villages. This rose to 933 tons by 1921, then trended downward to a low of
682 tons in 1940. By 1950 the deficit had been restored roughly to its
earlier level, where it remained through 1960. Demand grew sharply in the
1960s and 1970s and surpassed 2,000 tons in 1980. The boost in productivity that chemical fertilizers gave Chilapa's resident farmers, combined with
a gradual shift in consumption away from maize in favor of wheat and
animal products, led to a substantial reduction in the city's maize deficit in
1990 to below 1,200 tons. An accelerated rate of population growth, fed by
heavy rural-to-urban migration, reversed the decline after 1990, and in
2000 the city's maize deficit again topped 1,500 tons.

At the turn of the twentieth century, and presumably in the last decades
of the nineteenth, those who likely supplied the city with the quantities of
maize its consumers required were farmers who controlled expanses of
valley temporal in Zone 2, especially those in the middle Atempa and

TABLE 3.Maize budget (potential supply minus demand, in metric tons)
for select areas of the Atempa basin, 1900–2000

| | Deficit in Chilapa[a] | Potential surplus from valley fields | | | | | Surplus from Areas 1–3 | Surplus from Areas 1–5 | Probable areas of commercial production |
		Area 1	Area 2	Area 3	Area 4	Area 5			
1900	(905)	750	288	331	67	(3)	464	527	Areas 1–2
1910	(904)	532	215	287	21	(51)	129	99	Areas 1–3
1921	(933)	491	350	274	36	16	182	234	Areas 1–3
1930	(867)	490	210	255	68	108	87	264	Areas 1–3
1940	(682)	406	163	247	(3)	187	133	317	Areas 1–3
1950	(932)	243	116	228	(19)	(31)	(345)	(395)	Areas 1–3, uplands
1960	(912)	90	88	265	(52)	144	(469)	(377)	Areas 1–3, uplands
1970	(1,278)	(70)	72	112	(100)	4	(1,164)	(1,260)	Areas 2–3, uplands
1980	(2,102)	(240)	114	61	(188)	(103)	(2,166)	(2,457)	Areas 2–3, uplands
1990	(1,157)	686	592	431	112	234	551	898	Entire region
2000	(1,515)	543	545	315	27	184	(112)	98	Entire region

Sources: Table data based on estimated per capita consumption amounts given in chapter 3 and agricultural productivity estimates in appendix 2.

Notes: Chilapa deficit arrived at after deduction of potential output from all fields farmed by residents of the city and the agricultural suburbs of La Ciénega, El Paraíso, Acazacatla, and Zinenenzintla, comprising 441 hectares of valley temporal, 375 hectares of upland temporal, and 118 hectares of tlacolol, all situated in Zone 1. After 1950, the potential output of an additional 70 hectares of tierra de riego that had previously been sown in sugarcane is included.

Area 1 includes the 1,205 hectares of valley temporal and, after 1950, the 49 hectares of tierra de riego in the middle Atempa and Ajolotero valleys and in the lower reaches of Barranca Coapala. This includes land associated with the villages of Chautla, Amate Amarillo, Lodo Grande, Ayahualco, Nexapa, Atempa, and Trigomila. The land is located along the outer edges of Zone 1 and in Zone 2.

Area 2 includes 649 hectares of valley temporal farmed by households in Acatlán. Another 52 hectares of irrigated fields associated with Acatlán were sown in sugarcane before the 1950s and maize, flowers, and truck crops beginning in the 1960s. The area is located in Zones 2 and 3.

Area 3 includes 483 hectares of valley temporal found in the vicinity of Pantitlán. The land is located in Zones 3 and 4.

Area 4 includes 342 hectares of valley temporal in the upper Atempa valley (held by residents of Teomatatlán and Atzacoaloya). The land is located in Zones 2 and 3.

Area 5 includes 706 hectares of valley temporal in the lower Atempa valley (held by residents of Zitlala). It is located in Zones 3 and 4.

Ajolotero valleys, portions of the lower Atempa valley, and the lower reaches of Barranca Coapala, referred to as Areas 1 and 2 in table 3. This includes farmers in the villages of Trigomila, Atempa, Nexapa, Ayahualco, Acatlán, Lodo Grande, Amate Amarillo, and Chautla. In 1910 the output from the valley temporal held by farmers in these villages fell short, by 157 tons, of the amount needed in Chilapa. The area to which commercial maize production most likely spread was onto the plain at Pantitlán, referred to as Area 3 in table 3. Pantitlán itself is in Zone 3, but much of its valley temporal is in Zone 4, substantially farther from Chilapa than the fields worked by farmers in the original eight villages of commercial maize suppliers. There was a considerable amount of valley temporal nearer to Chilapa than the plain at Pantitlán, in the upper and lower Atempa valleys, for example, but even in 1910 one can see in these areas a problem that would only grow worse in later decades. Atzacoaloya (Area 4 in table 3) had the capacity to supply only 21 tons. Still less could be expected from Zitlala (Area 5 in table 3), whose 1910 population had exceeded the numbers that could be sustained from its high-quality land alone. Pantitlán, in contrast, had the wherewithal to supply the urban market with 287 tons. Among villages controlling valley temporal, there is a sharp distinction between these nine settlements, which through the first half of the twentieth century had a very favorable man-to-land ratio, and all others, in which the balance between population and arable land left far less scope for commercial agriculture.

This man-to-land ratio did not remain quite so favorable, however. Population growth in the nine villages of commercial grain producers gradually reduced the amount of maize that could be delivered to the urban market. The decline in Chilapa's population in the 1920s and 1930s offset the growing problem, but when the city reversed its demographic course and added nearly 1,250 consumers in the 1940s, the stark new reality came to a head. The only plausible scenario that I have found to eliminate a projected deficit for 1950 (of 345 tons if the only suppliers were farmers in the nine communities identified above) is not by moving outward to incorporate more of the communities that controlled valley temporal but instead by moving into the uplands. The existing demand for maize in Chilapa in 1950 could have been supplied (though with only 2 tons to spare) had the potential surplus from all of the arable land in Zones 1 and 2 been added to the amounts produced by the nine villages that had earlier specialized in commercial grain production (see table 4). In 1960, all of the arable land in Zones 1 through 3, together with the land held by Pantitlán in Zone 4,

TABLE 4. Maize budget (in metric tons) for the Atempa basin, 1900–2000

| Year | Supply-and-demand balance in Chilapa, Areas 1–3, and uplands | | |
	Zones 1–2	Zones 1–3	Zones 1–4
1900	1,323	2,427	4,116
1910	792	1,788	3,196
1921	904	1,817	3,471
1930	688	1,488	3,219
1940	668	1,328	2,903
1950	2	420	1,663
1960	(22)	485	1,928
1970	(1,069)	(784)	302
1980	(2,456)	(2,753)	(2,193)
1990	2,580	5,323	9,420
2000	1,902	4,515	7,568

Note: Data derived by adding the potential surplus from upland communities to the amounts produced in Areas 1–3 (from table 3). The surplus from upland communities is derived by deducting consumption requirements of upland villagers from the potential maize output that could be obtained from upland fields. Estimates of per capita consumption are from chapter 3, agricultural productivity estimates from appendix 2, and the arable upland surface estimates from table 2.

would have been needed to provision the city; by 1970, the potential surplus from all arable land in Zones 1 through 4 would have been required to provision the region. I have failed to find a scenario that would satisfy the demand that existed in 1980. It can be no coincidence that Chilapa's growth beyond a threshold that could be supported by grain production in Zones 1 through 3 (that is, by the land within a twelve-kilometer radius of the city) occurred only in the 1960s, at the precise historical moment when local roads were constructed and vehicular transportation systems were introduced. This represents the first traces of the direct physical dependence by any portion of the Atempa basin's population on industrial technologies.

Careful scrutiny of the calculations in tables 3 and 4 will reveal that the urban supply problem tipped from problematic to acute in the 1940s and that this change had next to nothing to do with population growth in Chilapa. The city's population had actually fallen in the 1920s and 1930s; even in 1950, the urban appetite for maize was effectively identical to what it had been fifty years earlier. The problem was instead caused by a slight but shockingly consequential rise in the numbers of people living in a handful of outlying communities. To be precise, it was a rise in the numbers of people living in nine of the fifty-eight communities that appear in the 1950 census in the area covered by Zones 1 through 4. Commercial maize production may have presented itself to rural households as just another economic alternative, but for the region as a whole, it was much more than this. The reproductive decisions made within households in these nine communities altered the flow of grain through the region's commercial exchange networks just enough to initiate a chain reaction that brought the urban economy, and with this the regional economy, to the brink of total collapse. This chain reaction continued to reverberate decades later, when the unsuccessful search for some stable foundation upon which to build a new regional economy ended with the onset of the region's industrial revolution.

FOOD AND THE FATE OF THE REBOZO INDUSTRY

Observers of the Atempa basin's economy in the mid-twentieth century found problems but did not point to the region's grain supply as the underlying culprit. Instead, they fixated on the difficulties faced by Chilapa's rebozo producers, difficulties that had become sufficiently acute to trigger the first wave of migration out of the Atempa basin since 1844. The problems were seen as specific to the rebozo industry, as though this occupied some sort of ethereal space isolated from the balance of the regional economy. The most detailed and insightful of such accounts was written in 1947 by Eicandro Ruiz Hernández, Mariano Acevedo, and Juventino Pineda y Ortega, all residents of Chilapa (two schoolteachers and a physician, respectively). These three wrote their analysis of the region six years after a brief visit to Chilapa by two anthropologists who noted that Chilapa's woolen industry was in wholesale decline (*plena decadencia*) but made no such representation regarding rebozo manufacturing (see Weitlaner and Weitlaner 1943:146). This observation about the state of Chilapa's woolen industry is odd, given that the city never had enough of a woolen industry to warrant mention by anyone else. In any case, any difficulties faced by rebozo producers before 1942 seem to have been defused through out-migration, something that escaped the attention of the visiting anthropologists but was noted by the city's residents (see Ruiz et al. 1947:24) and documented in its broad statistical outlines in the 1940 census (see table 1).

A more complete portrait of the textile industry's decline can be achieved with reference to occupational information recorded in Chilapa's civil registry.[4] In years prior to 1947, reboceros comprised 35–50 percent of Chilapa's adult males who appear in the marriage records. As had been the case with the 1791 census, the occupational information reported in the twentieth-century marriage records pertains only to the reporting individuals' primary occupations and omits mention of secondary or part-time pursuits and work done in households by women and children. Ruiz and his colleagues give some sense of the scope of part-time participation in the rebozo industry in their estimate that 95 percent of all households in Chilapa had some economic involvement in the rebozo industry in 1947 (Ruiz et al. 1947:24). Thus, the decrease in Chilapa's population to 6,152 persons in 1940, down from 7,143 in 1930, indicates that there was a measurable decline through this decade in the number of reboceros and in the volume of rebozo production. As a percentage of the population, reboceros held fast at just under half of the city's adult males, but the decline in the number of households in the city indicates that their numbers dropped in absolute terms.

The most fateful moment for the rebozo industry arrived between 1947 and 1950, a three-year stretch through which reboceros fell from 45 percent of the adult male population to 27 percent. The slide then slowed but continued until the number flattened at 22 percent from 1955 to 1960. The reprieve did not last long. Reboceros' representation as a percentage of the workforce fell to single digits by 1965 and slipped from 7 percent to 2 percent between 1965 and 1980. They then evaporated into statistical irrelevance. In 1990, I found five households headed by reboceros, two or three of which remained in 2004. At some point before 1960, reboceros ceased producing significant numbers of rebozos finos (Muñoz 1963:95–96). This was an important threshold because rebozos finos had previously formed the underpinning of interregional commerce. The loss of work in the textile industry left more than unemployment; it left the region as a whole with a severe balance of trade problem.

Sounding like good fighting socialists, Ruiz and his colleagues pointed an accusatory finger squarely at Chilapa's elite merchants in their explanation for the industry's decline. They noted that the industry had first grown through the efforts of independent artisans but asserted that in recent years, avaricious merchants had gained leverage over weavers and had reorganized the industry along the lines of a classic put-out system. Weavers were leaving the industry and the region because merchants had greedily reduced rates of remuneration to below subsistence levels. They recommended a government takeover. Weavers would be organized into cooperatives that could be extended credit to purchase thread and dyes and to modernize looms. Cooperative members would somehow be guaranteed sufficient income to cover their subsistence needs (Ruiz et al. 1947:24). Well, the government did not bite, and the industry, already on a two-decade-long decline, lost purchase completely and entered the free-fall that I describe above.

In retrospect, it is now clear that the analysis offered by Ruiz and his colleagues falls short in their failure to identify the constellation of forces that lay behind the industry's recent reorganization and the resulting hardships suffered by reboceros. That reboceros of the 1940s had lost the ability to acquire raw materials without resorting to credit extended by merchants indicates either or both of two things: Chilapa's reboceros might have suffered a decline in income because their rebozos were fetching lower prices in the markets in which they were sold, or production costs in Chilapa might have risen. With regard to the first possibility, I have found no evidence of a simultaneous disruption in rebozo production, distribution, or consumption elsewhere in Mexico (Davis 1991; Velázquez 1981; see Stephen 1991:119–23 for a discussion of Mexican textiles generally through this period). Neither the worldwide economic depression of the 1930s nor the rapid industrial growth in Mexico in the 1940s and early 1950s (see Hansen 1971) seem clearly related.

In regard to local production costs, however, the evidence is compelling. First, there is the evidence presented in the previous section showing that food production and marketing costs increased substantially through the twentieth century. I cannot show that these higher costs were passed on to consumers in the form of higher market prices, but any other possibility would be contrary to the most basic of economic principles. The only force the city commanded to induce farmers to engage in commercial grain production was of a pecuniary nature; higher grain prices were essential to induce farmers at progressively greater distances and with progressively lower-quality land to shift their attention, their labor, and their land to commercial grain production.

Second, there is the matter of the patterning of the rebozo industry's decline. Although the industry clearly struggled in the 1930s and 1940s, the episodic pattern of decline thereafter, with periods of slow contraction or even stability punctuated by moments of precipitous decline, has the distinct look of a sector of the economy that was extremely sensitive to the vagaries of summer rainfall. Recall the point made in the previous section regarding the increased volatility of the grain supply as commercial maize production pushed into the uplands. For urban consumers, the result was increasingly frequent and severe spikes in food prices. Rainfall records are available only for years following 1953, so I cannot correlate the initial episode of rapid decline in manufacturing, between 1947 and 1950, to a spike in maize prices owing to some sort of adverse climate event. During the second period of rapid contraction, between 1960 and 1965, rainfall was heavy in all years except 1962 and was remarkably heavy in 1960 and 1965. The monthly rainfall records tell only part of the story, however. They do not capture the precise temporal distribution of precipitation, and this can matter a great deal (as much as the gross rainfall amounts). Rainless periods of sufficient duration to cause devastating yield reductions in many upland fields can occur even in a year in which the monthly rainfall amount appears unremarkable; likewise, a single torrential downpour, especially one falling on already saturated fields, can (and regularly does) trigger mud slides and wash plants out of upland fields. While the circumstances in distant markets seem not to offer much explanation for the rebozo industry's collapse, the evidence for rising and unstable food prices is compelling and is itself sufficient to account for the behavior of merchants and reboceros alike.

As for the aftermath, we are presented with an illustration of the dictum that what goes up must come down. As rising food prices in the city reduced its principal industry to a shriveled ruin, disposable income among urban consumers fell, partly a result of a loss of employment and partly because higher food prices absorbed a steadily larger share of the disposable income that remained. Rural producers of commodities other than food — commodities once produced in response to demand among urban consumers — faced reduced demand and falling prices. Seeing only the effect that this had on their own households' budgets, rural producers almost certainly attempted to offset the resulting loss in income by intensifying production, by bringing more goods to the market. For the regional economy as a whole, this response could only have compounded the problem by contributing to an already oversupplied market and driving prices down still further. Only one commodity, maize, was immune to the general deflationary pressure that reverberated through the region, but not everyone could produce it in quantities large enough to matter. Ruiz and his colleagues rightly saw the heavy migration out of Chilapa in the 1930s as cause for alarm. It was an indication that severe imbalances had developed in commercial supply-and-demand relationships; it was an indication that an economic collapse had begun and that the regional economy was coming unraveled.

SIX

THE RETURN OF THE FOREST

There is a treadmill-like feel to the decades following the 1940s, to the efforts that were made to stanch the economic decline and reestablish some stable foundation on which to rest a regional economy. The desired end proved elusive; there simply was no preindustrial fix to the urban provisioning issues that lay at the core of the region's difficulties. As long as Chilapa relied on local farmers for its maize supply, any new industry that took root in the city had to enable urban households to cope with rising and ever-more-volatile food prices. It is not clear to me that any preindustrial industry or city could long survive under these circumstances. Making matters worse, producers in the Atempa basin went casting about for a new export industry even as the pace of industrial development elsewhere in Mexico was rapidly accelerating. This created unprecedented instability in the markets in which the products of any new export industry would have to compete. As with people the world over, Mexicans' consumer habits were radically changing in the mid-twentieth century; the steady and reliable demand that had characterized the market for Chilapa's rebozos became more exceptional with each passing year. Though the specific problems that confronted the Atempa basin may have been unique, its residents were hardly alone in crossing the threshold of midcentury and finding only frightening economic uncertainty on the other side (Hobsbawm 1994).

The third quarter of the twentieth century was a desperate time in the Atempa basin, a time when the prospect of the urban center sliding back to its agrarian roots sat like a great dark cloud over the region. Against this backdrop, the Mexican state made its first meaningful gestures in the direction of active involvement in the regional economy. This began modestly, with investments in basic infrastructure such as road construction and electrification, and gathered pace thereafter. Far from offering immediate relief, these early movements were highly destabilizing by breaching the region's isolation and opening the Chilapa market to outside suppliers. This would not have been so bad had the new imports been balanced by a simultaneous increase in exports. Instead, consumers in the Atempa basin found more use for imported goods than consumers elsewhere found for goods produced in the basin; the result was a net outflow of specie and, increasingly, paper currency. The government stepped in to right the balance, funneling money into the region through two main channels. First, money was distributed in rural communities by subsidizing producers of woven palm goods, which emerged as the most promising of the export industries to arise in the wake of the rebozo industry's decline. Second, money was directed into the city in the salaries of legions of workers employed to maintain the industrial infrastructure, staff an expanded school system, and administer the government's various policies and programs. These new sources of income were sufficient to keep most rural and urban households solvent, to lubricate commerce in the region generally, and to support greater rates of consumption of newly imported manufactured goods.

What was missing from these early interventions was any direct effort to address the region's central economic problem, that of its food supply. By the late 1970s, the problem had become so acute that it could no longer be left unattended. No local options remained, and thus the task fell to government planners. At the time, the prevailing sentiment among policymakers favored national self-sufficiency over reliance on imports, and there followed, through the 1980s, a brief experiment with supplying industrial agriculture technologies to poor farmers. Although producers in the Atempa basin came nowhere near to matching the productivity of farmers in fully industrialized settings, with government support they did manage to produce an amount of food well in excess of the regional demand. Then came neoliberalism and the ideological conversion of key policy makers from the populist credo of Cárdenas to the gospel of "free trade." Consistent with the new rhetoric, the subsidy programs that had propped up agriculture in the Atempa basin were restructured and partly withdrawn. Inconsistent with the new rhetoric, the old programs were replaced by a new batch of subsidy programs, one of which stands out for its consequences; for a brief period in the mid-1990s, the government directed monstrous quantities of imported grain to Chilapa. The grain was not simply subsidized and priced below the local product; it was given away to urban consumers free of charge. The irony here is as superb as the consequences were devastating. Neoliberalism is generally a keyword signaling a reduced role for government in local economic affairs, but in the Atempa basin, the onset of neoliberalism actually witnessed a marked increase in the degree and scope of government intervention in the local economy.[1] One of the by-products of these new forms of state intervention was a final economic detachment of urban consumers from rural producers. With this, the destruction of the regional economy was complete.

This chapter addresses the final days of the Atempa basin's preindustrial regional economy. The discussion centers mostly on government actions and the impact these had on the underlying economic relationships that linked urban consumers to rural producers. In the course of the discussion, we will be carried slightly beyond the main subject of this book and into the first decade of the Atempa basin's industrial era. I do this for two reasons: first, it brings us into the present day; and second, my angle of approach to neoliberalism differs from that followed in most recent discussions of the topic, and it suggests hitherto unconsidered but potentially productive avenues of inquiry.

THE PALM INDUSTRY

With the rebozo industry's midcentury decline, producers in and around Chilapa found a partial replacement for the lost work and income by devising a new industry involving woven palm goods. Sombreros, petates, sandals, coaxtlis, soyates, and perhaps *bolsas* (literally, bags), baskets, and other storage containers had long been produced in the communities scattered through the environmental zone that supports the growth of *zoyate* (north of Chilapa). Before the late 1930s, palm products were woven from individual palm leaves that were dried and bleached but otherwise unprocessed. The hallmark of the new industry was the use of "fabric" woven from cinta, or braided strands of bleached zoyate leaves, using techniques that were innovated by an entrepreneur from Chilapa in the mid-1930s (see Casarrubias 1989:35; Mastache and Morett 1982:40–41; Ruiz et al. 1947:25). The basic repertoire of finished goods came to include new types of sombreros, placemats, *tortilleros* (i.e., baskets used to hold warmed tortillas), handbags (bolsas), and baskets and storage containers, all made in a variety of sizes and styles.

At least in the early years, the manufacture of cinta-based palm goods was, for two reasons, a perfectly tailored solution to the difficulties that confronted the regional economy. First, the industry was directed primarily toward external markets, not local consumption. It thus sidestepped the problem of the embarrassingly low level of consumer demand and disposable income within the Atempa basin and simultaneously supplied the region as a whole with a source of revenue to replace that lost from the decline in rebozo exports. This is another instance of producers in the Atempa basin extending the life of the regional economy by piggybacking atop industrialization elsewhere in Mexico. The low unit value of individual palm goods made them rather more difficult and costly to transport to external markets than rebozos had been. From its beginnings in the late 1930s, the new palm industry relied on vehicular transportation to move goods to markets. In the very earliest years, some palm goods may have been moved by arrieros to Chilpancingo and from there transported by truck or bus to the nearest railhead, in Iguala, Guerrero. From Iguala they were shipped to distant markets, in the central highlands and the United States. After 1939, palm goods were transported using vehicles, either buses or cargo trucks, directly from Chilapa to Iguala.

A second way in which the new palm industry met the needs of the Atempa basin's regional economy involves the industry's internal structural features. From its beginnings, and more so as the industry evolved, the production process was highly differentiated, involving multiple steps executed by households scattered throughout the basin. To some extent, this had been the case among rebozo producers as well, with households, including some in rural communities, specializing in different stages of the overall production effort; by comparison, this attribute was much more developed in the cinta-based palm industry. Prior to the 1930s, producers of palm goods harvested the raw materials they needed from the stands of zoyate that surrounded their villages; there was, at most, a limited commercial market for raw or bleached palm leaves. With the rise of cinta production, this changed, and there arose a robust commercial market for palm leaf (see GEA 2003). Households in villages both within and beyond the areas of the basin where zoyate grows began braiding cinta to supplement income from preexisting forms of commodity production. Cinta production had apparently become ubiquitous in rural areas of the basin as early as 1940, only a few years after the braiding and weaving techniques were invented (Weitlaner and Weitlaner 1943:148–49). In these early years, braided cinta was sold to manufacturers in Chilapa, where the actual weaving or sewing and the final assembly of products were done in small workshops, the largest employing no more than a dozen or so people (Mastache and Morett 1982:40–50; Muñoz 1963:87–88, 93).

All of the products were made in multiple steps, from harvesting and bleaching or dyeing of zoyate leaves to braiding cinta, weaving "fabric" of cinta, cutting the fabric, and sewing or otherwise assembling the basic product. From this point, the steps varied from one product to the next but involved one or more of the following: sewing hems, adding decorative elements (most fashioned from dyed zoyate leaves or acrylic yarn), and attaching hardware such as handles, hinges, clasps, and the like. Within a few years of the industry's appearance, portions of the production process beyond harvesting and processing zoyate and braiding cinta began to be doled out from Chilapa's workshops to households in rural villages. Those elements of the manufacturing process that involved the use of sewing machines were the last to be done by full-time workers in urban workshops. By the 1950s, the relocation of the cinta-based palm industry into the countryside had become well established and would be nearly complete soon after (Mastache and Morett 1982:35–37, 40–50). Villages to the west of Chilapa, where households had previously derived income from seasonal work in the rebozo industry and as empuntadoras, were among the first to take up tasks beyond braiding cinta. People there wove cinta into sheets of fabric measuring just under a meter in width by perhaps twenty-five meters in length. Rolls of the fabric were then sold in Chilapa, where it was cut and assembled into bolsas or some other product. Households in other villages gradually took up other aspects of the manufacturing process. Some became specialists in adding hinges and clasps to bolsas, others in sewing decorative "flowers" of dyed palm leaves or yarn onto bolsas and tortilleros. A few communities developed distinctive products of their own, the most notable a form of bolsa made only in Santa Catarina. By the 1960s, the production of practically any item made of palm had come to involve residents of at least three villages and often far more. There were villages that specialized in harvesting and processing zoyate and people everywhere in the region who braided cinta; other villages specialized in weaving palm fabric, others cut and assembled the basic products, and still others added decorative elements and hardware. At the completion of each step, the items were sold in Chilapa, either to middlemen or directly from specialists in one phase of the operation to those in another. The industry thus generated both manufacturing and commercial work.

The ledger is mixed in regard to the industry's overall impact on the regional economy. On the plus side, palm goods were exportable commodities that could replace rebozos and the industry provided an enormous amount of part-time work that could be readily scheduled around farming and could thus complement subsistence production in the countryside. On the down side, the industry had no real impact on the problem of the urban food supply that was eating away at the region's core. Furthermore, although it initially provided full-time employment in Chilapa's workshops, and to increasing numbers of petty and some not-so-petty merchants in the urban center, the increased participation of rural households in production and assembly work put such serious pressure on rates of labor compensation that the industry's embryonic urban proletariat was shortly driven to extinction by swarms of cheaper, self-subsidizing laborers in the countryside.

This point warrants expanded consideration, as it would soon affect other types of work that had once been the exclusive purview of urban households. A household of farmers in the countryside could produce all or most of its annual food supply with something on the order of one hundred man-days of labor, plus or minus thirty or forty depending on the quality of its land. This left most rural households with a substantial amount of time and labor that could be applied to some sort of commercial activity aimed at obtaining enough currency to purchase items that could not be produced in the household. The needs of rural dwellers were modest and the time at their disposal abundant. Absent alternatives, even an activity compensated at a scandalously low rate might nevertheless be worthwhile insofar as the rate of compensation sufficed to generate the small amounts of needed currency. In contrast, urban households depended completely on the market for subsistence as well nonessential consumer goods. In consequence, the rate of labor compensation had to be much higher to support a household in the city, where food had to be bought, than in villages, where food could be grown.

The discrepancy between the rates of compensation required to support rural and urban households had existed for as long as Chilapa had been an urban settlement but grew steadily wider through the twentieth century. This is a feature of the regional economy that had earlier pushed the work of empuntadoras out of Chilapa and into communities west of the city and that had induced farmers in Chilapa to draw labor from rural rather than urban households to help harvest and process sugarcane. Indeed, a bit later, the city's labor market would suffer its mightiest blow from this quarter with the introduction of vehicular transportation in the 1960s. By dramatically reducing the friction of distance, vehicular transportation placed urban and rural laborers into direct competition (see Kyle 1996a). It should go without saying that urban workers were at a profound disadvantage anytime they found themselves competing against commuters from the countryside. Once the public transportation system became sufficiently reliable, a whole host of traditionally urban pursuits were thrown open to rural households, driving base wages for workers in many sectors of the economy to below the levels needed to support an urban household.

Of all the manifestations of this displacement of work from city to country, a phenomenon noted many years ago by Jane Jacobs (1969), the earliest and most dramatic example is provided by the cinta-based palm industry, which by the early 1960s had shifted almost entirely to the countryside. Part-time participation by urban households persisted, and persists today, though mostly in the industry's commercial facets. Following its initial appearance as an urban industry in the mid-1930s, the production of cinta-based palm goods gradually spread from city to country, but it left the urban center one fragment at a time and thus became ever more differentiated as it went. Rural communities carved out specialized roles in what swiftly became an enormously complex, panregional production process. For the region as a whole, the growth and elaboration of this industry was enough to stave off a catastrophic collapse; however, problems remained, particularly in the city, where the new industry failed to generate employment to replace the work lost with the decline in rebozo production.

As had representatives of an earlier generation with respect to the rebozo industry, an observer in the early 1960s identified avarice among merchants dealing in palm goods as the principal cause of the economic difficulties found in and around Chilapa (Muñoz 1963:86–93; also Mastache and Morett 1982:19–23). Again, proposals for a government takeover were issued. This time the government bit. In 1973 — the same year that construction on the Chilpancingo–Chilapa leg of Highway 93 was completed — a presidential decree was issued nationalizing elements of the Atempa basin's cinta-based palm industry by means of a government-owned and -financed corporation, known as the Fideicomiso de la Palma (FIDEPAL). FIDEPAL intervened in the industry in several ways. First, it purchased cinta from producers at subsidized prices,[2] exporting much of the palm goods to factories elsewhere in Mexico (in the states of Puebla, Oaxaca, and Jalisco, and México). The corporation also built a factory in Chilapa where bolsas and sombreros were produced. Finally, FIDEPAL personnel organized and subsidized purchasing and marketing cooperatives in rural communities — the sort of organization that Ruiz and his colleagues had envisioned for rebozo producers (see Mastache and Morett 1982:19–23). The cooperatives were housed in enormous warehouses built in the center of most of the basin's rural communities.

No sooner had all of this infrastructure been constructed and the cooperatives formed than a budget crisis in 1982 forced the federal government to dramatically reduce its funding of FIDEPAL. By the mid-1980s, FIDEPAL had ceased purchasing cinta, the factory in Chilapa had all but halted production, the rural cooperatives had disappeared, and the rural warehouses had been abandoned, left to stand as unsightly monuments to the federal government's good but overly enthusiastic intentions. Middlemen in Chilapa, and by this time in larger rural communities, regained whatever position in the industry they had lost during FIDEPAL's brief reign. Here things stood for the next decade (through the late 1980s and into the early 1990s), by which time the government had reorganized, regrouped, and returned. In the late 1990s, the government once again became a major player in the region's palm industry, this time acting through proxy NGOs (see below).

THE MEXICAN STATE AND URBAN EMPLOYMENT

The first significant state involvement in the economic affairs of the Atempa basin was not the appearance of FIDEPAL but instead the construction of a transmission line and related access roads to Chilapa from a hydroelectric plant on the Río Azul at Colotlipa in the late 1940s (Catalán 1947). This was followed in the 1960s and 1970s by rural electrification and road construction projects and the founding of rural schools and health clinics. Simultaneously, a multitude of federal agencies (FIDEPAL among them) established regional offices in Chilapa. Some of these ventures made an impact on social life in the basin in terms of their intended functions (e.g., the Comisión Federal de Electricidad) while others did not (e.g., the Comisión Federal Electoral). Where they had their most profound effect was in creating a great host of salaried employees, many with expense accounts in addition to their salaries, who directed unprecedented amounts of money into the urban economy. Salaries for government employees were set according to federal pay schedules and were higher than the potential earnings of most alternative forms of local employment—dramatically higher in most cases.

A sense of the magnitude and scope of the new forms of work introduced by the federal government can be inferred from the occupational data in Chilapa's civil registry. For example, between 1960 and 1970, day-laborers (i.e., *jornaleros*) fell from a twentieth-century high of 23 percent of Chilapa's adult males in 1960 to 12 percent in 1970. Simultaneously, teachers increased from 5 percent to 14 percent,[3] and *empleados,* a substantial percentage of whom were employees of various government agencies, increased from 5 percent to 19 percent. Between 1970 and 2000, teachers and salaried employees remained unchanged as a percentage of Chilapa's adult male workforce (together, about 33 percent), but their absolute numbers rose sharply alongside the growth of Chilapa. If one adds to the numbers of teachers and salaried employees those who called themselves engineers, agronomists, medical doctors, operators of heavy machinery, and miscellaneous other occupational categories associated with government agencies, the total share of the urban workforce employed directly by the government since 1970 stands at about 40 percent.

I cannot leave this topic without drawing special attention to a trend that accompanied the growth of salaried employment by government agencies in Chilapa. In marriage records from years prior to the 1970s, women were so consistently assigned to the occupational category of *labores domesticas* (domestic labor), if an occupational category was mentioned at all, that I did not bother recording this information in my notes. There was the occasional teacher, secretary, or nurse, but not enough information was recorded for women for these outliers to make a statistical impact. This began changing in the 1970s; during the 1980s, substantial numbers of brides were listed as teachers and salaried employees. By 1985, occupational information for women had begun to be collected regularly. Women citing labores domesticas in this year amounted to 50 percent of the total while teachers and empleadas stood at 23 percent and 15 percent, respectively. Half of the remaining women were secretaries (a group that might easily have been reported as empleada), and the others included nurses, students, and one *obrera* (wage laborer). Between 1985 and 2000, the number of brides who cited labores domesticas as their occupation dropped further, from 50 percent to 38 percent of the total, while most other categories held constant and new occupations were added. As of 2000, there remained many occupations restricted to men, including most forms of manual or skilled labor, and only two exclusive to women (labores domesticas and nursing). The more striking employment trend was not this, however, but instead the movement of both men and women into the new occupational categories that were created with the arrival of the federal government in the local employment market.

No later than 1970, government services had become nearly as dominant a slice of the city's employment profile as the textile industry had been before 1947 (and as freighting service had been in 1791). While compensation rates varied by standing within this new industry, even low-paid government employment was compensated at rates far higher than the earnings of the earlier textile producers.

TRANSPORTATION CHANGE

The creation of branch offices of government bureaucracies, the proliferation of schools and health clinics, and the construction of (and subsequent maintenance work on) basic electrification, telecommunications, and transportation infrastructures combined in Chilapa to solve the problem of urban employment and earnings just as the palm industry had in the countryside. It is a good thing they did, too, because not far behind these new arrivals there came a mighty tide of cheap, mass-produced tonnage that sealed the fate of most alternative means of making a living in the region.

Bus service over a road from Chilpancingo to Chilapa was first established in 1937. The earliest report of travel by this means that I have seen was based on an experience in 1941, when an anthropologist noted that it was a two-hour trip over a *"buena carretera"* (good road) (Winning 1941:330). Those living in Chilapa gave the road less-glowing reviews. For example, in 1947 the curmudgeon Eicandro Ruiz Hernández and his colleagues ranked the poor quality of the road alongside merchant avarice as a central impediment to local economic development (Ruiz et al. 1947:24–26). Besides being steep and winding, the road subjected travelers to lengthy delays and seasonal disruptions in access because of mud, mud and rock slides, and flash flooding. In 1990 I interviewed several people about their travel experiences in the late 1950s and early 1960s, and I heard repeatedly of harrowing four-hour or aborted trips to Chilpancingo.

In the course of interviewing on the general topic of transportation, I was treated to some delicious stories that had faded into family lore among a prominent branch of the Silvas, the family that a generation earlier had fought expropriation of their hacienda at Tlaxinga and Axopilco. Through the twentieth century, the Silvas operated a tienda mestiza on the southwest corner of the zocalo, and they owned Chilapa's first car and cargo truck. They were representatives of a social class that is not often renowned for its populist impulses, but the privilege of being the first in town to own vehicles had apparently kindled in them a little ember of civic obligation. For a small cash consideration, the Silvas would treat their less-fortunate neighbors to rides around the zocalo in their open-top car. This they did at least for a time, until the family offered the city a glimpse of a different and darker side of the industrial era when Chilapa's first car and truck collided in the region's first automobile accident.

Using the ill-fated car as a sort of carnival piece might seem like an awful waste, which it arguably was, but through the early 1960s there were hardly any roads or other surfaces in the city or region that could handle automobile traffic. Even city streets paved with cobblestones generally had ceramic water pipes or drainage channels running down their centers that either would be crushed by the weight of an automobile or would interfere with the vehicle's operation. Perhaps the best perspective on the limited role played by vehicles within the basin can be gained by looking at the fuel supply that powered it all. A service station operated by Petróleos Mexicanos (PEMEX), the government-owned oil conglomerate, was built on the outskirts of Chilapa sometime after 1960. Any vehicle arriving in the region before the station was built had to haul enough fuel to power an entire round trip to and from the region, first from Chilpancingo and later from Tixtla. In interviews, I was told that a few merchants banded together to purchase and stock a gasoline tank as a private reserve, but this did little to alleviate the problem: there was not enough fuel in the Atempa basin to support purely local vehicular transportation until after 1960. For the Silvas of the 1940s, the only real alternatives to going in circles around the zocalo were to leave their car parked or to drive it back the way it had come, over the road to Chilpancingo. This was the route taken by the cargo truck, which the family used to haul palm goods to the Iguala railhead and import merchandise for their tienda. In this, it was not long before the Silvas were joined by other merchants.

Even in the case of long-distance, interregional travel, vehicles made inroads slowly, and arrieros were able to compete through the 1940s (Ruiz et al. 1947:23–25). The limited information on bus fares and freight-hauling rates that survives, included in Maurilio Muñoz's study from the early 1960s (1963:29–32), shows that even at this late date, vehicular travel for either passengers or freight remained only modestly less expensive than foot travel and animal portage (Kyle 1995:250). Photographic records from the 1960s show that consumer goods such as Coca-Cola, Del Prado cigarettes, and Bimbo bread products were advertised on the store-fronts of tiendas, while mountains of colorful plasticware, glassware, and aluminum buckets and cookware were arrayed in the tianguis (and proba-bly in tiendas as well) as attractively as their garish presentations allowed.[4] In addition to vehicles owned by local tienda owners, others operated by itinerant merchants were likely responsible for importing merchandise as well. Some of these can be seen in the photos, parked along the edges of the zocalo on market days. In later years, after the 1970s, itinerant merchants who passed through Chilapa as part of a regular weekly circuit through market towns became commonplace, but these earlier arrivals have more the look of opportunistic peddlers who followed no set schedule, promis-cuously pursuing opportunities wherever these led. This sort of itinerant merchant remains common in the region today, particularly in rural vil-lages, where they peddle odd lots of cheap home furnishings, seasonal produce, medicinal substances, children's toys, and a further miscella-neous collection of modern consumer goods.

Many of the new consumer goods that arrived on cargo trucks were just that, new consumer goods, that met no real competitors in a mar-ketplace that was steadily more flush with earnings from the expanding palm and service industries. Aside from glassware and aluminum cook-ware, which sometime shortly after 1962 put sufficient competitive pres-sure on Chilapa's thirty households of potters to drive them out of the business, the only product that I can show to have had a measurable impact on the regional economy before the 1970s was the metal plowshare, the use of which spread through the basin beginning in the 1950s (Kyle 1995:157–61). But bubbling below the surface, there were clearly many small battles taking place. One of the earliest battles probably pitted imported cooking oils against locally produced lard. Similarly, worn tire tread and leather replaced zoyate as raw materials for men's footgear. Apparently never a great favorite, aguardiente too seems to have disappeared from the local economy under the onslaught of imported alcohol. These were all early tastes of much more far-ranging and momentous battles to come.

The construction of the PEMEX station and roads in the decade fol-lowing Muñoz's study opened the floodgates to vehicular transportation. Most of the rural roads that exist in the region today were built between 1960 and 1970, and Highway 93, which followed a new and somewhat flatter route to Chilpancingo, was completed in 1973. The highway was notable not so much for its flatness but for its paved surface, its firm roadbed, and its supporting bridges and drainage features, all of which combined to make the road much more resistant (though not entirely immune) to the seasonal disruptions caused by the rock and mud slides and flash flooding that had plagued the earlier route. It gave more-reliable and faster access to the region; as a result, passenger and freight hauling costs plummeted. Exactly how much these costs fell is difficult to ascertain with precision. The savings were more dramatic for freight, where haulage costs fell to a fifth or less of what they had been a decade earlier (Kyle 1996a). For passengers and those carrying small loads within the basin, there often was no savings at all; thus, much foot travel and animal portage persisted. It all depended on one's location relative to the handful of privileged transportation corridors shown in map 3.

Even with the survival of preindustrial transportation systems, it would be hard to overemphasize the impact of the changes that had occurred prior to the 1970s. Even before Highway 93 was completed in 1973, competition between local and imported products extended to virtually everything produced in the region except palm goods and foodstuffs. Although relatively few local products subjected to this new pressure ceased to be produced altogether, the rate of return on nearly all of them diminished. As the region's only significant export industry, the production of palm goods alone benefited from the changes. Lower marketing costs, the simultaneous creation of FIDEPAL and its subsidy programs, and the sharp decline in earnings from alternatives combined to create widespread dependence among rural households on the palm industry. This degree of dependence on a single branch of commercial activity had no precedent in the countryside, nor did the economic vulnerability that it created.

After 1973, reduced interregional transportation costs and the influx of earnings from the palm industry and from salaries and wages combined to substantially tighten the integration of the Atempa basin into the broader national economy. Though there is little way of demonstrating this today, the new money flowing into the region must have fueled an unprecedented cycle of inflation in the local market. The consumption of new imported goods would have bled off much of this pressure, draining the region of currency, but the regional economy's food sector as yet remained insulated from the growing connections to the outside. Here the inflationary pressure was unchecked, driving food prices to unprecedented heights.[5] It was against this backdrop that FIDEPAL fell victim to the fiscal crisis that beset the federal government in 1982. FIDEPAL's subsidies evaporated, its producer cooperatives were abandoned, and only a skeleton staff was left manufacturing sombreros in the factory in Chilapa. The blow would have been devastating to rural households had there not been the simultaneous introduction of a whole new set of government bureaucracies and initiatives.

FOOD AND FERTILIZERS

As I indicate above, the increased integration of the Atempa basin into broader national markets had yet to have a significant impact on the flow of grain in the region through the 1970s. Neither had an altered commercial environment created changes in the urban diet. By 1950, commercial grain production had spread into the uplands; by 1970, it had pushed outward, beyond Zone 3. New metal plowshares simultaneously relaxed the workload associated with cultivating heavy vertisols of the plains and enabled farmers to engage in more-intensive plow agriculture in steeper upland terrain, but this did not substantially alter the productivity of farm labor (see Wilken 1987:15–17). Improvements in the local transportation infrastructure had a bigger impact on labor productivity, at least as applied to transportation, easing the spread of commercial maize production past the twelve-kilometer threshold and into Zone 4 (and perhaps beyond). This bought the city an extra decade. The real unpleasantness arrived in the 1970s, which opened with a deadly bang in the form of the worst drought in the Atempa basin's recorded history.[6] This was followed by five consecutive years of below-average rainfall.[7] For a city already poised on the brink of nutritional insolvency, this could not have been a welcome twist of fate. The drought put an emphatic punctuation mark on the urgent need for a whole new system of urban supply.

Looking back, we can clearly see two distinct phases in the process of devising a new means of delivering food to Chilapa: both drew on industrial techniques and technologies, and both were subsidized by the Mexican government. In the first (roughly from 1980 through 1991), industrial inputs, mostly chemical fertilizers, were made available to local farmers, who were thus endowed with the capacity to continue in their historic role as suppliers of the region's stock of basic foodstuffs. My initial research in the Atempa basin was conducted in the last years of this phase. In the second, which began in the early 1990s and is ongoing as I write, the government first dismantled the existing programs, then cobbled together a package of alternatives to aid rural households while it simultaneously saturated the urban market with imported foodstuffs. Farmers thereby found a once-reliable consumer market sated by imported grain priced below anything they could match. It was during this second phase that any semblance of an integrated regional economy in the Atempa basin finally disappeared.

After the introduction of metal plowshares and cargo trucks, the next application of industrial technologies to the problem of the regional grain supply came shortly after the completion of Highway 93. Sometime in the mid-1970s, a small amount of maize was imported to the Atempa basin by the Instituto Nacional Indigenista (INI) (Díaz 1976:67), a government agency established to promote economic development among Mexican Indians. Aside from arriving in insignificant amounts, the INI maize was distributed exclusively in rural villages distant from Chilapa, not in the city where it was most needed, and was almost certainly fed to poultry and swine (see Fox 1992:113). A slightly more significant development was the 1979 construction in Chilapa of a regional distribution facility for CONASUPO, the government-owned company established to distribute basic foodstuffs at subsidized prices.[8] Goods imported to the Atempa basin by CONASUPO were distributed through a network of rural stores, which in 1989 numbered thirty-six. I was able to obtain records only for 1989, when CONASUPO distributed about 730 tons of maize in the Atempa basin.[9] This came at a time when the regional demand surpassed 13,000 tons (much more if animal consumption is considered). The CONASUPO maize, much of it in the form of preground meal, was of a quality that was universally scorned. As had INI before them, CONASUPO shipped maize out of Chilapa to rural villages, where it too mostly wound up as feed for poultry and swine. Still, the CONASUPO maize was so cheap that it probably freed a small amount of the more valuable local product for distribution to the city.

CONASUPO's biggest impact in the Atempa basin actually had little to do with any direct contribution to the region's food supply. Aside from arriving in limited quantities, the timing was off; CONASUPO did not import maize to the Atempa basin until after 1979, when a separate batch of government agencies had arrived at a different and more successful (if short-lived) fix for the region's food issues. Where CONASUPO did make a difference was in the price of the grain in Chilapa. CONASUPO maize was available earlier and in larger quantities elsewhere in Guerrero, especially in the north in areas linked by paved roads to the railhead at Iguala, through which the grain was shipped. The market price of maize in northern Guerrero fell sharply as a result. With the completion of Highway 93, merchants in Chilapa were for the first time able to import maize. To ensure that merchants had no incentive to do this, and to preserve a position in the local market, maize producers in the Atempa basin were compelled to lower the selling price enough to at least match the cost of purchasing and importing maize. In this way, the activities of CONASUPO in neighboring regions altered the commercial environment and reduced grain prices in the Atempa basin, without CONASUPO's actually having much of a direct presence in the region.

The merchants I interviewed in 1990 reported that they and others regularly held cheap, low-quality, and often insect-damaged maize from northern Guerrero in reserve, releasing it onto the market as local supplies tightened and prices threatened to rise. In addition to providing visible notice to local farmers of what might come if they asked too much for their grain, the presence of even small amounts of imported grain in Chilapa had another effect on pricing. As recently as 1978, maize prices in Chilapa immediately prior to the harvest were more than double what they had been during the previous harvest season (Matías 1982:109–10). Seasonal fluctuations of this sort, once common, ceased to exist before I began documenting maize prices in 1990. The actions of CONASUPO in nearby regions had exerted a strong stabilizing effect in the Atempa basin as well as a deflationary one. Like the maize imported by INI and CONASUPO, the small amounts that merchants brought to Chilapa from northern Guerrero mostly ended up as feed for livestock. Nevertheless, interregional transportation costs had fallen sufficiently by 1980 to make it impossible to understand Chilapa's grain market without reference to nearby regions. The industrial noose on the regional food supply was tightening.

What enabled the Atempa basin's farmers to continue producing maize commercially, and even to profit in the face of falling prices, was a massive productivity spurt that accompanied the sudden availability of great quantities of chemical fertilizers. Fertilizers were first brought to Chilapa in the late 1960s by affluent merchants returning with merchandise from the railhead at Iguala. All fertilizers distributed in Mexico in these years were sold by Fertilizantes de México (FERTIMEX), a subsidiary of PEMEX. Although FERTIMEX sold fertilizers at subsidized prices from their warehouses, until the mid-1970s the nearest such facility was in Iguala and transport costs beyond that point had to be borne by private merchants and farmers (see Ahrens and Shields 1973). Fertilizers were heavy and bulky relative to their value, and thus the same transport constraints that prevented grain from being imported to the Atempa basin before the early

Figure 17. Farmer transporting a load of fertilizer to his field by horse.

1970s kept fertilizers out as well. After hauling only a couple of loads and finding no meaningful profit, Chilapa's merchants (including a different branch of the Silva family) abandoned the trade altogether. Smaller-scale traders gradually stepped into the vacuum, especially after transport costs fell in 1973 and after a FERTIMEX warehouse and distribution facility was built in Chilpancingo. This extended the government subsidy on transporting fertilizers nearer to Chilapa, though still not near enough to warrant importing more than small amounts (fig. 17).

There was a factor in addition to high retail prices that operated to retard the adoption of chemical fertilizers by farmers in the Atempa basin in the 1970s. The only fertilizers that were imported to the basin before 1980 were various forms of nitrogen (mostly ammonium sulfate and urea). Nitrogen deficiency was universal in the region's arable soils, but many areas were deficient in phosphorus also; there, nitrogen alone had a limited impact on maize yields. I listened patiently as the elite merchants who initially dabbled in the fertilizer trade told me how a lack of knowledge about the proper uses of chemical fertilizers among farmers and a general reluctance to experiment with novel technologies had limited local demand (and drove the merchants from the trade). I think that high transport costs, marginal returns to both merchants and farmers, and the inappropriateness of the available chemical formulas probably played a larger role in inhibiting the use of fertilizers than had either ignorance or the inherent conservatism of farmers.

Neither ignorance nor conservatism was much in evidence, at least not among farmers, in the years that followed. All of the economic and technical problems that limited demand for fertilizers in the 1970s were abruptly resolved in the early 1980s when a FERTIMEX warehouse was built on the outskirts of Chilapa. The warehouse was part of a fleeting (and failed) national initiative to achieve self-sufficiency in the production of basic foodstuffs (Austin and Esteva 1987; Fox 1992; Sanderson 1986), known as the Sistema Alimentario Mexicano (SAM). Unlike most earlier agricultural modernization efforts, which directed subsidies and technical support to already commercialized, capitalized, and often export-oriented farmers in northern Mexico, SAM was aimed at increasing access to modern farming technologies by poor farmers in the south, a group defined in a way that comfortably accommodated all farmers in the Atempa basin. The basic ingredients to the program involved extra subsidies for industrial inputs, technical assistance, and low-interest loans. The effort spanned government agencies, drawing resources and expertise from, among others, FERTIMEX, SARH, and the Banco de Crédito Rural (BANRURAL), this latter a government-run lending institution for farmers. Nationally, the retail price for chemical fertilizers, the most important industrial input, dropped by as much as 30 percent in 1980 alone (Austin and Fox 1987:69–71). In the Atempa basin, the effective subsidy was far larger because in building a FERTIMEX warehouse in Chilapa, the government for the first time absorbed the entire cost of transporting fertilizers into the region. Also for the first time, significant quantities of mixed-formula fertilizers reached the basin.

Two years after it began, in 1982, SAM fell victim to the same government budget crisis that had done in FIDEPAL. Fertilizer prices reverted to their pre-SAM levels, and the BANRURAL loan fund dried up. To farmers in the Atempa basin, this was not entirely a bad thing; the farmers who followed the advice of the SARH technical experts generally came to regret their docility. As an institution, SARH was famous for its lack of respect for indigenous agricultural systems; its agronomists worked tirelessly to convince farmers to forsake all that they knew about farming and to use new seed-stock, to plant commercial crops other than maize, and generally to adopt the latest fashions in scientific agriculture (Matías 1997). As Exhibit A in the case against the SARH agronomists, I submit a

BANRURAL loan that was urged on ejidatarios of Pantitlán. The loan was intended to underwrite a switch from maize to commercial potato production, an activity that had no precedent in the region or anywhere nearby. The result was one small potato crop, a second crop lost to a fungus that I was unable to identify, a default on the BANRURAL loan, and a reversion back to maize production. After 1982, the SARH agronomists were hobbled by a lack of resources and became a mostly harmless presence, as notable for the consumer demand generated by their comparatively fat salaries as for any role they played in local farming. They remained tireless advocates for hybrid and "improved" seed varieties and for the latest recommended fertilizer treatments,[10] but they lacked the resources to do much more than talk.

Despite the brevity of its existence and the often-inappropriate advice of its experts, SAM stimulated great changes in the Atempa basin by establishing the necessary infrastructure to distribute cheap fertilizers to the region's farmers. The FERTIMEX warehouse remained in operation after 1982 and received regular and steadily larger shipments of fertilizers through 1991. Fertilizer prices probably rose when the SAM program ended, but fertilizers remained far cheaper than they had been before the FERTIMEX warehouse was constructed. The effect on the regional economy was nearly instantaneous. By the mid-1980s, chemical fertilizers had come to be applied to more than 95 percent of the basin's cultivated surface (SARH 1987). In 1990 and 1991, I did not find a single crop growing in the basin absent chemical assistance. With the specter of imported grain lurking just outside the basin and with grain prices in Chilapa driven to historic lows as a result, a tremendous productivity boost was required to keep imported grain out and maize farming alive in the Atempa basin after 1980. This is just what chemical fertilizers provided. Fallowing even the most marginal upland fields to restore fertility was made unnecessary, and maize yields everywhere in the basin tripled and in some areas quadrupled. By 1990, maize had come to be produced in such prodigious quantities that finding markets had become the principal concern. Perhaps what saved local farmers was the high quality of what they produced. This was no hybrid maize bred to feed poultry or cattle or to be disassembled at the molecular level into starches, sugars, and oils. It was instead maize bred to be eaten, bred to be enjoyed. Most urban Mexicans had by 1990 acclimated to the flavorless product of modern industrial agriculture, but in and around Chilapa, people spent the 1980s and early 1990s awash in what we would today consider boutique maize varieties. The Atempa basin was even able to share its bounty, shipping quantities of high-quality maize to the more discriminating consumers who remained in Chilpancingo and Acapulco.

NEOLIBERALISM, SEDESOL, AND NGOS

About this same time, neoliberalism and a set of development prescriptions that became known as the Washington consensus (in recognition of their popularity among U.S. trade negotiators and lending institutions) arrived in the basin. Neoliberalism conjures up images of heartless bureaucrats, an image that in Mexico was once personified by president Carlos Salinas de Gortari (1988–94) until his term ended, the depth of the corruption that pervaded his administration was revealed, and his public persona was transformed from efficiency expert to miscreant. His bespectacled successor, Ernesto Zedillo Ponce de León (1994–2000), was much truer to type; lacking even an iota of charisma, the man is today recalled for his sincerity and competence. The beginnings of Mexico's implementation of the relevant policies, though not then known as "neoliberalism," can be traced to the aftermath of the 1982 debt crisis when Salinas's predecessor, Miguel de la Madrid Hurtado (1982–88), was forced to accept bailout terms dictated by international lenders. Salinas greatly accelerated the scope of neoliberal policies and the pace of their implementation; subsequent presidents, including Zedillo, Vicente Fox Quesada (2000–2006), and Felipe de Jesús Calderón Hinojosa (2006–present), have likewise been disciples of the creed.

From a rhetorical standpoint, the hallmark of neoliberalism is a commitment to reducing the role of government in the national economy as much and as fast as is politically feasible. This meant trimming government employment rosters, reducing barriers to international trade, privatizing government-owned industries, and deregulating as many sectors of the domestic economy as possible. The apparent intention of those designing Mexico's neoliberal policies was to draw to a close programs that granted universal access to subsidies and price supports (Cornelius 1994:xv–xvi); increasing numbers of Mexicans, it was felt, could well afford to pay their way through life at fair market prices rather than relying on subsidies that the government could ill afford. Furthermore, many policymakers questioned the wisdom of subsidizing existing production patterns; in remote and impoverished regions such as the Atempa basin, the programs seemed to perpetuate rather than alleviate poverty. Against this background, some among those shaping the government's agricultural policy began thinking of the programs they administered as issues of social welfare rather than economic development (Fox 1994:247–48).

In the Atempa basin, where rural producers had long depended on heavily subsidized forms of commodity production, urban employment rested on government services, and access to fertilizers, fuel, transportation, and even basic foodstuffs was shaped by government price controls, there had never been a meaningful distinction between "welfare" and "development" programs. If the intent of government planners had been to help undercapitalized producers establish a presence in national markets — to allow producers to compete in the market without government assistance — then no program introduced in the basin can be said to have been remotely successful. Even in the years of maximum fertilizer availability and use, in the late 1980s, farmers depended on fertilizer subsidies and other price supports, and still they fell far short of matching the productivity of fully industrialized (albeit themselves heavily subsidized) farmers. For example, in 2000, average maize yields in Iowa, in the core of the U.S. grain belt, came to a bit over 9 tons per hectare, more than double the highest average yield ever recorded in the Atempa basin. Whereas a farmer in the Atempa basin could count himself lucky if he had the land and fortitude to get a maize crop from 2 or 3 hectares of land, an average Iowa maize farmer worked thirty or forty times more land (about 90 hectares) and still ran a risk of growing obese from want of exercise. In 2000, Chilapa had 22,511 residents, a population that would have consumed 4,165 tons of grain if industrially produced and processed foodstuffs had not previously altered the composition of the typical diet. This amount could be produced by five average Iowa maize farmers.[11] Even factoring in the cost of transporting maize from Iowa to Chilapa, the import still came out cheaper than maize produced locally.

Neoliberal reform can be traced to the early 1980s, but President Salinas's contributions of the early 1990s were what created the most radical break with the paternalism inherited from the Mexican Revolution and the Cárdenas administration. The new Agrarian Code of 1994, the liberalization of international trade (including the passage of the North American Free Trade Agreement [NAFTA] and Mexico's entry into the General Agreement on Tariffs and Trade [GATT]), the privatization of key industries, the reduction or outright elimination of price controls on vital goods and services, and the euphemism "structural readjustment" to refer to the resulting economic carnage, were all legacies of Salinas's administration.

In the Atempa basin, the change that posed the most immediate threat was the 1991 privatization of FERTIMEX. Fertilizer prices abruptly rose and fertilizer deliveries abruptly fell. I have no data specific to the Atempa basin, but in the state of Guerrero as a whole, fertilizer sales fell from 127,910 tons in 1987 to 54,429 tons in 1992 (Espinosa and Meza 2000:89). Most of the fertilizer that was delivered to Guerrero in 1992 went to the state's more-commercialized farmers in the north and on the coast. Reports from the Atempa basin make clear that this was not one of the areas to which meaningful quantities were shipped (e.g., Illsley et al. 2003:12). Maize yields accordingly plummeted.

Recognizing that Mexico had large numbers of poor whose livelihood and well-being depended directly on the various government programs and policies that were to be phased out or eliminated, President Salinas's package of neoliberal reforms included a new program, the Programa Nacional de Solidaridad (National Solidarity Program, or PRONASOL), that was charged with maintaining the most vital government interventions in local economies. Under PRONASOL, many funding decisions were removed from the portfolio of entrenched federal bureaucracies; municipios and local civic organizations were instead given unprecedented responsibility for identifying development priorities. Ayuntamientos and NGOs were felt to be more responsive to local needs and potentialities. The recipe proved effective, at least if measured in the electoral success of the program's architects, and in 1992 PRONASOL was expanded and made into a government ministry, known as the Secretaría de Desarrollo Social (Ministry of Social Development, or SEDESOL). As had PRONASOL before it, SEDESOL served as a granting agency that provided funding to support a myriad of initiatives proposed by local governments and NGOs (Fox and Aranda 1996; Rodríguez 1997; Yaworsky 2002, 2005).

Were it possible to give a full accounting of federal expenditures in the Atempa basin, I am confident that it would reveal that the era of neoliberal reform has witnessed a substantial increase in government involvement in the local economy rather than the reverse, which the rhetoric of neoliberalism might lead one to anticipate. The fact that the government has generally acted through proxies changes nothing in this regard. SEDESOL had divided the country into administrative regions that were lumped into funding-eligibility categories based on the scope and breadth of poverty found within them (Yaworsky 2002:50–51). The Atempa basin easily qualified for the highest levels of support; in consequence, resources have poured into the basin. Much of the SEDESOL money has been funneled through the ayuntamiento, one of the few conduits for which the flow of funds is documented in public records. On the eve of neoliberalism's arrival in Mexico, in 1982, Chilapa's ayuntamiento had receipts and expenditures that were the equivalent of $172,800 in U.S. dollars. By 1990 this had grown to $1,673,000, a near-tenfold increase.[12] Early the following year, President Salinas made an appearance in Chilapa. With a great deal of fanfare, he bestowed on the ayuntamiento a new dump truck, expanding the fleet from two to three. He also announced that a new market building would be constructed to relieve congestion in the center of town. Thirteen years and one small riot later,[13] the project was finally completed and the congestion in some ways relieved,[14] though many in town, not least merchants with storefronts on the zocalo, still consider this a source of regret. The final initiative that Salinas announced in 1991 was a road-paving project on the road north to Zitlala, a project that provoked only slightly less controversy;[15] it was completed in a year or two. What Salinas did not announce was that the ayuntamiento budget was to be augmented. It rose from $1,673,000 in 1990 to $2,638,000 in 1991. Expenditures then held steady for the next seven years before climbing abruptly to $9,323,000 in 1999 and to over $13,000,000 in 2000 and beyond. The first twenty years of neoliberalism thus witnessed a seventy-seven-fold increase in annual spending by the local government. Most of the new money came from the federal government, whose contribution to the ayuntamiento's revenue stream rose from 66 percent in 1982 to 96 percent in 2001.

In 2001, Chilapa's presidente municipal published an *Informe,* a sort of state-of-the-municipio report, in which he gave a detailed accounting of the uses his administration had made of the federal largess (Miranda 2001). A substantial amount, 18 percent, funded a tremendously expanded and well-equipped police force — the same force that a few years later was called out to quiet rioting merchants, among other things. A much larger share was spent on infrastructural projects, especially in the burgeoning city; streets were paved, potable water systems were built or expanded, and a modern landfill was built (replacing a ravine above Nexapa) to handle the city's growing output of garbage, which in 2001 amounted to thirty-two tons daily. In the countryside, engineers fitted roads with culverts and drainage systems to improve access in the rainy season. Comisarías, basketball courts, schools, and health clinics were built or refurbished, and new electrification projects were undertaken. Then there were amounts transferred directly to households and individuals, both in cash and in kind. In 2001, 33,000 daily food rations were distributed to families and 45,700 free breakfasts were served to schoolchildren. Housing construction materials were likewise widely distributed. Over $700,000 was dispersed in cash, most to women in outlying villages. Notably, by the late 1990s, the ayuntamiento had become the basin's largest distributor of fertilizer, which was sold to farmers at about half the price charged by merchants (Yaworsky 2002:56–58). In 2001, the amount of fertilizer distributed by the ayuntamiento came to 10,231 tons (worth $1,600,000), more than 20 percent of the quantity sold in the entire state in 1992. Another $44,000 was dispersed among 632 farmers as unsecured, low-interest loans (of $50 to $100 each); $66,000 was spent on feed, medicines, and other goods to support animal husbandry; and $16,500 went to purchase electric mills and sewing machines that were given to rural women. And in perhaps the most flagrant defiance of the basic tenets of neoliberalism, the ayuntamiento dipped into the public coffers to purchase and distribute 20,900 toys to the basin's children.

The ayuntamiento was not the only player involved in dispersing federal funds. Indeed, several federal bureaucracies in addition to SEDESOL maintained or even expanded their operations; in terms of urban employment, the federal government's health and education bureaucracies were of major importance. INI, too, emerged from the reorganization of government bureaucracies intact, finding many new partners (both in and out of government) to sustain established programs. As it had since its arrival in the region in the 1960s, INI funded a constellation of social welfare and development programs in rural communities that were similar, if more limited in scope, to those administered by the ayuntamiento in 2001. Perhaps the most important administrators of SEDESOL funds, second only to the ayuntamiento, were NGOs that emerged in tandem with the growth of PRONASOL and SEDESOL in the early 1990s (Yaworsky 2002, 2005). The largest and best funded was Sanzekan Tinemi, an organization that grew from "community food councils" that had served as local consultative groups for CONASUPO in the 1980s (Meza 2000). NGOs came in many shapes and sizes, and some received portions of their funding from other government agencies and even from international donors, including the Inter-American Development Bank and the Commission for Environmental Cooperation. Even so, such an overwhelming portion of the resources supporting NGOs in the Atempa basin came from SEDESOL that it is not unreasonable to think of them as adjuncts to SEDESOL itself (Yaworsky 2002:65–66, 2005).

The diverse uses to which SEDESOL funds have been put by NGOs

and by SEDESOL have been catalogued by William Yaworsky (2002).
One that has reached perhaps the largest number of people has been Sanzekan Tinemi's resurrection of certain efforts pioneered years earlier by
FIDEPAL. Having reprised the old argument that the economic benefits of
the palm industry were unduly concentrated in the hands of Chilapa's
monopolistic merchants, Sanzekan Tinemi obtained SEDESOL funds to
organize production cooperatives and to establish itself as a purchasing
agent and marketing firm. In the late 1990s, Sanzekan Tinemi orchestrated
sales of palm goods to a Dutch nonprofit company (known as Fair Trade
Organisatie) that specializes in marketing artisanal products made by indigenous peoples of developing regions of the world. The relationship
was short-lived but solidified Sanzekan Tinemi's position in the palm industry. Though lacking the resources to subsidize producers to the extent that FIDEPAL had, Sanzekan Tinemi has nevertheless transferred
substantial amounts of money to producers in the form of unsecured low-
interest loans, cash payments, and marketing assistance.[16] A similar program involved mescal. Sanzekan Tinemi spearheaded an effort to expand
maguey production from the traditional mescal-producing stronghold of
Tepehuisco to surrounding communities and to introduce the resulting
product in national and international markets. The project entailed a detailed market analysis, environmental studies, the introduction of modern
distilling technologies, and the formal incorporation and licensing of the
enterprise. What had once been a thoroughly preindustrial and illicit cot-
tage industry serving only local demand was thus transformed into a small
but modern and industrialized operation (GEA 2002).

Another notable program, administered directly by SEDESOL, was
known as the Programa Nacional de Jornaleros Agrícolas (National Program for Agricultural Laborers). This was ostensibly aimed at "improv-
ing" the lives of seasonal agricultural laborers, but in practical terms, the
program simply provided organizational structure and support to facilitate
seasonal migration; the result was a substantial increase in human yield for
labor contractors seeking seasonal workers for agribusiness concerns in
northern Mexico. Before the early 1990s, seasonal migration from rural
villages in the Atempa basin had generally involved relatively small numbers of men who struck out in any of a number of directions following the
maize harvest. In 1990 and 1991, I knew people who did seasonal work in
construction trades in coastal tourist centers, others who picked tomatoes
in northern Mexico, and still others who picked fruits and vegetables in
California and Oregon. I also knew of households in Chilapa in which

money remitted by people who had left more permanently, to Mexico City
or to the United States, had become a significant source of earnings. But
before 1990–91, there had existed nothing so systematic and nothing that
involved as many people or as much money as the migration stream that
SEDESOL would shortly organize. Under the new program, contractors
from industrialized farms in northern Mexico, mostly in the state of Sina-
loa, came to a SEDESOL facility in Chilapa to negotiate contracts with
village representatives and organize transportation to work sites. The number of farmers who participated was massive. In 1998, about 10,000 laborers, drawn from every village in the Atempa basin outside of Zone 1,
were transported from Chilapa to northern Mexico. Many whole families
accompanied those who signed contracts; in most villages, between half
and two-thirds of the entire population came and went seasonally.

A fair number of those who remained year-round in their natal villages
participated in the region's premier make-work project. Beginning in 1993,
Sanzekan Tinemi and other NGOs, using SEDESOL funds, joined with the
Secretaría de Medio Ambiente, Recursos Naturales, y Pesca (Ministry of
Environment, Natural Resources, and Fisheries) to organize reforestation
projects. Workers were paid 90 percent of the legal minimum wage in what
amounted to full-time, year-round occupations (Yaworsky 2002:215–21).
The most complete data come from the Sanzekan Tinemi records for
the year 1999, when this group employed 972 individuals to plant some
500,000 plants on at least 300 hectares of land. Other workers were employed seasonally and by other NGOs. While I have no data on the total
area in the basin that has been newly reforested, it almost certainly runs
into the thousands of hectares.

FOOD AND THE FATE OF THE REGION

Reforestation in the Atempa basin's uplands has been made possible
by a relaxation in pressure on the landscape occasioned by depopulation of
the uplands and a simultaneous shift among urban consumers to a more
thorough dependence on industrial food production and distribution systems. Though the basin's overall population has grown since 1990, it has
become more concentrated in Chilapa and in the largest towns and villages; thirty-five of the seventy-nine rural villages that existed in both 1990
and 2000 lost population, and many others barely held steady. Meanwhile,
urban consumers began drawing a substantial share of their food and fuel

directly from outside suppliers rather than through the more indirect route of importing and distributing fertilizer and allowing local farmers to supply the market. Reforestation of land that had earlier been cleared to provide fuel and expand the cultivated surface signals a relaxation in the intensity of local land use and a displacement of the environmental footprint of the Atempa basin's population to locations outside of the basin. In short, it signals the final dismemberment of the internal division of labor that once defined and gave structure to the regional economy.

The trigger that set in motion the final moments of the region's pre-industrial history was the 1991 privatization of FERTIMEX. Fertilizer use fell to practically nothing in 1992, and maize yields reverted to pre-industrial levels.[17] Although fertilizer had begun trickling back into the basin by 1993,[18] it did not arrive in quantities equal to the late 1980s until 1999 or 2000, when the ayuntamiento assumed control of its distribution. In 2001, local farmers used record amounts, which they obtained at heavily subsidized prices, and maize yields had likely returned to their earlier highs. By the time this happened, however, the local consumer market had been profoundly changed.

I was unable to travel to the Atempa basin for several years after my dissertation research was completed in the late summer of 1991. When I next returned in the summer and fall of 1997, I found Chilapa to be almost unrecognizable. The most obvious change involved the city's spectacular growth and the resulting congestion that this had caused in the narrow streets of its inner precincts. Vendors had spilled out of the daily market and had overrun the arterials in the center of town. New retail outlets were everywhere, and ambulatory vendors worked the streets in numbers far greater than before. The tianguis had grown, too, spilling out of the zocalo into the streets for several blocks in all directions. The number of auto-mobiles had grown to a point at which passage through the city's narrow streets was practically impossible even on weekdays, the traza not having been designed to accommodate automobiles. There were no parking facili-ties; vehicle owners were forced to devise solutions that impeded both vehicular and pedestrian movement. By 2000, the local government had restricted certain streets to one-way traffic but liberty, improvisation, and gridlock reigned in 1997.

These were my first impressions of the city in 1997. A few days passed before I came to appreciate that another change, more fundamental to the city's underlying nature, went beyond mere scale and volume. In 1991, Chi-lapa supported only two *tortillerías* (a store where tortillas are made and sold). In both, *nixtamal* (maize soaked in lime solution to remove the pericarp) was first prepared in large troughs, then ground into *masa* (dough) using the same sort of mills that could be found scattered throughout the town and that were patronized by neighborhood women who made their own nixtamal and tortillas. In the tortillerías, the masa was fed into a machine that converted it into tortillas. Machine-made tortillas were not especially popular, and the tortillerías were patronized by the small numbers of people who, for one reason or another, found it inconvenient to make tortillas in their households and opted not to buy them from *tortilleras* (women who sold homemade tortillas from their homes or street corners in the center of town). What practically all of the tortillas made in Chilapa in 1990 and 1991 had in common, no matter where or by which means they were produced, was that they were made of locally produced grain that was first processed into nixtamal, then ground into masa, and then made into tortillas. To the best of my knowledge, I did not knowingly eat a single tortilla in Chilapa that was made from anything other than locally produced grain. The alternatives, including grain imported by merchants and CONASUPO, were considered suitable only for animals. This was especially the case for the preground tortilla mix sold under the brand names of Maseca and Minsa. Both of these products were available in 1991 in limited quantities in a few tiendas (especially CONASUPO tiendas), but I knew of no one who ate them.

When I arrived in 1997, I found that resistance to the consumption of imported grain and other foodstuffs had gone the way of the city's sleepy streets. There were at least eighteen new tortillerías scattered about the city, and all were outfitted with new machinery that streamlined tortilla production; one merely added Maseca (or Minsa) and water, and the machines handled the rest. How, I asked, had people's tastes changed so dramatically in six years? This was nothing, I was told. To see something truly noteworthy, I should have been there a couple of years earlier. In 1995, the federal government distributed thousands of cards with magnetic strips that entitled the bearer to free tortillas when presented at new "authorized" tortillerías. These were stores that were allowed to participate in a subsidy program through which store owners were reimbursed by the government for the tortillas they distributed. All of the participating tortillerías were equipped with card-scanning devices and with the new machinery that used only preground tortilla mix. The older machines, the ones that converted masa made from nixtamal into tortillas, had ceased operations, those tortillerías not having been invited to participate in the program. In other words, tortillas made of imported and processed maize were distributed free, while those made from local grain were not. The cards were apparently distributed by the fistful to everyone in town; I was assured that I would have received a stack of them had I been there at the time, my income and immigration status notwithstanding. Subsidized food distribution programs, particularly covering tortillas, had been introduced among the poor in more-industrialized and urban areas of Mexico years earlier, but nothing like this had existed in the Atempa basin until the mid-1990s.

Upon hearing all of this, I immediately began surveying the new tortillerías in an effort to determine the quantities of maize they were distributing. In 1997, I managed to collect information on ten of eighteen tortillerías. As my other informants had reported, employees and owners of the tortillerías claimed that tortilla sales had fallen in the last year or two as the supply of the magnetic cards diminished. Even so, about 950 tons of maize were distributed in 1997 from the ten tortillerías I surveyed; had the eight remaining tortillerías sold comparable amounts, the total amount of grain consumed in the form of mass-produced tortillas (made from imported, preground tortilla mix) would have come to 1,710 tons. This is an amount equal to about half of the maize that would have been consumed in the city had consumption rates remained at preindustrial levels. More likely, the caloric contribution of maize in the diet of Chilapa's residents had fallen, replaced by small but gradually increasing amounts of wheat products, fats and oils, and meat and dairy products, such that the new tortillerías were probably the source of substantially more than half of the city's tortillas in 1997.

Similar inquiries that I conducted in 2001 covered nine of the twenty tortillerías that then existed. Sales had dropped slightly from 1997, to something in the neighborhood of 1,250 tons of maize. Tortilleras, the women who made tortillas using locally produced grain, had captured a conspicuously larger market share than they had held in either 1991 or 1997. What is surprising is that they had not captured an even larger share and that the new tortillerías survived at all. After all, this came on the heels of the 2000 maize harvest, which had benefited from the record amounts of fertilizer distributed by the ayuntamiento. That there was not a still-more-pronounced movement back to the consumption of locally produced grain was a testament to the thoroughness with which the earlier subsidy program had led to a displacement of tortilla making from the households of consumers. As women entered the workforce in ever-larger numbers, the work of preparing food in households had became progressively more streamlined and homemade tortillas increasingly rare. Pressure in this direction certainly existed in 1991, but the combination of reduced local grain production (caused by the disruption in fertilizer availability in the early 1990s) and the simultaneous appearance of tons of free tortillas made from Maseca and Minsa was what tipped the balance in favor of importation. Once tipped, even the restoration of the local grain supply was not enough to restore the region to its earlier configuration. Urban consumers had joined their urban brethren elsewhere in having acclimated to imported and industrially processed food products.

For those in the countryside, newly cast adrift, the restoration of fertilizer supplies in the late 1990s held the promise that they might recapture a market in which they had once had no competitors. It was not to be. Relative to agricultural production costs, and especially labor costs, maize prices had lost so much ground that even production for subsistence looked steadily less sensible. Indeed, the new tortillerías had spread into rural villages alongside their proliferation in Chilapa; I know of at least six, and I suspect that there are many more, that appeared in villages in the mid- to late 1990s. Labor invested in subsistence maize production had for some years yielded a rate of return lower than prevailing wages, but when there was no wage work to be had, it nevertheless made sense for farmers to use their otherwise-idle hours and their land to secure a supply of food. The expanded opportunities created by NGOs, the arrival of labor contractors from the north, and the construction and commercial boom in Chilapa that accompanied the flood of SEDESOL money into the region had combined to tip the economic balance away from farming. As recently as 2002, I found farmers using their land as intensively as ever (see Appendix B), applying the record amounts of fertilizers that were distributed by the ayuntamiento to produce what was likely a bumper crop. Two years later, the futility of it all had apparently settled in, and the intensity of land use fell accordingly. Though I heard some, mostly men, complain of the foul taste of the modern tortilla and I heard many express regret at the steadily rising cost of living, I have heard none mourn the passing of the economic and ecological unit that I have called a region. Preoccupied by the immediate problem of making a living in a newly interconnected world, no one noticed that the region had slipped quietly into history.

CONCLUSION

In Memoriam

For roughly two hundred years, from the early 1790s to the early 1990s, living in the Atempa basin entailed carving out a niche in a broader regional economy that encompassed households scattered throughout the basin. Exactly how scattered and how thoroughly a household's productive efforts were oriented toward the broader whole varied through time and space. At the center of it all was Chilapa, a settlement that spent most of the colonial period as a sleepy and distant agrarian backwater, the sort of place to which junior government administrators might be sent to prove their worth or to which older ones whose star had fallen were exiled. In the second half of the eighteenth century, a shift in the broader colonial economy transformed Chilapa and its immediate surroundings into a strategic location from which to exploit commercial opportunities associated with New Spain's textile industry. This drew a handful of entrepreneurs and a larger retinue of arrieros, craftsmen, and others of central Mexico's working class into the basin, where they planted the seeds of a city. After incubating quietly for a few decades, Chilapa roared to life in the early 1790s as a full-blown urban manufacturing center. For those living in Chilapa's shadow, life would never be the same.

Residents of the urban center required consumers for their products and suppliers to satisfy their needs. Consumers of urban products were found in the city, in local villages, and, especially, in distant markets. With respect to the needs of urban households, topping the list was food. Owing to transport constraints, food could be supplied only by farmers who lived and worked in the surrounding countryside. It was a countryside populated mostly by Indians, descendants of those who had occupied the basin "from time immemorial" and had watched, or had tried to watch, from the margins as Chilapa underwent its urban transformation. If there had been an initial effort by Chilapa's residents to induce their rural neighbors to par-

203

ticipate voluntarily in a regional economy, it fell flat and was swiftly replaced by brutality and coercion organized by the city's economic and
political elites. Had Chilapa been larger, wealthier, and better connected to
a network of outside urban centers upon which elites could draw for support, they might have managed to pull it off. However, Chilapa's elites
overplayed their hand — which became fatally clear in 1842 when the relative balance of power between city and country, between rich and poor,
was briefly put to a test.

Having failed in the effort to design an urban hinterland to their liking
and in the service of their interests, the masters of the Atempa basin moved
on and left their misshapen creation to its own devices. The regional economy came close to collapsing entirely as substantial numbers from the
urban working class abandoned urban life and headed to the countryside to
join Indian villagers and try their hand at farming. Yet they did not completely severe their links to the city, which shrank but survived in a fashion,
and the Indians they met in the countryside were eventually lured into
maintaining or expanding their participation in local commerce. The bulk
of their nutritional needs supplied by their own efforts, those in the countryside participated in the regional economy on their own terms, driven by
self-interest and the tangible material benefits that came from doing so.
The benefits included improved access to consumer goods (clothing, ceramic cooking vessels, agricultural tools, and minor foodstuffs, among
other things) and the added security that came from maintaining pigs,
poultry, specie, or some other exchangeable commodity with a value that
could be tapped in hard times.

Commerce among city folk, in contrast, was not merely a matter of
improved access to a minimal inventory of consumer goods or a means of
providing economic security in the face of an oftentimes capricious and
unforgiving world. For urbanites, participation in the regional economy
was obligatory, not voluntary. Like a brain's consumption of oxygen, a
constant and timely delivery of adequate amounts of maize was required to
cover the caloric requirements of Chilapa's residents. Using the proceeds
of the textile industry, those who remained in Chilapa after the 1840s
rebellion were able to draw the needed supplies from the countryside; with
this, the regional economy came of age. By the turn of the twentieth
century, it had hit a point of maturity, had begun showing signs of strain by
the 1920s, and had entered its twilight years by 1940. Through the decades
leading into the mid-twentieth century, the growth of population in households of commercial maize farmers led to a gradual shift from maize to

other commercial pursuits. The resulting increase in the cost of su
the flow of maize into the city ultimately set in motion a spiral of ec
decline that nearly toppled the city and with it the region.

Chilapa might not have survived as an urban center through the 1950s
without exploiting new economic opportunities that opened with the accelerating industrialization of central Mexico. Reduced transport costs occasioned by the spread of vehicular transportation systems allowed producers
and merchants in the Atempa basin to redirect their energies from the failed
textile industry to the production of palm goods. This temporarily halted
Chilapa's decline and allowed the region to maintain an approximation
of its earlier economic configuration. Lower transportation costs were a
mixed blessing, however, that acted as a slow-growing cancer eating away
at the pockets of economic vitality that survived in the region. Vehicles
enabled merchants to import a wide range of cheap consumer goods, creating direct head-to-head competition between outside industrialized and
local preindustrial producers. With the exceptions of food and palm products, the rate of return on the basin's surviving forms of commodity production tumbled as a result of the competition. Not all in the countryside
had the ability to produce food commercially, and there were limits to the
profit that could be earned in producing palm goods. In the 1960s, the
regional economy again faced imminent collapse. This time the end was
averted only by means of heavy government investments in infrastructure
and a transfer of public funds into the region as both salaries and subsidies.

Through 1992, government planners did relatively little to draw overt
attention to the depth of the control that their growing role in the economy
had created. A handful of overzealous agronomists notwithstanding, the
whole thrust of government intervention in the basin's economy was essentially conservative. Introduced technologies and subsidy programs had
merely enhanced the effectiveness of existing patterns of production and
distribution. The combination of fertilizers and cargo trucks (neither being
nearly as useful alone as in combination) boosted agricultural productivity
and extended the distances over which maize could be moved; subsidies
were offered to producers of palm goods to help rural households continue
practicing mixed-subsistence and small-scale commodity production; and
salaries of government employees supplied urban households with the
purchasing power they needed to continue drawing commodities to the
market from the surrounding countryside. Although many preindustrial
activities were allowed to disappear, the most important components of the
economy were propped up and made to continue.

The use of industrial technologies and the tightening of material link-ages to outside commercial networks increased steadily after the 1950s, received a mighty boost with the completion of the highway in 1973, and reached a point of abject dependence no later than 1980. This had different consequences and created different sorts of political and economic vul-nerabilities in the city and in the country. Urban households had been dependent on commercial suppliers for as long as the city had existed; whether the suppliers were ten or ten thousand kilometers away mattered little, so long as the needed goods and services arrived consistently and in adequate amounts. In 1992, the government policy makers who ensured that this was accomplished abruptly changed course and drew to an end the programs that in previous decades had kept Chilapa supplied by sustaining the broad outlines of the earlier preindustrial region. Rather than directing fertilizer to local farmers, the new managers of Chilapa's economy opted instead to cut local farmers out of the loop and to ship food directly to the city. This ruptured the final and most essential link that tethered Chilapa to its traditional hinterland.

Deprived of a market for their products, the doomed villagers were left to depend on a combination of migration and government-funded make-work projects. Many took up seasonal migration while some left perma-nently, moving to Chilapa, Acapulco, Mexico City, or the United States. Others were invited to stay behind, at least for a time, to plant trees in the devastated neighborhoods of their villages. Although few seem ready to admit this directly, the masters of Mexico's expanding industrial economy envision no role for people who remain scattered through remote and inaccessible locations such as can be found in the nooks and crannies of the Atempa basin. This settlement distribution that took shape in the course of feeding Chilapa, as a preindustrial regional economy crystallized, matured, and struggled to stay afloat. It is a settlement distribution that had lost its underlying rationale after 1992; the day when the distribution of arable land dictated the physical placement of villages and determined the loca-tions where there was work to be done had passed.

Today Chilapa no longer depends to any great extent on land or other resources found in the Atempa basin. No export industry has emerged to replace rebozos and palm goods. The city has instead become a ser-vice center that depends on transfer payments remitted by migrants and SEDESOL. A substantial portion of the work now done in the city involves services related to the ongoing "structural readjustment" in the coun-tryside. It is anyone's guess whether the city will survive once the trees are all planted and villagers all gone. Meanwhile, the city's hinterland has moved out of the Atempa basin and spread across the globe. Portions of it can be found in Iowa's maize fields, Southeast Asia's rubber plantations, South Africa's mines, the corporate boardrooms of North America and Europe, and many lesser and unknown places. Feeding Chilapa today involves fragments of the working lives of people scattered over the earth. To pursue the story further would require that we venture into the innards of the Mexican government, to the negotiation table of the World Trade Organization, and to the other similar venues where policies controlling the fate of households and communities in the Atempa basin have lately been formulated. Few of those who move in these circles are even aware of the Atempa basin's existence, yet the lives of those in and around Chilapa hang on the decisions they make. Not even don Manuel Herrera dared dream of power this vast. Nor could any who lived in the Atempa basin before the late twentieth century have envisioned a vulnerability so deep.

While unique in its details, in broad outline the story of the Atempa basin's regional economy is one that can be found repeated in scores of remote valleys through southern Mexico and beyond. Outside of the densely populated central Mexican highlands, preindustrial regions tended to be fragile economic entities that survived only by adapting to shifting patterns of interregional trade as well as to more purely internal forces that threatened to tip intraregional supply-and-demand relationships too far from balance. Yet when and where they existed, regions framed the economic decisions of the individuals, households, and communities of which they were composed. From a regional standpoint, households were the fundamental production and consumption units. Although communities oftentimes had a secondary economic role relating to the deployment of labor, they were more notable as political units that served to protect the territorial and other prerogatives of geographically concentrated clusters of households. In their economic relationships with others, households looked for opportunities not to their natal communities but to the region. Unlike communities, regions were bound together less by political than by economic means, by the interplay between supply and demand in a central marketplace.

Of course, economics and politics are thoroughly interconnected, and preindustrial regions were forums for the exercise of political power. Power in social affairs is generally understood to involve monopoly control over the potential or actual application of violence. What is less commonly noted is that power does not spring spontaneously into being, nor can it be sustained over time without resting on a foundation that confers economic leverage over people's lives and livelihoods. Within preindustrial regions, the typical foundation for political power was differential control over food. Other resources (sugar in the Atempa basin, for example) might be convertible into specie, into "wealth" as this word is generally understood, but wealth can be made into power only if it can be used to control food or other vital resources. Residents of the Atempa basin could, and most did, live without wealth; none, even the wealthy, long survived without eating. In the end, wealth remained harmlessly concentrated in Chilapa, but power was firmly vested in the countryside. This is where food was produced and where it was controlled by thousands of households scattered across several hundred square kilometers of mountainous terrain. Villagers parted with food on their own terms, in tiny transactions whose terms were decided through countless individual episodes of commercial haggling; in this way, villagers held the city in check.

Practically everything about preindustrial regions, from their internal structure and composition to their very existence, was conditioned by constraints on the movement of goods and services that resulted from the Mexico's rugged topography and the country's primitive systems of transportation. As such, it is hard to imagine something more certain to destabilize a preindustrial regional economy than the introduction of modern systems of vehicular transportation. This, incidentally, accounts for the divergent experiences of Atzacoaloya and Ayahualulco that I note in the introduction to this volume. Atzacoaloya was located along the path of the first transmission line to deliver electricity to the Atempa basin. A road built in conjunction with the electrification project passed through Atzacoaloya and made this among the basin's first rural communities with vehicular access to Chilapa. Smaller roads branching off the route leading through Atzacoaloya provided access to dozens of other communities and made Atzacoaloya a transportation hub through which practically all foot, animal, and vehicular traffic to and from the southeast portion of the region was funneled. This presented residents of Atzacoaloya with commercial opportunities that were quite rare among rural communities. Furthermore, it ensured that Atzacoaloya would be connected to Chilapa by a steadily expanding stream of cars, trucks, buses, and other vehicles. By the 1980s, this stream had become sufficiently reliable and had sufficient capacity to allow residents of Atzacoaloya to commute to jobs in Chilapa. A similar circumstance developed to the north of Chilapa, along the road to Acatlán and Zitlala; to the east, in the middle Atempa valley communities of

Atempa and Nexapa; and along Highway 93, especially in the middle Ajolotero valley to the west. In contrast, Ayahualulco was not among the communities with commuting opportunities. A road terminating in Ayahualulco was built in the 1970s, but topographic obstacles ensured that it followed a circuitous and lightly populated route. Few vehicles used the road, and the residents of the villages situated along it continued walking to Chilapa through the late 1990s.

Most of the Mexican communities that have been selected for study by ethnographers were once components of the sort of regional economy featured in this book. Through the 1950s, this was generally recognized, and anthropologists either conducted regional investigations or coordinated their research with cultural and historical geographers who investigated the region while ethnographers sampled the constituent parts. Unfortunately, this convention had mostly disappeared by the 1960s. Only Ralph Beals, a veteran of the earlier tradition of regional studies, together with graduate students working under his supervision, made an attempt to maintain a regional focus and examine a region's fate as the pace of industrialization intensified (see Beals 1975; Berg 1974; Cook and Diskin 1976). It was a lonely effort that had faded completely by the mid-1970s. Geographers had by that time gone their separate way, and anthropologists had become narrowly fixated on individual communities. The resulting ethnographies exposed researchers to the charge, heard frequently in the 1960s and 1970s, that they too-often portrayed communities as disembodied entities, disconnected from history and from the broader world. Anthropologists responded not by resurrecting the earlier regional research framework but by turning for insight to political economists, who at the time were much impressed by the global reach of industrial capitalism and the government policies and programs through which it was regulated. The result was a raft of studies of economic and political issues, including studies of land tenure and the ejido program (e.g., DeWalt 1979), the increased commercialization of household production strategies (e.g., Cancian 1972), migration and urbanization (e.g., Kemper 1977), and the impact of government policies and programs on all of these things (e.g., Warman 1980). By the 1980s, a notion of political economy that was weighted heavily toward the political but both light and highly selective on the economic had become firmly entrenched in the discipline. Given that anthropologists' preferred unit of analysis, the community, was primarily a political entity and only secondarily (and oftentimes superficially) an economic one, the comparative neglect of economics was perhaps inevitable.

The failure to appreciate the role played by regions in shaping patterns of economic activity has had significant consequences for our understanding of rural Mexico. Arguably, the progressive dismemberment of one preindustrial region after another has been among the central economic trends in Mexico in the past fifty years. In overlooking these processes, anthropologists have been left without the explanatory tools needed to understand conundrums such as that presented by the divergent experiences of Ayahualulco and Atzacoaloya. The result has been an unfortunate tendency to fill the void by adopting the explanatory framework of the actors. Building on the postrevolutionary political narrative outlined in chapter 4, researchers often take the political claims and counterclaims about the Mexican state, and the extent to which the state has upheld its revolutionary ideals, as a starting point for analysis.

One popular but strained approach to finding meaningful research questions in the premises set forth by political protagonists is to begin by asserting that the simple fact of peasant survival in the modern world is a puzzling occurrence. From my perspective, peasant survival in the modern era can be made to appear puzzling only by ignoring the transportation constraints that preserved remnants of preindustrial economies into the mid- to late twentieth century and looking none too closely at the manner in which peasants have been subsidized and otherwise supported in the face of steadily mounting ecological and economic imbalances. Strip away an awareness of these elemental matters of fact, and the continued existence of peasants reasonably appears problematic. This is only a beginning point, however; arguing that peasant survival is problematic serves as a rhetorical prelude to the assertion that peasant survival is nothing to take for granted and rests on determined and deliberate political resistance. The next step is to identify the parties against whom this "resistance" is directed. The lead candidates include the state (e.g., Warman 1980), international capital (e.g., Chevalier and Buckles 1995), and, more recently, neoliberalism. Viewed from the Atempa basin, these are all paradoxical selections given that government subsidies and the selective exploitation of commercial opportunities in national and international markets were for many years the only things that kept the region afloat. What seems to matter more than the facts is that the arguments about resistance sound good and conform to the prejudices of at least one side in ongoing political disputes.

Nowhere have researchers internalized the premises of political actors more thoroughly than in the contemporary Chiapas highlands, which surely ranks among the earth's most popular venues for community-based ethnography. Here the resistance thesis has evolved its most elaborate story line, complete with a cast of expertly crafted characters adapted from the pages of Mexican folk history. Rather than seeing irony in demands for local autonomy issued in the name of the rural masses (see Esteva 2003) — against a material backdrop of overpopulation and growing dependence on industrial food production and delivery systems (Collier 1975, 1994) — the possibility of living autonomously in rural villages and the probability that this will come to pass as a result of resistance seems to be taken at face value. Scholars have gone to great lengths to validate the political rhetoric by affirming that it describes a realistic alternative to industrial capitalism and liberal democracy (e.g., Nash 2001; Speed 2005).

Facts can be stubborn, however, and I think they will prove especially unforgiving to arguments that credit peasant survival to resistance. Indeed, the evidence against the suggestion was strong even before it was refined into an acceptable academic position. Michoacán's preindustrial farmers, for example, had mostly abandoned farming and decamped to Mexico City or to the United States well before the 1970s, when these arguments began to take shape. Farmers from Michoacán were joined by those from Oaxaca's Mixteca just as researchers began writing in earnest about the resistance that peasants were mounting. This same thesis also withstood the destruction of the peasant economy in the state of Morelos. There, peasants fell victim to urban sprawl and the spread of industrial agriculture even as the ink was drying on Arturo Warman's pioneering study of resistance in Morelos (1980), in which he wrote of the inevitability of peasant survival in rural Mexico. In the Atempa basin, peasants outlived those of these other regions and are only now following the well-trod path to cities and across the northern border. Still, the point remains: where, amid the devastation left by the successive collapse of preindustrial regions, is evidence that resistance, or political action of any sort, has any meaningful consequence?

When I think of the role resistance has played in shaping the recent history of the Atempa basin, it brings to mind an experience I had back in August 1998. One evening I was in a car riding with friends to Zitlala when we came upon a roadblock at the entrance to Acatlán. A hundred or more people had organized an impromptu community assembly in the middle of the road to discuss the high bus fare that was being charged for travel to and from Chilapa. Enforcement of government-regulated fares had been ignored, and riders found themselves paying nearly double the authorized rate. The specific target of the assembled crowd's ire was a man from

Zitlala who held a concession granting exclusive rights to operate buses
between Chilapa and Zitlala. The concession holder was one of a handful
of wealthy and politically connected residents of Zitlala who had apparently used his political clout to circumvent official price controls. Like that
of Atzacoaloya, since the 1960s Acatlán's economy had gradually shifted
from solidly agricultural to a hybrid farming and bedroom community that
was tightly linked to Chilapa's labor market. It was a commuter town, in
other words, and people relied on the buses to get to work. The impending
onset of the school year lent additional urgency to the cause. Students from
Acatlán matriculated at schools in Chilapa, and the high fare for bus passage threatened their educational opportunities.

At the assembly, it was agreed that the following morning a group from
Acatlán, in league with representatives of other affected communities,
would block the road leading north of Chilapa to protest the high fares.
Early the next morning, a large group of demonstrators, some armed with
machetes, duly assembled at the designated spot and placed small boulders
in the road to prevent vehicles from passing. To travel by vehicle from
Chilapa to Acatlán, Zitlala, Ayahualco, La Mohonera, Topiltepec, Pochahuisco, and a number of smaller villages, people had to go from Chilapa to
the roadblock, cross the barrier on foot, then board another vehicle on the
far side to continue the trip. Several hours after the protest began (with
police sitting idly by, while an altercation with an annoyed truck driver
escalated to violence), Chilapa's presidente appeared and summarily announced a solution to the crisis. The authorized fare would be respected; as
a special bonus, students would be granted passage at half the regular fare.

At first glance, the roadblock near Acatlán might seem an inspired
instance of popular mobilization and resistance. But upon close examination, the episode takes on more ambiguous shades. The most obvious loser,
the concession holder, was prevented from extorting money from those
who had become captive to industrial technologies through their dependence on jobs and services in Chilapa. Yet there were other, less obvious
losers, including members of Chilapa's working class. In restraining commuting costs, the presidente ensured that employers in Chilapa would not
need to pay higher wages to attract cheap labor from the countryside.
Among the beneficiaries of this act of resistance, one must surely include
the presidente, who found in the event a forum in which to demonstrate that
his administration was responsive to people's needs. Chilapa's employers
and consumers also emerged in fine shape, narrowly avoiding the necessity
of paying higher wages and higher retail prices for goods sold by Acatlán's

petty merchants. As an alternative avenue of resistance, protesters from Acatlán might have pushed for higher wages in Chilapa, though with commuters dispersed through Chilapa's labor market this would have been more difficult to organize. The bus fare was the easiest point of attack. In any case, this was not resistance of a sort that did much to hinder the destruction of the Atempa basin's preindustrial regional economy; indeed, the objective of the entire exercise was to *increase* access to industrialized sectors of the economy.

Genuine resistance to the expansion of industrial capitalism is rare and almost wholly ineffectual even where it is found. I can point to exactly one instance in the Atempa basin (mentioned in the introduction), involving the household in La Ciénega whose members grew their own food and cooked with wood even as their house compound and farm were engulfed by urban sprawl. They could resist full incorporation into Mexico's expanding industrial economy by growing their own food, selectively exploiting Chilapa's abundant commercial opportunities, and accepting the stable but modest lifestyle that this combination of activities enabled. Not many others in the Atempa basin have found themselves in a position that would make combining the first two of these things a possibility; thus, the third is mostly a moot point. The basin's inhabitants have instead been forced to accept that they are finely adapted, culturally, socially, and in most every conceivable way, to making some form of contribution to the survival of a region that no longer exists. Setting aside Chilapa and a handful of bedroom communities, towns and villages in the basin have been transformed from settlements situated near strategic production sites to settlements that have the feel of refugee camps. A solid majority of the basin's inhabitants have come to depend on the benevolence of government-financed relief organizations that struggle to help equip people with the cultural and financial tools needed to facilitate a transition into the industrialized world. With each passing year, more of the able-bodied make their escape, leaving behind the aged, the infirm, and the socially encumbered. There was never a realistic way to resist the complex sequence of events that led to the region's collapse. No action (or lack of action) by the state, by international capital, or by the architects of neoliberalism could have done anything to avert it. Rather, the Atempa basin's regional economy had a natural life cycle, and in the late twentieth century it drew to an end.

Twentieth-Century Settlements by Transportation Zone

TABLE 5. Atempa basin communities, 1900–2000

Community	Distance (km)	Population										
		1900	1910	1921	1930	1940	1950	1960	1970	1980	1990	2000
Zone 1												
Chilapa	0.00	7,399	7,339	7,510	7,143	6,094	7,336	7,368	9,204	13,326	16,332	22,511
El Paraíso	1.66	144	161	138	166	137	206	278	289	320	309	446
El Zoyatal	2.00							128	112	315	245	
Flor Morada	2.06											154
La Ciénega	2.19					58	96	132	142	147	241	112
Acazacatla	2.52	138	169	157	194	190	179	203	243	290	335	396
El Terrero	2.80								65	80	129	222
Zinenenzintla	2.86	146	156	134	122	147	156	150	184	211	233	97
Agua Zarca	3.54										102	329
Barranca Honda	3.60								110	149	155	115
Other (number)											46 (1)	72 (5)
Subtotal		7,827	7,825	7,978	7,625	6,626	7,973	8,259	10,349	14,838	18,127	24,454
Zone 2												
Tlapizaco	4.13	107	110	145	177	156	162	186	313	277	215	149
Ayahualco	4.29	465	557	583	540	717	708	931	947	1,004	634	531
Los Magueyes	4.39									20	436	560
Ocuituco	4.48	215	339	298	346	328	490	296	432	535	531	609
Lodo Grande	4.70	254	337	379	475	550	698	547	607	711	860	867
Maquiscoatlán	4.77	227	200	369	361	201	318	364	577	760	816	806
La Providencia	4.82							262	284	319	310	388
Amate Amarillo	4.98			213	158	286	374	451	609	794	867	919
Miraflor	5.11								140	155	169	162
Atempa	5.14	102	361	406	373	307	602	745	933	1,211	1,028	970
Nexapa	5.40	337	621	750	772	842	1,047	1,448	1,737	1,930	2,573	3,007

216

Santa Catarina	5.94	532	1,320	502	596	660	771	887	948	1,297	1,259	1,231
Chautla	5.98		84	98	100	130	208	226	286	342	318	350
Trigomila	6.21		172	128	144	186	261	327	399	409	446	548
Cuadrilla Nueva	6.23	207	174	117	100	146	144	232	261	336	436	512
Tlacoaxtla	6.50		227	182	232	302	378	406	415	579	769	576
Tepetlacingo	6.58					152	227	393	307	472	404	466
Teposcuautla	6.87	136	198	250	340	345	338	358	423	551	813	914
La Mohonera	6.95	195	293	255	360	431	520	610	868	1,023	1,022	1,181
Los Amates	7.13	73	200	128	172	201	259	255	352	461	561	360
El Limón	7.26	116	121	137	206	238	250	235	276	244	278	317
Terrero	7.36										115	96
Acatlán	7.58	1,251	1,644	916	1,671	1,925	2,181	2,438	2,525	2,299	2,628	2,885
Teomatatlán	7.61	60	95	83	67	106	127	189	216	254	323	355
Zoquitipa	7.76	146		164	257	260	356	423	569	661	672	231
Santa Ana	7.76	266	241	233	233	290	345	197	477	598	697	645
Cuautenango	7.87	155	214	158	163	225	293	398	506	651	597	776
Zinzintitlán	7.88			177	229	194	293	316	595	770	659	628
Agua Fria	7.91											119
Other (number)												46 (1)
Subtotal		4,844	7,508	6,671	8,072	9,178	11,350	13,120	16,002	18,663	20,436	21,204
Zone 3												
Coaquimisco	8.10	379	373	256	349	316	337	357	388	536	441	419
Lamazintla	8.14	162	223	164	144	190	210	222	229	275	311	368
El Refugio	8.42	114	107	153	184	187	253	233	247	384	303	379
Xochitempa	8.69	57	109	139	187	207	266	303	357	391	527	480
Rancho Coaquimisco	8.74										78	116
Zinantla	9.06										352	217
Ahuihuiyuco	9.12	169	303	295	358	445	434	563	693	910	1,073	1,298

TABLE 5. Continued

Community	Distance (km)	Population										
		1900	1910	1921	1930	1940	1950	1960	1970	1980	1990	2000
El Calvario	9.16								144	145	110	232
Tlanipatla	9.24	499	654	508	491	504	576	592	538	665	484	656
Atzacoaloya	9.42	1,059	1,270	1,201	1,043	1,391	1,455	1,570	1,801	2,240	2,350	2,401
Tetitlán	9.54					69	214	18	64	79	89	96
Tepehuisco	10.10	182	227	269	305	355	315	317	320	439	550	534
Xulchuchio	10.23	181	207	176	180	165	239	353	453	541	448	536
El Peral	10.40	104		208	284	235	405	275	302	289	337	161
Tlaxinga	10.42			253	343	434	603	740	846	1,105	1,183	735
Topiltepec	10.50	857	800	872	948	1,042	1,194	1,188	1,139	1,619	1,745	1,945
Zizicazapa	10.51	83	248	207	98	87	225	387	398	804	980	1,174
Axopilco	10.59	87		131	144	198	263	312	345	406	435	408
Santa Cruz	10.97								327	354	386	
Pochahuisco	11.02	625	793	841	963	1,171	1,314	1,639	2,007	2,188	2,534	3,465
Calhuaxtitlán	11.08							165	178	261	332	464
Mazatepec	11.10									413	532	
Teyapa	11.15										130	214
La Laguna	11.17								48	99	103	4
Ahuacuotzintla	11.19		685							127		166
Pantitlán	11.42	298	540	607	712	753	857	657	1,154	1,276	1,463	2,308
Acalco	11.85	124	164	183	288	415	483	646	708	923	1,066	819
Coatzingo	11.85								104	184	197	249
Other (number)												157 (5)
Subtotal		4,980	6,703	6,463	7,021	8,164	9,643	10,537	12,790	16,653	18,539	20,001
Zone 4												
Ayahualulco	12.11	847	1,192	892	1,088	1,247	1,356	1,740	1,928	2,275	2,426	2,377
Zitlala	12.36	3,071	3,329	2,969	2,469	2,044	3,220	2,275	3,034	3,609	4,555	4,731

Location	Distance											
Viramontes	12.79		149	73	74	134	170	188	230	288	282	348
Tenexatlajco	13.76	20		91	132	197	223	249	290	268	264	221
Papaxtla	13.92									104	174	192
Ahuehuejitic	13.94									311	364	368
Colotepec	14.10					89	134	185	212	262	314	346
El Jagüey	14.20	249	237	332	377	442	510	548	739	827	1,206	2,091
Xicotlán	14.29							74	124	153	241	348
Zompeltepec	14.48						105	260	283	355	464	616
Ahuexotitlán	14.66	408	218	318	378	492	571	537	474	800	1,024	896
San Marcos	14.69							141	200	226	278	307
Mexcaltepec	15.13								136	638	274	372
Llano Grande	15.50										55	65
El Pinoral	15.60										201	440
Samacingo	15.61										74	71
Atenxoxola	15.70	196	105	161	180	214	243	323	377	459	527	
El Ahuejote	15.85											291
San Jerónimo	15.88	246	395	229	123	419	450	557	595	496	496	439
Tonalapa	15.94							106	90	153	125	143
Other (number)									39 (1)		63 (2)	199 (8)
Subtotal		5,037	5,625	5,065	4,821	5,278	6,982	7,183	8,751	11,224	13,407	14,842
Summary												
Zone 1	0–4	7,827	7,825	7,978	7,625	6,626	7,973	8,259	10,349	14,838	18,127	24,454
Zone 2	4–8	4,844	7,508	6,671	8,072	9,178	11,350	13,120	16,002	18,663	20,436	21,204
Zone 3	8–12	4,980	6,703	6,463	7,021	8,164	9,643	10,537	12,790	16,653	18,539	20,001
Zone 4	12–16	5,037	5,625	5,065	4,821	5,278	6,982	7,183	8,751	11,224	13,407	14,842
Total		22,688	27,661	26,177	27,539	29,246	35,948	39,099	47,892	61,378	70,509	80,520

Sources: National censuses (DGE 1905b, 1912, 1934, 1943, 1952, 1963, 1973; DEN 1927; INEGI 1989, 1991, 2002).
a Recalculations, using INEGI imagery and ArcGIS 9.2, of the length of trails that I originally measured using a pedometer or odometer (Kyle 1995).

Preindustrial Maize Production in the Atempa Basin

At several points, the arguments in this book hinge upon certain assumptions about the productivity of preindustrial maize farming in the Atempa basin. Any estimate of the amount of maize produced in the basin, or in geographically restricted portions of it, must rest upon estimating the values of three separate variables: the extent of the arable surface, the intensity with which the arable surface was used, and the annual yield of the cultivated portions. Of the three, only the first, the extent of the basin's arable surface, is known with a fairly high degree of precision (see summary data in table 2). Using ArcGIS 9.2, I measured the basin's arable surface by plotting individual fields atop orthorectified digital images created by INEGI. The images, taken in 1995, show fields that were cultivated in the 1980s and early 1990s, when pressure on the landscape was at a historical maximum. I calculated the area of 30,954 fields within a sixteen-kilometer radius of Chilapa. To distinguish between valley and upland surfaces, and to segregate the latter into the categories of "upland temporal" and "tlacolol," I used 1:50,000 topographic maps (INEGI 2000, 2001) to determine the approximate slope of fields — an admittedly crude procedure. Fields situated in valleys and with an average slope of less than seven degrees were deemed "valley temporal." Much of the area receiving the "valley" designation I know from ground surveys; accordingly, I have substantial confidence in the accuracy of this figure. Likewise, the area designated "tierra de riego" is an approximation based on ground surveys. Upland fields with a slope of less than thirty degrees were deemed "upland temporal" and those above thirty degrees "tlacolol." I have rather less confidence in the accuracy of this line of demarcation, though not so little as to substantially affect my conclusions.

The second and third variables are more problematic; relatively little information is available on the percentage of the arable surface that was sown in maize in any given year, and only scattered reports on maize yields could be found. Regarding land-use patterns, I collected data in three tracts of valley temporal (near Lodo Grande, Atzacoaloya, and Chilapa) in the years 1990, 1991, 2001, and 2004. In the first three of these years, 70–90 percent of the arable surface in all locations was intercropped with maize, beans, and squash in the summer growing seasons. A secondary crop, which might have been beans, jicama, or peanuts, was sowed on 5–10 percent, and another 3–11 percent was fallowed. In 2004, I measured a sharp decline in the area sown in maize and secondary crops (60–65 percent of the overall area) and a corresponding increase in the area left in fallow (35–40 percent).

The pattern of land use that I observed first in 1990 had taken shape in the years immediately following the 1982 introduction of chemical fertilizers. An indication of the impact this new technology had on land-use patterns can be seen in data collected by the SARH during the critical years of the 1980s. Within the municipio of Chilapa (which for present purposes can serve as a proxy for the Atempa basin), 8,366 hectares of maize was reportedly sown in 1982 and 16,915 hectares in 1986 (SARH 1987). In unpublished records of the SARH covering the years from 1987 through 1990, the area sown in maize roughly matched the amounts reported for 1986 (see Kyle 1995:177–79). If the area sown in maize in 1986 was 90 percent of the arable surface of the municipio, the 1982 figure would represent 45 percent of the arable surface. Unfortunately, the SARH estimates make no allowance for variation in the type of arable land, something known from other sources to have profoundly shaped land-use patterns.

Marcos Matías Alonso (1997:81–82, 258–63) has published data from his studies of individual fields scattered through the Atempa basin and adjacent regions in years between 1982 and 1985. These show several land-use patterns, most of which alternate between monocropped maize, beans, maize intercropped with beans and squash, and fallow. For example, in a field near Zitlala, maize and squash were planted in 1982 and 1984, and beans were monocropped in 1983 and 1985. In a field near Cuautenango, maize, beans, and squash were planted in 1982, 1984, and 1985, and the field was fallowed in 1983. Similarly, a field near Atlixtac, just east of the Atempa basin, was planted in maize, beans, and squash in 1982 and 1984 and was fallowed in 1983 and 1985. If these patterns were extended through the arable lands associated with each of the communities, then 100 percent, 75 percent, and 50 percent of the lands of Zitlala, Cuautenango, and Atlixtac, respectively, would have been sown annually. Unfortunately, Matías gives no information about the properties of the soils, the slope, and the agricultural technologies used by farmers in the fields to which he refers. Furthermore, at least some of the fields documented by Matías, like those in the areas that I documented, were likely "contaminated" by the growing use of chemical fertilizers.

General descriptions of agricultural practices in the Atempa basin (Kyle 1995; Matías 1982, 1997) and adjacent regions (e.g., Muñoz 1963) and ethnographic reports from elsewhere in Mexico (e.g., Collier 1975; Kirkby 1973; Wilken 1987) are consistent in showing a fundamental difference in land-use strategies by farmers cultivating level valley and sloping upland fields, particularly when the valleys are worked with plows and the uplands with hand tools. All else being equal, soils in valleys are sufficiently fertile to sustain near-continuous cropping, very similar to the pattern that I documented in the three areas that I have monitored over the years and that Matías reported for Zitlala and Cuautenango. Though fertilizers were used in each of these areas, they likely had a bigger impact on yields than on fallow patterns. In contrast, in the absence of chemical fertilizers, fields on sloping surfaces would have required regular fallowing. This seems to have been the case in the field Matías described in Atlixtac, a town located much farther than either Cuautenango or Zitlala from the new fertilizer distribution facilities that were established in Chilapa in the early 1980s. How frequently unfertilized fields were fallowed depended on a combination of factors, including overall soil fertility, the production technologies used, and the nature of ecological succession patterns in fallowed fields. In general, the higher the fertility, the less frequent the fallowing. Where plows were used, fallow periods were kept shorter than the period required for invasive woody plants to become established, because the fields would have to be cleared by hand before plowing. Woody plants can emerge in two to five or more years, depending on a host of local environmental variables. In contrast, where hand tools were used, farmers sought to extend fallow periods as long as was necessary for woody species to overtake herbaceous plants, especially grasses, as these are extremely difficult to remove from fields without the use of a plow. Again, the time required for woody species to become established varies, though it would rarely be fewer than four to five years; reports of fallow periods of fifteen or more years are not unknown.

In terms of my tripartite division of the Atempa basin's arable land prior to the introduction of chemical fertilizers, the admittedly slim evidence nevertheless points to a comparatively intensive use of valley lands. As occurred elsewhere in Mexico, the Atempa basin's valley temporal was likely kept in production nearly continuously, with maize sown in 75 percent or more of all fields in any given year. As an average, I base my estimates of maize production in the basin on the assumption that 80 percent of valley fields in the Atempa basin were sown annually. In the more-variable upland fields, I assume that 60 percent and 40 percent of the upland temporal and tlacolol, respectively, was cultivated annually. The introduction of steel plowshares in the uplands in the 1960s all but eliminated tlacolol agriculture. Thus, for years beginning in 1960, I have lumped the fields of tlacolol together with upland temporal, and I assume that 60 percent of all upland fields were sown in maize annually. With the adoption of chemical fertilizers in the 1980s, the distinction between land-use patterns in valley and upland settings largely disappeared. Thus, in estimating potential production in 1990 and 2000, I assume that 80 percent of all of the basin's arable surface was sown in maize.

With respect to yields, finding in the available data a solid basis on which to rest estimates is nearly as frustrating as attempting to determine preindustrial fallow patterns. I have measured yields in the Atempa basin, in 1990 and 1997, that range from just over 100 kilograms per hectare (an amount so low as to count as a total loss) to 6,500 kilograms per hectare. All of my measurements were done in fields that received chemical fertilizers, without which productivity would have been far lower. Yields responded very closely to the quantities of fertilizers that farmers apply, and this has depended on the erratic funding of government subsidy programs. My 1990 measurements (Kyle 1995:377–79), made at a time when fertilizer use was at an all-time high, can be taken to represent the peak productivity achieved in the basin. The average yield in fields of valley temporal ($N = 26$) and upland temporal ($N = 29$) was 3,968 and 3,403 kilograms per hectare, respectively. My sample was much smaller in 1997, but yields were consistently lower: 2,382 kilograms per hectare in valley temporal ($N = 5$) and 1,749 kilograms per hectare in upland temporal ($N = 7$). Rainfall was near normal in both years, such that the difference can be attributed entirely to reduced fertilizer use in 1997 as compared to 1990.

A broader sense of the impact that these and other industrial inputs have had on yields can be seen in statewide statistics collected by the SARH (cited in Matías 1997:38). From 1960 to 1977, the average yield in Guerrero was reportedly 930 kilograms per hectare. The highest annual yield, 1,140 kilograms per hectare, was reported in 1977, while the lowest,

735 kilograms per hectare, was reported in 1973. Average yields jumped sharply after 1977, a reflection of the increased use of industrial inputs in the state as a whole. The final year for which these data are available is 1989, when the average statewide yield was 1,920 kilograms per hectare. With regard to the variation from one type of field to another, Matías has published a limited amount of yield information from his and other un-published studies of unfertilized fields. His data show a range from 657 kilograms per hectare in Cuautenango to 2,200 kilograms per hectare in Acatlán (Matías 1997:78). Studies done elsewhere in the broader Montaña region of Guerrero, which includes the Atempa basin, record yields as low as 500 kilograms per hectare (cited in Matías 1997:78).

For present purposes, what is more important than the yield in a year of average rainfall is the amount that farmers could anticipate producing in a year with adverse weather conditions. As I note in chapter 5, a substantial amount of the grain produced in the Atempa basin was fed to animals. I assume that the difference between the minimum obtainable yield and the average yield roughly matches the amount that was directed to domes-ticated animals. Thus, in attempting to calculate the maize supply that was available for human consumption, I use figures that assume adverse weather conditions and minimum yields. Adverse weather conditions can be quite localized, and thus the aggregate statewide averages cited above smooth over much underlying variability. Nevertheless, the difference be-tween the cumulative annual average yield (930 kilograms per hectare) and the lowest recorded annual yield (735 kilograms per hectare) can be taken as a starting point in considering year-to-year variation in output. A better sense of the magnitude of weather-induced variation in maize yields can be seen in a study of agriculture in Alcozauca, east of the Atempa basin. Researchers found that fields of tlacolol yielded 800 kilograms per hectare in a normal year but only 500 kilograms in a bad year. The difference was still greater in fields of upland temporal, where yields fell to 700 kilograms per hectare from the normal yield of 1,600 kilograms per hectare. Irrigated land in Alcozauca, in contrast, yielded 2,000 kilograms per hectare irre-spective of rainfall (Matías 1997:77).

Further confusing the issue is the fact that the two poorly documented variables — fallow periods and maize yields — are likely interrelated in ways that I touch on in the discussion of intensification in chapter 3. Farmers fallow fields to restore soil fertility. The longer this process is allowed to continue, the greater the overall fertility gain; conversely, the shorter the fallow period, the lower the annual maize output. Population growth induces farmers to strike a balance between the two variables in a way that should drive average annual yields down as more land is brought into production and fallow periods shortened. There are no available long-term data that could be used to illustrate this relationship, not from the Atempa basin or from anywhere else in Mexico. Nevertheless, this is a widely recognized dynamic that few specialists would question. All of the data summarized above, on land-use patterns and yields, were collected in years when there was acute population pressure on the landscape in the Atempa basin. Several centuries of intensification had likely shortened fallow periods and lowered yields as much as could be sustained through time (and in some locations beyond this point). The data thus provide a grainy snapshot of the circumstances found at the end of a long sequence of preindustrial agricultural intensification.

Such a snapshot suits my purpose insofar as my concern is mostly restricted to agricultural productivity in the middle and late twentieth century, the period of maximum pressure on the landscape in the Atempa basin. Accordingly, my estimates of average maize yields contain no provisions for the probable decline in yields that resulted from population growth and intensification. I note merely that in the earliest decades of the twentieth century, fallow periods are likely to have been somewhat longer, and yields somewhat higher, than my estimates suggest.

With these considerations in mind, I turn to the task of estimating yields for the three types of arable land found in the basin. For fields of valley temporal, I assume that farmers were able to achieve an average yield of 1,000 kilograms per hectare with a high degree of confidence (i.e., irrespective of rainfall). Matías cited 2,200 kilograms per hectare as the yield of unfertilized fields in Acatlán in 1982 (1997:78), but this amount is far higher than anything reported by others — higher even than Matías reported for Acatlán in an earlier publication (see Matías 1982). As an average yield, a substantially lower figure of 1,200 kilograms per hectare seems more appropriate, dropping to 1,000 kilograms per hectare in a bad year. What made valley temporal such a desirable agricultural resource was the predictable yields it offered, not extraordinarily high yields. In the uplands, there was much less predictability. For fields of both upland temporal and tlacolol, I assume that farmers could minimally average 700 kilograms per hectare, substantially less than the yield they would obtain in a year with normal rainfall, when yields would have approached or matched the 1,200 kilograms per hectare obtained from valley temporal. An estimate of 1,000 kilograms per hectare in the valleys and 700 kilograms per hectare in the uplands results in an estimated average for the Atempa basin as a whole of 835 kilograms per hectare. This is less than the cumulative statewide average yield for preindustrial agriculture that I cite above (930 kilograms per hectare) but substantially more than the minimum recorded statewide average (735 kilograms per hectare).

Tables 3 and 4 in chapter 5 relating to maize output are based on the land-use and productivity estimates outlined here. Again, the amounts are derived based on the assumption that 80 percent, 60 percent, and 40 percent of fields of valley temporal, upland temporal, and tlacolol, respectively, were planted annually through 1950. I further assume that farmers obtained yields of 1,000 and 700 kilograms of maize per hectare in the valleys and uplands, respectively. To account for the decline in tlacolol agriculture after 1950, I lump the area of tlacolol together with upland temporal in estimating the output beginning in 1960, when irrigated land began to be taken out of sugarcane and sown in maize. I thus lump irrigated fields with valley temporal in estimating output after 1960. The use of chemical fertilizers starting in the early 1980s led to a near-total elimination of fallowing in upland fields and a substantial rise in yields. My estimates of maize production in 1990 and 2000 are based on the assumption that 80 percent of the entire arable surface in the basin was sown in maize and that fields in the valleys and in the uplands yielded 2,000 and 1,500 kilograms per hectare, respectively. There has been substantial variation in fertilizer availability from one year to the next, causing this factor to join, and probably surpass, rainfall as a determinant of productivity.

In both table 3 and table 4, I combine these land-use and productivity estimates with estimates of human consumption requirements (see discussion of table 1 in chapter 3) to examine the balance between supply and demand in particular portions of the basin through the twentieth century. The tables show the amounts (including negative amounts) of maize that remain in particular areas once the consumption needs of the resident population are deducted. As I note in chapter 5, my goal is to identify areas of the basin where farmers had sufficient productive capacity to engage in commercial maize farming.

NOTES

CHAPTER 1. A LAND OF OPPORTUNITIES

1. See http://www.chowhound.com/topics/112112 (accessed February 27, 2007). Kennedy also had problems with Chilapa's hotels (see Kennedy 1998:359).

2. I refer here to a somewhat arbitrarily demarcated area within sixteen kilometers (traveling on foot) of Chilapa's zocalo. The relationship between this area and the notion of a "region" is discussed in chapter 3. A complete list of settlements in the study area, their distance from Chilapa, and their population as recorded in national censuses appears in Appendix A.

CHAPTER 2. THE CITY

1. The municipal administration in office in 1983 sponsored a grand celebration of the town's 450th anniversary, thereby demonstrating the superior political connections of the 1533 faction. Municipio administrations serve three-year terms, and factionalism among both the historians and their political allies almost ensures that the town's "official" founding date will periodically shift.

2. Archaeological investigations in the Atempa basin are in their infancy (see Schmidt n.d.).

3. A 1591 directive prohibited local officials from obligating Indians from Chilapa to work in mines near Zumpango, an indication that in the years leading up to the directive, some Indians were under such obligation. See AGN-I, vol. 5, exp. 848.

4. Documents go both ways on this point. In 1591, local officials were enjoined from requiring Indians to support movement along the camino real as part or all of their tribute obligation (AGN-I, vol. 5, exp. 637). Officials were later

directed to supply labor in support of troop movement over the trail, in 1616 (AGN-I, vol. 7, exp. 27, fol. 10), 1651 (AGN-I, vol. 16, exp. 142, fol. 134), and 1691 (AGN-I, vol. 31, exp. 13, fol. 9).

5. Most tribute from Chilapa was paid to an *encomendero,* a recipient of a royal grant to the tribute collected from a particular jurisdiction, well into the eighteenth century. The original grantee was Diego de Ordaz. The grant was passed to successive descendants thereafter. A handful of villages in Chilapa's political jurisdiction paid tribute to Chilapa's caciques, the descendants of the preconquest ruler.

A small amount of the jurisdiction's tribute payments were made in kind rather than in specie, particularly in maize (Paso y Troncoso 1905a:181–82), firewood, and, in at least one documented instance, uncompensated labor (AGN-CRS, vol. 2, exp. 2). Payment in kind was limited partly by law but also by a general lack of useful ends to which large quantities of locally produced goods or even labor could be applied.

6. Cacao beans exchanged at a rate of 80 to 100 per real or 640 to 800 per standard silver peso (Simpson 1950:188). The most important coins in circulation were reales, medio reales, and pesos, valued at eight reales. The medio real, one-sixteenth of a peso, represented a value far too large to handle small day-to-day transactions, hence the continued use of cacao beans. For a discussion of failed efforts to introduce fractional coinage in New Spain, see Hamilton 1944.

7. The census covered only racial groups other than Indians. For non-Indians, it gives a house-by-house enumeration that includes name, age, gender, and civil status for each individual. The entries for most males include a note on the person's occupation and physical condition. Beyond this, the individual entries contain an assortment of inconsistently recorded miscellanea. Households of Indians are noted, but beyond their street address, no details are given.

8. In 1791, Chilapa's sirvientes de arrieros ranged from 12 to 76 years in age, though most were young adults; on average, they were 27 years old. Arrieros ranged from 18 to 60, but most were in their thirties and forties; on average, they were 36 years old, 9 years older than sirvientes. A few sirvientes were older men, probably former arrieros who no longer owned their own mules and were easing into retirement without the financial means to do so.

9. In the late 1770s, the *alcalde mayor* of Chilapa (i.e., the head administrative officer of the alcaldía mayor based in Chilapa) monopolized the sale of mules in the Chilapa region as a perquisite of office. Most of these mules were likely sold on credit. Payment for mules took a variety of forms, including specie, panela, honey, wax, cochineal, and cotton (New York Public Library 1777:10). Government reforms in subsequent years removed the alcalde mayor's monopoly and

allowed wealthy merchants to enter the trade. For an example, see AGN-G, vol. 121, exp. 2-1.

10. There is some uncertainty here in that the census entry for a few individuals merely notes that they owned an *atajo* of mules but cites no specific number. An atajo was generally between thirty-five and forty-five pack animals, plus five or six riding animals. My estimate of the mule population assumes that an atajo was composed of forty mules.

11. This group owned between two and twenty-one mules. The average among them was eight, the standard deviation just over four.

12. For example, don José de Vique served as an employee in Chilapa's *aduana* (customs office) in 1791. In 1803, he appeared in Tepecoaquilco as an arriero and a viandante looking to sell a load of cloth valued at 681 pesos (Amith 2005:379–80).

13. Much less commonly, arrieros might travel to Cruz Grande for salt or to Acapulco if they sought cacao or Asian products. In the 1770s, Chilapa's arrieros were heavily involved in trade through Acapulco, but this had been taken over by arrieros from Tepecoaquilco by the 1790s (Amith 2005:330–31) while those from Chilapa devoted themselves more fully to the cotton trade.

14. By economic sector, and in order of numerical importance, these include transportation workers, including arrieros (83) and sirvientes de arrieros (264); farm workers and administrators, including labradores (63), ranchers (*vaqueros*) (12), hacendados (5), farm administrators (*mayordomos*) (2), and a hacienda administrator; textile workers, including weavers (33), tailors (29), and spinners (6); other artisans and service trades, including shoemakers (15), ironsmiths (10), butchers (7), bakers (6), silversmiths (6), feather workers (*plumarios*) (5), barbers (3), saddle makers (3), soap makers (3), kettle makers (3), carpenters (3), painters (2), a sculptor, a potter, and a wax worker; service professionals, including government officials (10), priests (6), scribes (3), teachers (3), musicians (2), a surgeon, and a court interpreter; merchants, including *comerciantes* (6) and *mercaderos* (2), store clerks (*cajeros*) (2), viandantes (3), a shopkeeper (*tendero*), a petty sugar dealer (*azucarero*), and 12 vagrants (*vagos*), some of whom were probably petty viandantes in a slump; servants and a residual category of laborers. A total of 32 males are listed as servants (*criados*), most being adolescent orphans and only a few grown adults for whom this was a full-time occupation. A similarly vague category was *operario,* cited by 39 men. These were workers employed in agriculture or artisanal trades. The term lumped together forms of work that in later years would be broken into separate categories, including *peones, jornaleros, obreros,* and *empleados.*

15. See AGN-H, vol. 122, exp. 2, fols. 38–43.

16. See AGN-H, vol. 122, exp. 2, fols. 38–43.

17. For prices in Chilapa, see AGN-H, vol. 122, exp. 2, fols. 38–43. For prices in Puebla, see Thomson 1989:271. Richard Salvucci (1987:157–58) cites manta prices as high as ten to twenty-one reales per vara in the central highlands. These figures may refer to markets removed from the immediate Puebla vicinity, where retail prices reflect transport as well as manufacturing and marketing costs.

18. The following paragraphs draw in part on research done as part of a senior honors project by Monyka Salazar de Weaver (see Salazar and Kyle n.d.).

19. Some manta from Chilapa did find its way into markets outside of the Atempa basin during the boom years around the turn of the nineteenth century. Chilapa became a main supplier of manta to the Tepecoaquilco-Iguala region in the first decade of the nineteenth century (Amith 2005:379–82), but violence associated with the War of Independence and competition from suppliers from the central highlands combined thereafter to pressure the northern fringes of the market for Chilapa's textiles.

20. For a time in the late 1880s, things became so bad that merchants were often kidnapped and ransomed as well as assaulted and robbed (Salazar 1987:58).

21. On the use of machine-made thread in rebozo manufacturing, see Keremitsis 1987:108.

22. In 1953, there was a rebocería called La Flor de Chilapa ("The Flower of Chilapa") in Toluca, located in the same area as the earlier La Chilapeña (*Catedral,* September 20, 1953, p. 91; Velázquez 1981:74). The relationship between these establishments, if any, and the years in which they operated are, unfortunately, not known.

23. Data on surnames represented in the community in 1791 are contained in the census of that year, cited above. For 1840, the data are from church burial records, discussed in Kyle 2003 and in the following chapter. For 1990, the data come from a sample of marriage records found in Chilapa's civil registry (see chapter 5, note 4). In 1791, 1840, and 1990 the twenty most common surnames account for 50 percent, 48 percent, and 55 percent of the population, respectively.

CHAPTER 3. RURAL GROWING PAINS

1. I refer here to an area of some 470 square kilometers that lies within a 16-kilometer radius of Chilapa.

2. The average rainfall amount is derived from unpublished records of the Comisión Nacional del Agua (CONAGUA) in Chilpancingo. It is the average of annual rainfall totals collected at a weather station in Chilapa from 1953 to 1997.

3. Soil maps published by the Instituto Nacional de Estadística, Geografía, e Informatica (INEGI 1997) show areas within the basin with the following soils: regosols, vertisols, rendzinas, phaeozems, lithosols, cambisols, kastanozems, luvisols, and fluvisols.

4. In a study of comparable agricultural systems in Guatemala, Stadelman (1940) presented data on labor requirements for plowed temporal and tlacolol agriculture. Averages derived from his data are 75 and 118 man-days per hectare for plow and tlacolol agriculture, respectively. Were it possible to extend this work over a full year, one person could thus cultivate nearly five hectares of land using a plow but only three using hand tools.

5. If opportunities to rapidly improve a lifestyle exist, then people will obviously rise to the occasion. This discussion presumes that the rare historical circumstances presenting such opportunities do not exist, as they did not (and do not) for most villagers in the Atempa basin.

6. In some soils, the end result of concerted efforts to intensify production is not physical exhaustion on the part of laborers but rather the physical destruction of the arable surface. Reducing fallow periods can cause devastating erosion, stripping soils from hillsides and depositing it in the valleys below. The Atempa basin has many highly eroded areas, many likely a result of ill-advised efforts at intensification.

7. Among other things, the burro or porter's transport capacity was almost always unused on the return trip from the market. This contrasts with the cotton trade, in which goods of some sort would be hauled to help defray the cost of each leg of an arriero's journey, even if each leg of the trip was not equally profitable.

8. In 1990–91 I measured travel speed of porters and burros and found both to average about four kilometers per hour (Kyle 1995:222), a figure used as a basis for calculations throughout this book.

9. For example, Ayahualulco is twelve kilometers from Chilapa. When I first began working in the region, people from this town regularly attended the Sunday market, but they often arrived Saturday afternoon and spent the night with their goods on the edge of the zocalo or on the porch of the palacio municipal.

10. The overall area of the territories shown in map 6 are as follows: Acatlán, 4,006 hectares; Atzacoaloya, 9,524 hectares; Ayahualulco, 7,213 hectares; Chilapa, 22,627 hectares; San Jerónimo Palantla, 9,979 hectares; Santa Catarina, 1,385 hectares; and Zitlala, 15,579 hectares. These are only rough approximations of the communities' actual holdings, which is all that can be achieved with the surviving records.

11. At least seventeen royal grants were issued in and near the Atempa basin (both Santos and Álvarez 1990 and Amith 2005 provide itemized lists of the

transactions). Most of these were held by the Jesuits from the mid-seventeenth century until the early to mid-eighteenth century. A total of some 13,500 hectares is a reasonable estimate of the total Jesuit holdings in the general vicinity of the Atempa basin. At least some of the grants involved land west of the Atempa basin, however, beyond the area with which I am concerned. Very roughly, the Jesuits probably held something in the neighborhood of 8,000 to 10,000 hectares in the Atempa basin, an amount that is a third or more of the area attributed to Chilapa in map 6.

12. For the sale of a portion of the Augustinian lands, see AGN-T, vol. 1514, exp. 6, fol. 3. On other matters related to the Augustinian withdrawal, see AGN-CRS, vol. 30, exp. 2. See also Álvarez 1845:43–44.

13. The earliest reference to panela production in the region dates to 1652, when the Moctezuma heir was granted a license to build a *trapiche* (mill) on holdings south of the Atempa basin (AGN-T, vol. 2676, exp. 3, fol. 13; see also Santos and Álvarez 1990:94). This was an exceptional petition for its time, and nothing like it appears again until 1735, when licenses were issued authorizing the operation of a trapiche in Tecoyutla (AGN-IC, vol. 4, exp. 2, fols. 15–25) and on land leased from Atzacoaloya (AGN-T, vol. 2075, exp. 4, fol. 12; AGN-M, vol. 72, fol. 226).

14. For more on the Mezas, see AGN-T, vol. 2075, exp. 4, fol. 12; AGN-T, vol. 1156, exp. 1, fol. 137; AGN-M, vol. 72, fol. 226; AGN-M, vol. 67, fol. 185v; Álvarez 1845:141–42.

15. The 1791 census enumerates the Spaniards, mestizos, castizos, and pardos living in outlying settlements as well as in the city. Most of the outlying settlements had only a mestizo or Spanish *mayordomo,* or labor boss, to oversee the sugar operations. Two exceptional cases were Mimistla and Topiltepec. Both of these settlements had unenumerated Indians, but the first was also populated by a contingent of twenty-two Spanish and mestizo arrendatarios and the second by a group of fifty-seven mestizo labradores and vaqueros.

16. In the previous chapter, I estimate that about 22 percent of Chilapa's households were headed by farmers, about half labradores and the other half the town's remaining Indians. Some of the Indians might have bought land and become labradores, while others were likely peones and arrendatarios. Members of many other households, especially the sirvientes de arrieros, probably worked as seasonal farmers, an activity that would have complemented the seasonality of work in the transportation sector.

17. Estimates based on parish burial records appear in Kyle 2003:106. I have since worked with tax records dating to 1825 and 1826. These show numbers of taxpayers that are consistent with the previously published estimates.

18. A few dispersed homesteads were found in Zones 1 and 2 by tax collectors in the 1820s. In 1825, they numbered something under seventy households, or about 350 people. Most had Spanish surnames, an indication that they were gente de razón and either arrendatarios or, more likely, labradores.

19. For examples, see AGN-I, vol. 69. exp. 294, fols. 193–94; AGN-HH, leg. 441.

20. Peter Guardino has suggested that don Manuel came from a family that was prominent in the late colonial period in the Chilapa region (1996:151). To my knowledge, the earliest Herrera in the region was don Ignacio, who wisely resigned his position as the subdelegado of Chilapa when José María Morelos brought his army and the War of Independence to town in 1811 (see AGN-S, vol. 37, exp. 14, fols. 86–98). He was probably the father of Manuel and Mariano Herrera, both of whom appear in tax records of the 1820s (e.g., AGN-TC, vol. 24, exp. 8, fols. 327–423) and in burial records of the 1840s (LDS, Reel 603363, libro 4, fols. 30, 52).

21. I am grateful to Peter Guardino for providing me with a copy of the pertinent bill of sale. The original is held at the Archivo General de Notarías del Distrito Federal (not. 169, 6/9/1838). For a discussion of the elements of don Manuel's purchase and claims, see Guardino 1996:150–51.

22. The Moctezumas' claim to these areas apparently rested on the assertion that the colonial *encomienda* rights to tribute collected within Indian communities had not been tribute at all but were instead rent payments to the original Moctezuma cacicazgo. The Moctezuma cacicazgo and the Ordaz encomienda had by this time been merged through intermarriage. By this legal theory, the holdings of the comuneros of other congregaciones — among them Santa Catarina, Ayahualulco, Acatlán, Zitlala, and San Jerónimo Palantla — should have been included in the purchase alongside Atzacoaloya. That they were not suggests that the Moctezuma brothers and Herrera well knew that their legal theory was flawed. The move on Atzacoaloya was probably a reflection of role the community had come to play as a refuge (see Kyle 2003).

23. There are several published studies of the 1840s rebellion, including a number of early studies published in Mexico (e.g., Meyer 1973; Ochoa 1968; Reina 1980, 1983) and a three-way exchange between John Hart (1988, 1995), Peter Guardino (1995a, 1995b, 1996), and myself (Kyle 1996b, 2003). This account draws from all of these works and mostly parallels the arguments found in Kyle 2003.

24. Local officials had been ordered to collect the new tax by authorities in Mexico City. Nevertheless, it was, and to some extent still is, customary for local officials to use discretion in implementing directives from above.

25. Parish burial, baptismal, confirmation, and marriage records are relatively sensitive indicators of the state of tension in the region in that priests were gente de razón who were generally identified with Chilapa's elites. Thus, a hiatus in the parish records demonstrates those times when it was too dangerous for members of this group to travel to a given community. In Ayahualulco, the hiatus began with the initial killings at San Sebastian Buenavista in March 1842 and ended in January 1847. In Santa Catarina, the records cease in October 1842 and begin anew late in March 1846. My records for Atzacoaloya are incomplete and prevent me from dating the onset of the hiatus; I know only that it concluded in January 1846. In Chilapa, the hiatus lasted only from August 1844 to March of the following year.

26. I know of only one subsequent incidence of violence that can be linked to the 1842 rebellion. In 1854, a group of nationally prominent politicians and generals (led by Álvarez) met in Ayutla and there proclaimed themselves to be outside of the peace of President Santa Ana. Santa Ana responded by mustering federal troops that converged on Chilapa, the gateway to Ayutla, from Mexico City, Oaxaca, and Michoacán. Skirmishes between these troops and supporters of Álvarez were fought just south of Chilapa, in the vicinity of the long-suffering community of Ayahualulco. Amid the turmoil, one Juan Abarca of Ayahualulco took the opportunity to lead a group of Indians in torching what remained of the trapiches at Tlaxinga, Nancintla, and Atenxoxola. Not to be outdone, Coronel Miguel Navarro, the heir to the hacienda of Topiltepec, led a contingent of the visiting troops in pursuit of Juan Abarca, who was found and executed, his head being mounted atop a stake in the center of Ayahualulco (Andrade 1911:25). Don Miguel lived another three years before he was killed while fleeing Chilapa before the advance of troops loyal to Álvarez (LDS, Reel 603365, libro 5, fol. 165).

CHAPTER 4. HERE BE DRAGONS

1. For those unfamiliar with the reference, this was a convention used by medieval European cartographers to label areas beyond the known world.

2. The archives of the district and municipal governments in Chilapa were regularly destroyed by armies that came and went from the city in the years between the 1842 rebellion and the 1927 Cristero uprising. The state archive fared little better; it was destroyed while in transit from Tixtla to Chilapa in 1870 (Salazar 1998:189). Unfortunately, we cannot know what these repositories once contained. However, if the lamentations of Guerrero's governors are any guide (e.g., Arce 1872), there was precious little in the way of local government in the region.

3. The following discussion is based on data that I extracted from microfilm copies of the archives of the Parroquia de El Sagrario Chilapa that are held by the Church of Jesus Christ of Latter-day Saints (LDS). Specifically, I have worked with the following: records pertaining to the cemetery at Atzacoaloya dating to the years 1807–10 and 1845–57 (Reels 603359 and 603364); records of the cemetery of Ayahualulco dating to 1815–23 and 1837–57 (Reels 603359 and 603360); records of the cemetery of Santa Catarina dating to 1815 and 1837–59 (Reels 603359 and 603362); and records from Chilapa, divided between burials of gente de razón in the years 1840–59 (Reels 603363 and 603365) and indios between 1840 and 1855 (Reels 603360 and 603363). I have also examined records of baptisms in Atzacoaloya in 1844–45 (Reel 603296) and marriage records (involving residents of the entire parish) for 1850–51 (Reel 604351), 1860–63 (Reels 603457 and 603459), and 1879–80 (Reels 603388).

4. For an ethnographic description from Oaxaca of the integration of panela production into household subsistence strategies, see González 2001:175–94.

5. Don Manuel Herrera could not have looked upon Atzacoaloya as a potential source of surplus maize. Much more likely, the town had become a refuge that he sought to dismantle to redeploy the labor to his many vacant properties.

6. To cite one example, John Gunther (1941:81), a prolific political journalist and popular author of the interwar years, compared Cárdenas to India's Mahatma Gandhi.

7. Following Cárdenas's term of office, decrees were issued to a number of communities in the Atempa basin that confirmed existing ownership claims. I have records of seven such awards, issued between 1947 and 1981, totaling 28,508 hectares of land. These grants do not amount to redistribution, however.

8. On the halting and generally unsuccessful efforts to apply the 1856 laws in Guerrero, see Salazar 1998:179–85, 255–57.

9. *Diario Oficial,* January 9, 1947, and July 29, 1949.

10. Atzacoaloya is part of this group even though its corporate holdings were claimed by the Moctezuma heirs long enough to be included in the 1838 Herrera purchase. From the beginning, the Moctezuma/Herrera claim to this land was exceptionally weak, and it died a quiet death alongside don Manuel in 1843.

11. Zitlala is an exception in being one of the few communities in the basin where conflicts with hacendados persisted and even intensified after the 1842 rebellion. These conflicts came to a head in the Mexican Revolution (1910–21), which drew participants from Zitlala but not, as far as I can tell, from other communities in the region. Most of the land that was subject to dispute was well to the north of the area that concerns me, however. Zitlala's most important lands were those of the lower Atempa valley, control over which had remained in the

hands of the town's comuneros. For a discussion of Zitlala's conflicts with hacendados, see Salazar 1998:269–72.

12. For a native perspective on tenure relations in this group of communities, see an oral history from Topiltepec reported by Illsley and colleagues (2003: 12–13).

13. Investigators here confronted circumstances in which both of the affected parties had an interest in exaggerating the nature of landowners' territorial claims. Farmers could help their case for a dotación by emphasizing their poverty and their need for land. Landowners sought to ensure that they were indemnified for land they claimed to own. Thus, testimony that farmers paid rent to landowners, even where it was not, served the interest of both parties.

14. Where pequeños propietarios felt especially threatened by the claims of adjacent communities or other petitioners for land grants, they too submitted petitions for decrees that functioned like a confirmación. Perhaps the most notable was a petition filed by a landowner from Chilapa who claimed a portion of Las Huertas, near Acatlán (Matías 1997:109–14). Pequeños propietarios holding land in a contested zone between Santa Catarina, Chautla, and Amate Amarillo did the same (see *Diario Oficial,* July 2, 1956, and November 28, 1983), as did those of Topiltepec, where internal conflicts between pequeños propietarios and comuneros remain endemic to this day (Illsley et al. 2003:12–13).

15. Although public records in Chilapa dating to the relevant period had been destroyed by the time surveyors sought to disentangle property relations, oftentimes copies were preserved in family records.

16. This time-tested practice remains common in the Atempa basin. And it works not just with land. Today, automobiles illegally imported from the United States are made legal, at least legal enough to be registered and properly licensed, through sales that give a new owner evidence that the vehicle was purchased in Mexico.

17. See AGN-TC, vol. 24, exp. 8, fols. 327–423; AGN-TC, vol. 24, exp. 10, fols. 434–72; AGN-TC, vol. 24, exp. 11, fols. 473–507.

18. Teposcuautla is a sprawling settlement spread along a series of parallel ridges. I was walking up and down successive ridges searching for the home of an authority figure when a group of about a dozen machete-wielding men surrounded me and announced that my presence was upsetting the community's children. I had by this time been in the region long enough to be known by people in many rural communities, and through this network, I later heard that the men in Teposcuautla suspected that I had come to kidnap children. At the time, the Mexican press was widely reporting the apparent existence of North American kidnapping rings that aimed to deliver infants to the United States to be put up for adoption.

19. The only exception of which I am aware is an episode of factional strife in Topiltepec in the late 1930s that pitted would-be comuneros against pequeños propietarios. The Mexican military briefly occupied the town to keep the peace (see Illsley et al. 2003:10).

20. Chilapa was among the few locations in central Guerrero with an infrastructure capable of sustaining massed troops for more than a few days at a time. This made it a frequent target of both invading armies and rebels of varying denominations. By my count, troops holding Chilapa were violently dispossessed of control of the town on at least fourteen occasions: in 1811, 1812, 1813, 1820, 1833, 1844, 1855, 1857, 1867, 1870, 1911, 1912, 1914, and 1927. Only rarely did these events lead to changes in the district or municipal governments or otherwise disrupt life in the basin.

21. The argument set forth over the following pages parallels suggestions found in Muñoz 1963:57.

22. Other documented examples include Atzacoaloya (Gutiérrez 1988) and Topiltepec (see GEA 2003).

23. Anthropologists working in Chiapas (e.g., Bobrow-Strain 2007; Collier 1994:47–48; Stephen 1998:18–19) have lately documented cases of land invasions aimed at the holdings of absentee landowners or neighboring villages. To my knowledge, no one has looked at the sort of internal invasions that I am suggesting here.

24. In turn, this custom has given rise to today's legends of buried treasures, legends that are so pervasive in the Atempa basin (and probably throughout rural Mexico) that one cannot go far or spend much time in the region without hearing a sample.

25. Eyler Simpson (1937:551) cites these items in an inventory of imported merchandise for sale in a tienda mestiza in nearby Tlapa in the 1930s. Chilapa's tiendas mestizas would have been similarly stocked.

CHAPTER 5. MATURATION AND DECLINE

1. I have no relevant supporting evidence for these last few points. Yet I will, I hope, be forgiven for allowing my imagination a moment of license. Given the stupendous inefficiency of the earlier system of urban supply and the tremendous savings of effort that came from allowing the market and not an urban militia to shape land use patterns, my speculation here is not entirely without foundation.

2. Researchers working in Topiltepec recently found that households con-

sumed 60–70 kilograms of wood per week for fuel alone. This amounts to 2.8–3.4 metric tons annually (see GEA 2003:29).

3. A team of ethnobotanists working in and around the Atempa basin in the early 1990s recorded the use of 180 edible plant species (Casas et al. 1996). Not all species entered commercial networks, but many did. For a study of the commercialization of "weeds" in the Toluca vicinity, see Vieyra-Odilon and Vibrans 2001.

4. The richest source of occupational information is contained in marriage records, which includes occupational information on all adult males participating in a nuptial event. Most marriage records have occupational information for seven individuals (the husband, fathers of the newlyweds, and four others who stood as witnesses), fewer if the newlyweds' fathers were dead or otherwise absent. I have collected this information from records from 1937 (the earliest that survive), 1940, 1943, 1945, 1947, 1950, 1955, 1960, 1963, 1965, 1970, 1975, 1980, 1981, 1985, 1990, 1995, and 2000. A detailed breakdown of the data from 1937 to 1990 can be found in Kyle 1995:383–84.

CHAPTER 6. THE RETURN OF THE FOREST

1. Snyder (2001) and Stephen (1998:19–21) have likewise found contradictions between the rhetoric and the actual implementation of neoliberalism.

2. In early 1973, cinta producers sold eighteen-meter lengths of cinta to private merchants for $0.50 to $0.80 each. At year's end, FIDEPAL paid producers at least $2.50 for the same. A day's effort could yield up to two such lengths, and thus the potential daily earnings for braiding cinta rose from $1.00–$1.60 to at least $5.00, a three- to fivefold increase (see Mastache and Morett 1982:32).

3. Virtually all teachers in the region resided in Chilapa, though many worked in rural communities.

4. The Salmerón family of Chilapa has produced several generations of photographers whose photos circulate fairly widely in Chilapa and, more recently, on the Internet. A collection posted by Juan Francisco Salmerón Sánchez can be seen at http://members.tripod.com/chilapa _ gro.mx/fotos.html (accessed February 27, 2007).

5. However simple this sounds in general principle, it is virtually impossible to demonstrate. Aside from the absence of data on prices in Chilapa, the Mexican peso was unstable through the relevant period (roughly 1960–1980). Given that so many of the items brought to the market were imported, and priced in accordance

with supply-and-demand relationships in other parts of Mexico, everything about pricing mechanisms in Chilapa's daily and weekly markets was likely cast into turmoil. Nevertheless, unless economists have their general theory of pricing all wrong, the additional money flowing into the Atempa basin combined with a steadily tightening grain supply should have resulted in sharply rising grain prices.

6. A tremendous spike in deaths shows up in the civil registry in 1972, one of two years (the other being 1963) in the interval between 1928 and 1985 when more deaths than births were recorded. This followed the harvest of 1971, which was probably nearly as awful as had been the harvest of 1970. Though the total annual rainfall in 1971 was low but not too terribly so, rainfall in the critical month of August was just over 75 millimeters, less than half the forty-five-year average of 164 millimeters. This appears to have resulted in a poor harvest for a second consecutive year, creating something that from these records looks like a famine.

7. Against a forty-five-year annual rainfall average of 830 millimeters, the recorded rainfall totals for the first six years of the 1970s are 383, 680, 570, 798, 743, and 666 millimeters, respectively.

8. In some areas of Mexico (though not in or around Chilapa), CONASUPO also purchased agricultural commodities, including maize, at subsidized prices (e.g., Cancian 1972).

9. Unpublished records of CONASUPO, on file in Chilapa. The records I examined were handwritten ledgers, a sort of bureaucratic ephemera unlikely to survive today.

10. Far from being conservative, farmers with the resources to do so generally followed the agronomists' recommendations, although I did not find any clear economic rationale for doing so. Whereas SARH agronomists came forth with productivity estimates showing that fields planted with hybrid seed varieties yielded far better than fields of indigenous seed stock, my research (Kyle 1995:168–75) shows that the SARH estimates were based on a flawed method of calculating yields that consistently underestimated the yield of fields planted with indigenous seeds.

11. Data from the United States Department of Agriculture, National Agriculture Statistics Service, at http://www.nass.usda.gov/Statistics __ by __ State/Iowa/index.asp (accessed February 27. 2007).

12. To facilitate comparison, I have converted all monetary figures in this section to U.S. dollars, using the dollar's value in 2000 as the standard. Budget figures for 1982 are found in INEGI 1984:680. Those for other years can be found in SIMBAD, an online database maintained by the INEGI (http://www.inegi.gob .mx/). I converted the peso amounts found in these sources to U.S. dollars using the average exchange rate listed by the U.S. Federal Reserve (http://www.federal

reserve.gov/releases/h10/hist/) in the month of June in the specified year. I then adjusted the dollar amount using the Consumer Price Index (using the conversion utility found at http://eh.net/hmit/compare/) to fix the dollar's value at its level in 2000.

13. In 2004, the presidente municipal, Maclovio Ariza Acevedo, found himself in the middle of a bitter conflict pitting two of his brothers against each other. One was an organizer of merchants in the new market building, the other an organizer of a smaller group that remained in the old market building. Although the local government initially intended to move all merchants to the new building, substantial numbers of the town's residents favored leaving the old market alone. Thus, merchants with retail establishments in the old building had significant popular support behind their effort to stay put. The conflict erupted into violence in early 2004 when merchants from the new market, acting under the direction of the presidente's brother, attempted to demolish the old building. The presidente's other brother organized the resistance. The result, more of a melee than a proper riot, ended when the municipal police, acting on orders from the presidente, dispersed the crowd with teargas. When the air cleared, one corner of the old market building had been reduced to rubble, but the stalls within were intact. For more on the conflict, see Illsley et al. 2003:78–79.

14. The project did not so much relieve congestion as simply move it several hundred meters to the north. When originally designed, the new market was on the outskirts of town, but subsequent urban sprawl in the valley to the north has shifted the city's geographic center to such an extent that the new market is now nearly dead center, just as was the old one (see map 2).

15. Here the problem involved indemnification to farmers in Acatlán whose lands were in the right-of-way (Matías 1997:113–14).

16. The return to producers of palm goods has nevertheless fallen steadily since Sanzekan Tinemi became involved in the industry (Illsley et al. 2003:98).

17. Thus, Illsley and colleagues (2003:25) found average yields of 850 kilograms per hectare in Topiltepec in the late 1990s. My measurements consistently showed yields over 3,000 kilograms per hectare in the same area less than a decade earlier.

18. Sanzekan Tinemi managed to import 1,000 tons in 1993, 1,400 tons in 1994, and 1,500 tons in 1995. This was sold to farmers at roughly the same price charged by merchants. In contrast to the merchants, who expected payment at the time of delivery, Sanzekan Tinemi made a variety of financing arrangements and thus enabled farmers who otherwise might not have used fertilizer to do so (Meza 2000:389–91).

REFERENCES CITED

ARCHIVES AND ARCHIVAL COLLECTIONS

AGN. Archivo General de la Nación Document Collections
Clero Regular y Secular (CRS)
Gobernación (G)
Historia (H)
Histórico de Hacienda (HH)
Indios (I)
Padrones (P)
Industria y Comercio (IC)
Mercedes (M)
Subdelegados (S)
Tierras (T)
Tribunal de Cuentas (TC)
Archivo General de Notarías del Distrito Federal
LDS. Parroquia de El Sagrario Chilapa, microfilm copies held by the Church of
  Jesus Christ of Latter-day Saints
Registro Civil, H. Ayuntamiento Municipal de Chilapa de Álvarez

PERIODICALS

Catedral, Publicación Mensual. Chilapa, Guerrero.
Diario Oficial: Organo del Gobierno Constitucional de los Estados Unidos Mexi-
  canos Diario Oficial. Mexico City.

Revista Conmemorativa de la Fundación de la Escuela Secundaria Federal "General José de San Martín." Chilapa, Guerrero.
Revista Ehécatl. Chilapa, Guerrero.

PUBLISHED WORKS AND MANUSCRIPTS

Ahrens, Curtis L., and John T. Shields. 1973. *The Fertilizer Marketing System in Mexico.* Muscle Shoals, Ala.: National Fertilizer Development Center.

Álvarez, Juan. 1845. *Manifesto que Dirige a la Nación el General Juan Álvarez, con Motivo de la Representación Calumniosa que Unos Emigrados de la Villa de Chilapa Hicieron a la Augusta Cámara de Diputados en Febrero Áltimo.* Mexico City: I. Cumplido.

Amith, Jonathan D. 2005. *The Möbius Strip: A Spatial History of Colonial Society in Guerrero, Mexico.* Stanford, Calif.: Stanford University Press.

Anderson, Richmond K., Jose Calvo, Gloria Serrano, and George C. Payne. 1946. A Study of the Nutritional Status and Food Habits of Otomi Indians in the Mezquital Valley of Mexico. *American Journal of Public Health* 36:883–903.

Andrade, Vicente de Paula. 1911. *Chilapa: Estudios Sobre Esta Ciudad.* Mexico City: Escuela Tipo-Litografica Salesiana.

Annis, Sheldon. 1987. *God and Production in a Guatemalan Town.* Austin: University of Texas Press.

Arce, General Francisco O. 1872. *Memoria Presentada Ante La H. Legislatura del Estado de Guerrero.* Chilpancingo, Guerrero: Imprenta del Gobierno del Estado.

Austin, James E., and Gustavo Esteva. 1987. *Food Policy in Mexico: The Search for Self-Sufficiency.* Ithaca, N.Y.: Cornell University Press.

Austin, James E., and Jonathan Fox. 1987. State-Owned Enterprises: Food Policy Implementers. In *Food Policy in Mexico: The Search for Self-Sufficiency,* ed. James E. Austin and Gustavo Esteva, pp. 61–91. Ithaca, N.Y.: Cornell University Press.

Bazant, Jan. 1964. Evolution of the Textile Industry of Puebla, 1544–1845. *Comparative Studies in Society and History* 7:56–69.

Beals, Ralph L. 1945. *Ethnology of the Western Mixe.* Berkeley: University of California Press.

———. 1946. *Cherán: A Sierra Tarascan Village.* Washington, D.C.: U.S. Government Printing Office.

———. 1975. *The Peasant Marketing System of Oaxaca, Mexico.* Berkeley: University of California Press.

Beals, Ralph L., and Evelyn Hatcher. 1943. The Diet of a Tarascan Village. *América Indígena* 3:295–304.

Benedict, Francis G., and Morris Steggarda. 1936. *Food of the Present-Day Maya Indians of Yucatan.* Carnegie Institution of Washington, Contributions in American Archaeology 18. Washington, D.C.

Berg, Richard L. 1974. *El Impacto de la Economía Moderna Sobre la Economía Tradicional de Zoogochi, Oaxaca y su Área Circundante.* Mexico City: Instituto Nacional Indigenista.

Biskowski, Martin. 2000. Maize Preparation and the Aztec Subsistence Economy. *Ancient Mesoamerica* 11:293–306.

Bobrow-Strain, Aaron. 2007. *Intimate Enemies: Landowners, Power, and Violence in Chiapas.* Durham, N.C.: Duke University Press.

Borah, Woodrow. 1983. *Justice by Insurance: The General Indian Court of Colonial Mexico and the Legal Aides of the Half-Real.* Berkeley: University of California Press.

Boyer, Richard. 1981. Juan Vazquez, Muleteer of Seventeenth-Century Mexico. *Americas* 37: 421–43.

Burton, Anthony. 1984. *The Rise and Fall of King Cotton.* London: British Broadcasting Corporation and Andre Deutsch.

Cancian, Frank. 1965. *Economics and Prestige in a Maya Community: A Study of the Religious Cargo System in Zinacantan, Chiapas.* Palo Alto, Calif.: Stanford University Press.

———. 1972. *Change and Uncertainty in a Peasant Economy.* Stanford, Calif.: Stanford University Press.

———. 1992. *The Decline of Community in Zinacantan: Economy, Public Life, and Social Stratification, 1960–1987.* Palo Alto, Calif.: Stanford University Press.

Casarrubias Caballero, Jesús. 1989. *Chilapa.* Mexico City: Costa-Amic Editores.

Casarrubias Guzman, Magdalena. 1994. *El Arte Culinario de Chilapa, Guerrero.* Mexico City: Costa-Amic Editores.

Casas, Alejandro, María del Carmen Vázquez, Juan Luis Viveros, and Javier Caballero. 1996. Plant Management among the Nahua and the Mixtec in the Balsas River Basin, Mexico: An Ethnobotanical Approach to the Study of Plant Domestication. *Human Ecology* 24:455–77.

Catalán Guevara, Arquímedes. 1947. Sistema Hidroelectrico de Colotlipa, Guerrero. In *Revista Conmemorativa de la Fundación de la Escuela Secundaria de Chilapa* (pamphlet), pp. 70–74. Chilapa, Guerrero.

Chase, Stuart. 1931. *Mexico: A Study of Two Americas.* New York: MacMillan.

Chevalier, Jacques M., and Daniel Buckles. 1995. *A Land without Gods: Process Theory, Maldevelopment and the Mexican Nahuas.* London: Zed Books.

Cohen, Jeffrey H. 1999. *Cooperation and Community: Economy and Society in Oaxaca.* Austin: University of Texas Press.

——. 2004. *The Culture of Migration in Southern Mexico.* Austin: University of Texas Press.

Collier, George A. 1975. *Fields of the Tzotzil: The Ecological Bases of Tradition in Highland Chiapas.* Austin: University of Texas Press.

——. 1994. *Basta! Land and the Zapatista Rebellion in Chiapas.* Oakland, Calif.: Institute for Food and Development Policy.

Cook, Scott, and Martin Diskin, eds. 1976. *Markets in Oaxaca.* Austin: University of Texas Press.

Cordry, Donald. 1980. *Mexican Masks.* Austin: University of Texas Press.

Cornelius, Wayne A. 1994. Foreword to *The Politics of Economic Restructuring: State-Society Relations and Regime Change in Mexico,* ed. Maria Lorena Cook, Kevin J. Middlebrook, and Juan Molinar Horcasitas, pp. xi–xx. La Jolla, Calif.: Center for U.S.-Mexican Studies.

Cornelius, Wayne A., and David Myhre, eds. 1997. *The Transformation of Rural Mexico: Reforming the Ejido Sector.* La Jolla, Calif.: Center for U.S.-Mexican Studies.

Daltabuit, Magalí. 1988. *Ecología Humana en una Comunidad de Morelos.* Mexico City: Instituto de Investigaciones Antropologicas.

Davis, Virginia. 1991. Resist Dyeing in Mexico: Comments on Its History, Significance, and Prevalence. In *Textile Traditions of Mesoamerica and the Andes,* ed. Margot Schevill, Janet C. Berlo, and Edward B. Dwyer, pp. 309–35. New York: Garland Publishing.

Dehouve, Danièle. 1976. *El Tequío de los Santos y la Competencia Entre los Mercaderes.* Mexico City: Dirección General de Publicaciones del Consejo Nacional para la Cultura y las Artes; Instituto Nacional Indigenista.

DEN (Departamento de la Estadística Nacional). 1927. *Censo General de Habitantes, 30 de Noviembre de 1921: Estado de Guerrero.* Mexico City: Talleres Gráficos de la Nación.

DeWalt, Billie. 1979. *Modernization in a Mexican Ejido: A Study in Economic Adaptation.* New York: Cambridge University Press.

DeWalt, Billie, and Martha W. Rees. 1994. *The End of the Agrarian Reform in Mexico: Past Lessons, Future Prospects.* La Jolla, Calif.: Center for U.S.-Mexican Studies.

DeWalt, Kathleen Musante. 1983. *Nutritional Strategies and Agricultural Change in a Mexican Community.* Ann Arbor, Mich.: UMI Research Press.

DGE (Dirección General de Estadística). 1905a. *Censo General de la República*

Mexicana: Estado de Guerrero. Mexico City: Imprenta y Fototipía de la Secretaría de Fomento.

———. 1905b. *División Territorial de la República Mexicana: Estado de Guerrero.* Mexico City: Imprenta y Fototipía de la Secretaría de Fomento.

———. 1912. *División Territorial de los Estados Unidos Mexicanos: Estado de Guerrero.* Mexico City: Imprenta de la Secretaría de Fomento.

———. 1934. *Quinto Censo General de la Población, 15 de Mayo de 1930: Estado de Guerrero.* Mexico City: Secretaría de la Economia Nacional.

———. 1943. *Sexto Censo de Población: Guerrero.* Mexico City: Secretaría de la Economia Nacional.

———. 1952. *Séptimo Censo General de Población, 6 de Junio de 1950: Estado de Guerrero.* Mexico City: Secretaría de Economia Nacional.

———. 1957. *Tercer Censo Agricola-Ganadero y Ejidal de 1950: Guerrero.* Mexico City: Secretaría de Economia Nacional.

———. 1963. *VIII Censo General de Población: Estado de Guerrero.* Mexico City: Secretaria de Industria y Comercio.

———. 1973. *IX Censo General de Población, 28 de Enero de 1970. Localidades por Entidad Federativa y Municipio con Algunas Caracteristicas de su Poblacion y Vivienda,* vol. 1: *Aguascalientes a Guerrero.* Mexico City: Secretaría de Industria y Comercio.

———. 1975. *Quinto Censo Agricola-Ganadero y Ejidal de 1970: Guerrero.* Mexico City: Secretaría de Economia Nacional.

Díaz Nuñez, Ignacio. 1976. *Análisis del Tianguis en Chilapa, Guerrero, y su Repercusión en la Economía Indígena Regional.* Unpublished thesis, Instituto Politécnico Nacional, Mexico City.

Dollero, Adolfo. 1911. *México al Día: Impresiones y Notas de Viaje.* Mexico City: Librería de la Vda de C. Bouret.

Enge, Kjell I., and Scott Whiteford. 1989. *The Keepers of Water and Earth: Mexican Rural Social Organization and Irrigation.* Austin: University of Texas Press.

Espinosa Damián, Gisela, and Miguel Meza Castillo. 2000. Guerrero en Cifras: Las Dimensiones de la Pobreza. In *Crónicas del Sur: Utopías Campesinas en Guerrero,* ed. Armando Bartra, pp. 75–102. Mexico City: Ediciones Era.

Esteva, Gustavo. 2003. The Meaning and Scope of the Struggle for Autonomy. In *Mayan Lives, Mayan Utopias: The Indigenous Peoples of Chiapas and the Zapatista Rebellion,* ed. Jan Rus, Rosalva Aída Hernández Castillo, pp. 243–69. Lanham, Md.: Rowman and Littlefield.

Fedoroff, Nina V. 2003. Prehistoric GM Corn. *Science* 302:1158–59.

Food and Agriculture Organization of the United Nations. 2000. *The State of Food and Agriculture, 2000.* Rome: Food and Agriculture Organization of the United Nations.

Foster, George McClelland. 1948. *Empire's Children: The People of Tzintzuntzan.* Smithsonian Institution, Institute of Social Anthropology, Publication 6. Washington, D.C.

———. 1960. *Culture and Conquest: America's Spanish Heritage.* Chicago: Wenner-Gren Foundation for Anthropological Research.

Fox, Jonathan. 1992. *The Politics of Food in Mexico: State Power and Social Mobilization.* Ithaca, N.Y.: Cornell University Press.

———. 1994. Political Change in Mexico's New Peasant Economy. In *The Politics of Economic Restructuring: State-Society Relations and Regime Change in Mexico,* ed. Maria Lorena Cook, Kevin J. Middlebrook, and Juan Molinar Horcasitas, pp. 243–76. La Jolla, Calif.: Center for U.S.-Mexican Studies.

Fox, Jonathan, and Josefina Aranda. 1996. *Decentralization and Rural Development in Mexico: Community Participation in Oaxaca's Municipal Funds Program.* La Jolla, Calif.: Center for U.S.-Mexican Studies.

García y Cubas, Antonio. 1861. *Memoria Para Servir a la Carta General de la República Mexicana.* Mexico City: Imprenta de Andrade y Escalante.

GEA (Grupo de Estudios Ambientales). 2002. *Informe de Mercadeo, Maguey/Mescal.* http://quin.unep-wcmc.org/forest/ntfp/cd/7 _ Market _ reports/f _ Maguey-mezcal.pdf.

———. 2003. *Informe de Mercadeo, Palma Soyate, Guerrero, Oaxaca.* http://quin.unep-wcmc.org/forest/ntfp/cd/7 _ Market _ reports/e _ Palma _ soyate.pdf.

Gerhard, Peter. 1993. *A Guide to the Historical Geography of New Spain.* Rev. ed. Norman: University of Oklahoma Press.

Gibson, Charles. 1964. *The Aztecs under Spanish Rule: A History of the Indians of the Valley of Mexico, 1519–1810.* Stanford, Calif.: Stanford University Press.

Giles, Antonio. 1953. Parroquia de San Luis Acatlán. *Catedral* (September 20), pp. 89–90.

González, Roberto J. 2001. *Zapotec Science: Farming and Food in the Northern Sierra of Oaxaca.* Austin: University of Texas Press.

Good, Catherine. 1995. Salt Production and Commerce in Guerrero, Mexico: An Ethnographic Contribution to Historical Reconstruction. *Ancient Mesoamerica* 6:1–14.

Grijalva, Juan de. 1985. *Crónica de la Orden de N.P.S. Agustín en las Provincias de la Nueva España.* Mexico City: Editorial Porrúa. Originally published 1625.

Guardino, Peter F. 1995a. Barbarism or Republican Law? Guerrero's Peasants and National Politics, 1820–1846. *Hispanic American Historical Review* 75:185–213.

———. 1995b. Reply to Hart. *Hispanic American Historical Review* 75:751–53.

———. 1996. *Peasants, Politics, and the Formation of Mexico's National State: Guerrero, 1800–1857.* Stanford, Calif.: Stanford University Press.

Gunther, John. 1941. *Inside Latin America.* New York: Harper and Brothers.

Gutiérrez Gutiérrez, Donaciano. 1988. Los Nahuas de Guerrero. In *Estudios Nahuas,* ed. Cristina Suárez y Farías, pp. 83–125. Mexico City: Instituto Nacional de Antropología e Historia.

Hamilton, Earl J. 1944. Monetary Problems in Spain and Spanish America, 1751–1800. *Journal of Economic History* 4: 21–48.

Hansen, Roger D. 1971. *The Politics of Mexican Development.* Baltimore, Md.: Johns Hopkins University Press.

Hart, John M. 1988. The 1840s Southwestern Mexico Peasants' War: Conflict in a Transitional Society. In *Riot, Rebellion, and Revolution,* ed. Friedrich Katz, pp. 249–68. Princeton, N.J.: Princeton University Press.

———. 1995. Comment on Guardino. *Hispanic American Historical Review* 75:749–51.

Hassig, Ross. 1985. *Trade, Tribute, and Transportation: The Sixteenth-Century Political Economy of the Valley of Mexico.* Norman: University of Oklahoma Press.

Haswell, Margaret. 1973. *Tropical Farming Economics.* London: Longman.

Hernández, Mercedes, Adolfo Chavez, and Hector Bourges. 1983. *Valor Nutritivo de los Alimentos Mexicanos: Tablas de Uso Practico.* 9th ed. Mexico City: Instituto Nacional de la Nutrición.

Hobsbawm, Eric J. 1962. *The Age of Revolution, 1789–1848.* New York: New American Library.

———. 1968. *Industry and Empire: From 1750 to the Present Day.* New York: Penguin Books.

———. 1994. *Age of Extremes: A History of the World, 1914–1991.* New York: Random House.

Illsley Granich, Catarina, Jasmine Aguilar, Jorge Acosta G., Jorge Garcia B., Tonantzin Gómez A., and Javier Caballero N. 2001. Contribuciones al Conocimiento y Manejo Campesino de los Palmares de *Brahea dulcis* (HBK) Mart. en la Región de Chilapa, Guerrero. In *Plantas, Cultura y Sociedad: Estudio Sobre la Relación entre Seres Humanos y Plantas en los Albores del Siglo XXI,* ed. Beatriz Rendón Aguilar, Silvia Rebollar Domínguez, Javier Caballero Nieto, and Miguel Angel Martínez Alfaro, pp. 259–86. Mexico City: Universidad Autónoma Metropolitana.

Illsley Granich, Catarina, Tonantzin Gómez, Lucio Díaz, Grissell Velasco, Juana Flores, Pilar Morales, Jorge García, and Jasmín Aguilar. 2003. *Proyecto de Comercialización de Productos Forestales no Maderables: Factores de Éxito y Fracaso: Palma Soyate (*Brahea dulcis*), Comunidad Topiltepec, Municipio de Zitlala, Guerrero, México.* Mexico City: Grupo de Estudios Ambientales. http://quin.unep-wcmc.org/forest/ntfp/cd/8 _ Community _ reports/j _ Palma _ soyate _ Topiltepec.pdf.

Illsley Granich, Catarina, Tonantzin Gómez, Fabrice Edouard, and Elaine Marshall. 2006. Palma Soyate, *Brahea dulcis* (Arecaceae). In *Comercialización de Productos Forestales no Maderables: Factores que Influyen en el Éxito y Fracaso,* ed. E. Marshall, K. Schreckenberg, and A. C. Newton, pp. 47–50. Cambridge, U.K.: Centro Mundial de Vigilancia de la Conservación del PNUMA. http://quin.unep-wcmc.org/forest/ntfp/cd/1 _ CEPFOR _ Final _ project _ outputs/a/a _ Comercializacion _ de _ PFNM _ Esp.pdf.

INEGI (Instituto Nacional de Estadistica, Geografia, e Informatica). 1984. *Manual de Estadísticas Básicas del Estado de Guerrero.* Mexico City: Instituto Nacional de Estadística, Geografía, e Informatica.

———. 1989. *X Censo General de Población y Vivienda, 1980: Estado de Guerrero.* Aguascalientes, Mexico: Instituto Nacional de Estadística, Geografía, e Informatica.

———. 1991. *XI Censo General de Población y Vivienda, 1990: Guerrero.* Aguascalientes, Mexico: Instituto Nacional de Estadística, Geografía, e Informatica.

———. 1994. *VII Censo Agrícola-Ganadero: Guerrero,* vol. 2. Aguascalientes, Mexico: Instituto Nacional de Estadística, Geografía, e Informatica.

———. 1997. *Carta Edafologica,* series 1, *1:1,000,000* scale, *Cobertura Nacional.* Aguascalientes, Mexico: Instituto Nacional de Estadística, Geografía, e Informatica.

———. 2000. *Carta Topográfica,* 1:50,000 scale, *Chilapa de Álvarez, E14C29.* Aguascalientes, Mexico: Instituto Nacional de Estadística, Geografía, e Informatica.

———. 2001. *Carta Topográfica,* 1:50,000 scale, *Quecholtenango, E14C39.* Aguascalientes, Mexico: Instituto Nacional de Estadística, Geografía, e Informatica.

———. 2002. *Principales Resultados por Localidad: XII Censo General de Población y Vivienda, 2000: Estado de Guerrero.* Aguascalientes, Mexico: Instituto Nacional de Estadística, Geografía, e Informatica.

Jacobs, Jane. 1969. *The Economy of Cities.* New York: Random House.

Jaenicke-Després, Viviane, Ed S. Buckler, Bruce D. Smith, M. Thomas P. Gilbert,

Alan Cooper, John Doeblley, and Svante Pääbo. 2003. Early Allelic Selection in Maize as Revealed by Ancient DNA. *Science* 302:1206–1208.

Kaplan, David. 1965. The Mexican Marketplace Then and Now. *Proceedings of the 1965 Annual Spring Meeting of the American Ethnological Society, Seattle, 1965.* Seattle: University of Washington Press.

Kearney, Michael. 1996. *Reconceptualizing the Peasantry: Anthropology in Global Perspective.* Boulder, Colo.: Westview Press.

Kelly, Isabel, and Angel Palerm. 1952. *The Tajin Totonac,* part 1: *History, Subsistence, Shelter, and Technology.* Smithsonian Institution, Institute of Social Anthropology, Publication 13. Washington, D.C.

Kemper, Robert V. 1977. *Migration and Adaptation: Tzintzuntzan Peasants in Mexico City.* Beverly Hills, Calif.: Sage Publications.

Kennedy, Diana. 1998. *My Mexico: A Culinary Odyssey with More Than 500 Recipes.* New York: Clarkson Potter Publishers.

Keremitsis, Dawn. 1987. *The Cotton Textile Industry in Porfiriato, Mexico: 1870–1910.* New York: Garland Publishing.

Kicza, John E. 1983. *Colonial Entrepreneurs: Families and Business in Bourbon, Mexico City.* Albuquerque: University of New Mexico Press.

Kirchoff, Paul. 1952. Mesoamerica: Its Geographic Limits, Ethnic Composition and Cultural Characteristics. In *Heritage of Conquest: The Ethnology of Middle America,* ed. Sol Tax, pp. 17–30. New York: Free Press.

Kirkby, Anne V. T. 1973. *The Use of Land and Water Resources in the Past and Present Valley of Oaxaca, Mexico.* University of Michigan, Memoirs of the Museum of Anthropology 5. Ann Arbor.

Kyle, Chris. 1995. *The Ecology and Political Economy of Maize in the Upper Atempa Basin, Guerrero, Mexico.* Ph.D. Dissertation, Columbia University, New York.

———. 1996a. From Burros to Buses: Transport Efficiency and Economic Development in Guerrero, Mexico. *Journal of Anthropological Research* 52:411–32.

———. 1996b. Comment on Guardino. *Hispanic American Historical Review* 76:433–36.

———. 2003. Land, Labor, and the Chilapa Market: A New Look at the 1840s' Peasant Wars in Central Guerrero. *Ethnohistory* 50:89–130.

Kyle, Chris, and William Yaworsky. 2008. Mexican Justice: Codified Law, Patronage, and the Regulation of Social Affairs in Guerrero, Mexico. *Journal of Anthropological Research* 64:67–90.

Leatherman, Thomas L., and Alan Goodman. 2005. Coca-colonization of Diets in the Yucatán. *Social Science and Medicine* 61:833–46.

Lewis, Oscar. 1949. Plow Culture and Hoe Culture: A Study in Contrasts. *Rural Sociology* 14:116–27.

———. 1951. *Life in a Mexican Village: Tepoztlán Restudied.* Urbana: University of Illinois Press.

Logan, Michael H., and William T. Sanders. 1976. The Model. In *The Valley of Mexico: Studies in Pre-Hispanic Ecology and Society,* ed. Eric R. Wolf, pp. 31–58. Albuquerque: University of New Mexico Press.

Mastache Flores, Alba Guadalupe, and Elia Nora Morett Sánchez. 1982. *El Trabajo de la Palma en la Región de La Montaña, Guerrero.* Chilpancingo: Universidad Autónoma de Guerrero.

Mathewson, Kent. 1984. *Irrigation Horticulture in Highland Guatemala: The Tablón System of Panajachel.* Boulder, Colo.: Westview Press.

Matías Alonso, Marcos. 1982. Tlayolli: El Pan de los Indios en Acatlán, Chilapan de Álvarez, Guerrero. In *Nuestro Maíz: Treinta Monagrafias Populares del Maíz,* pp. 91–118. Mexico City: Museo Nacional de Culturas Populares.

———. 1997. *La Agricultura Indígena en la Montaña de Guerrero.* Mexico City: Plaza y Valdés, Dirección General de Culturas Populares, Unidad Regional Guerrero.

Matsuoka, Yoshihiro, et al. 2002. A Single Domestication for Maize Shown by Multilocus Microsatellite Genotyping. *Proceedings of the National Academy of Sciences* 99:6080–84.

McBryde, Felix Webster. 1945. *Cultural and Historical Geography of Southwest Guatemala.* Smithsonian Institution, Institute of Social Anthropology, Publication 4. Washington, D.C.

Meyer, Jean. 1973. *Problemas Campesinas y Revueltas Agrarias, 1821–1910.* Mexico City: SepSetentas.

Meza Castillo, Miguel. 2000. "Seguimos Estando Juntos": La Organización Campesina en Chilapa. In *Crónicas del Sur: Utopías Campesinas en Guerrero,* ed. Armando Bartra, pp. 375–411. Mexico City: Ediciones Era.

Miranda González, Gustavo. 2001. *Segundo Informe de Gobierno: Chilapa, Guerrero.* Chilapa: H. Ayuntamiento Constitucional, Chilapa de Álvarez, Guerrero.

Monaghan, John. 1995. *The Covenants with Earth and Rain: Exchange, Sacrifice, and Revelation in Mixtec Sociality.* Norman: University of Oklahoma Press.

Morse, Richard M. 1962. Latin American Cities: Structure and Function. *Comparative Studies in Society and History* 4:473–93.

Muñoz, Maurilio. 1963. *Mixteca-Nahua-Tlapaneca.* Mexico City: Instituto Nacional Indigenista.

Nash, June. 2001. *Mayan Visions: The Quest for Autonomy in an Age of Globalization.* New York: Routledge.

National Research Council. 1978. *Postharvest Food Losses in Developing Countries.* Washington, D.C.: National Academy of Sciences.

New York Public Library. 1777. *Yndice Comprehensibo de Todos los Gobiernos, Corregimientos, y Alcaldes Mayores de Mexico que Contiene la Governacion del Virreynato de México.* Phillips MS. Collection, 15796.

Ochoa Campos, Moisés. 1968. *Historia del Estado de Guerrero.* Mexico City: Librería de Porrúa Hnos. y Cía.

Oettinger, Marion. 1974. *The Voice of the Neighbors: A Study of Tlapanec Community Boundaries and Their Maintenance.* Ph.D. dissertation, University of North Carolina, Chapel Hill.

Olivera, Mercedes. 1979. Huemitl de Mayo en Citlala ¿Ofrenda Para Chicomecoatl o Para la Santa Cruz? In *Mesoamerica: Homenaje al Doctor Paul Kirchhoff,* ed. Barbro Dahlgren de Jordán, pp. 143–58. Mexico City: Instituto Nacional de Antropología e Historia.

Ortiz Hernán, Sergio. 1994. *Caminos y Transportes en México: Fines de la Colonia y Principios de la Vida Independiente.* Mexico City: Secretaría de Comunicaciones y Transportes, Fondo de Cultura Económica.

Parsons, Elsie Clews. 1936. *Mitla: Town of the Souls.* Chicago: University of Chicago Press.

Paso y Troncoso, Francisco del, ed. 1905a. Relación de Chilapa. In *Papeles de Nueva España,* series 2, *Geografía y Estadística,* vol. 5, pp. 174–82. Madrid: Rivadeneyra.

———. 1905b. Suma de Visitas de Pueblos. In *Papeles de Nueva España,* series 2, *Geografía y Estadística,* vol. 1. Madrid: Rivadeneyra.

Piperno, D. R., and K. V. Flannery. 2001. The Earliest Archaeological Maize (*Zea mays* L.) from Highland Mexico: New Accelerator Mass Spectrometry Dates and Their Implications. *Proceedings of the National Academy of Sciences* 98 (4): 2101–2103.

Plattner, Stuart. 1975. The Economics of Peddling. In *Formal Methods in Economic Anthropology,* ed. Stuart Plattner, pp. 55–76. Washington, D.C.: American Anthropological Association.

Ravelo Lecuona, Renato. 1987. Periodo 1910–1920. In *Historia de la Cuestión Agraria Mexicana: Estado de Guerrero, 1867–1940,* ed. Jaime Salazar Adame, pp. 81–220. Mexico City: Centro de Estudios Histórico del Agrarianismo en México.

Redfield, Robert. 1941. *The Folk Culture of Yucatan.* Chicago: University of Chicago Press.

Redfield, Robert, and Alfonso Villa Rojas. 1934. *Chan Kom, a Maya Village.* Washington, D.C.: Carnegie Institution of Washington.

Reina, Leticia. 1980. *Las Rebeliones Campesinas en México (1819–1906).* Mexico City: Siglo XXI.

———. 1983. *Las Luchas Populares en México en el Siglo XIX.* Mexico City: Casa Chata.

Rodríguez, Victoria E. 1997. *Decentralization in Mexico: From Reforma Municipal to Solidaridad to Nuevo Federalismo.* Boulder, Colo.: Westview Press.

Rubín de la Borbolla, Daniel, and Ralph L. Beals. 1940. The Tarascan Project: A Cooperative Enterprise of the National Polytechnic Institute, Mexican Bureau–Indian Affairs, and the University of California. *American Anthropologist* 42:708–12.

Rubinstein, Robert A., ed. 1991. *Fieldwork: The Correspondence of Robert Redfield and Sol Tax.* Boulder, Colo.: Westview Press.

Ruiz Hernández, Eicandro, Mariano Acevedo H., and Juventino Pineda y Ortega. 1947. Síntesis Económica del Municipio de Chilapa del Estado de Guerrero. In *Revista Conmemorativa de la Fundación de la Escuela Secundaria de Chilapa* (pamphlet), pp. 24–26. Chilapa, Guerrero.

Salazar Adame, Jaime. 1987. Periodo 1867–1910. In *Historia de la Cuestión Agraria Mexicana: Estado de Guerrero, 1867–1940,* ed. Jaime Salazar Adame, pp. 9–80. Mexico City: Centro de Estudios Histórico del Agrarianismo en México.

———. 1998. La Modernización. In *Historia General de Guerrero,* vol. 3: *Formación y Modernización,* ed. Elizabeth Jiménez García, pp. 147–333. Mexico City: Instituto Nacional de Antropología e Historia.

Salazar de Weaver, Monyka, and Chris Kyle. n.d. *Chilapa's Traza in 1791.* Unpublished manuscript.

Salvucci, Richard J. 1987. *Textiles and Capitalism in Mexico, 1539–1840.* Princeton, N.J.: Princeton University Press.

Sanders, William T. 1956. The Central Mexican Symbiotic Region. In *Prehistoric Settlement Patterns in the New World,* ed. Gordon R. Willey, pp. 115–27. Viking Fund Publications in Anthropology 23. New York: Wenner-Gren Foundation for Anthropological Research.

Sanderson, Steven. 1986. *The Transformation of Mexican Agriculture.* Princeton, N.J.: Princeton University Press.

Santos Carrera, Moises, and Jesús Álvarez Hernández. 1990. *Historia de la Cuestión Agraria Mexicana: Estado de Guerrero, Epocas Prehispanica y Colonial.* Chilpancingo: Universidad Autónoma de Guerrero.

SARH (Secretaría de Agricultura y Recursos Hidráulicos). 1987. *Diagnóstico General: Municipio de Chilapa.* Unpublished manuscript on file with the SARH, Chilapa, Guerrero, Mexico.

Sayer, Chloë. 1988. *Mexican Textile Techniques.* Princes Risborough, Aylesbury, Bucks, U.K.: Shire Publications.

Schjellerup, Inge. 1986. Ploughing in Chuquibamba, Peru. *Tools and Tillage* 5:180–89.

Schmidt, Paul. n.d. Surface Archaeology in the Chilapa-Zitlala Area of Guerrero, Mexico, Season 1. Report submitted to the Foundation for the Advancement of Mesoamerican Studies, Crystal River, Florida. http:///www.famsi.org/re ports/02009/index.html.

Schultze, Leonhard Sigmund. 1938. *Bei den Azteken, Mixteken und Tlapaneken del Sierra Madre del Sur von Mexiko.* Jena, Germany: Gustav Fischer.

Seeger, Martin L. 1978. Media of Exchange in 16th Century New Spain and the Spanish Response. *The Americas* 35: 168–84.

Simpson, Eyler N. 1937. *The Ejido: Mexico's Way Out.* Chapel Hill: University of North Carolina Press.

Simpson, Lesley Byrd. 1950. *The Encomienda in New Spain: The Beginning of Spanish Mexico.* Berkeley: University of California Press.

———. 1966. *Many Mexicos.* Berkeley: University of California Press.

Smith, Carol A. 1976. *Regional Analysis.* 2 vols. New York: Academic Press.

Snyder, Richard. 2001. *Politics after Neoliberalism: Reregulation in Mexico.* Cambridge, U.K.: Cambridge University Press.

Solano, Francisco de, ed. 1988. *Relaciones Geográficas del Arzobispado de México: 1743,* vol. 1. Madrid: Consejo Superior de Investigaciones Científicas.

Speed, Shannon. 2005. Dangerous Discourses: Human Rights and Multiculturalism in Neoliberal Mexico. *Political and Legal Anthropology Review* 28:29–51.

Stadelman, Raymond. 1940. *Maize Cultivation in Northwestern Guatemala.* Washington, D.C.: Carnegie Institute of Washington.

Steggarda, Morris. 1941. *Maya Indians of Yucatan.* Carnegie Institution of Washington, Contributions to American Archaeology, 531. Washington, D.C.

Stein, Stanley J. 1997. Tending the Store: Trade and Silver at the Real de Huautla, 1778–1781. *Hispanic American Historical Review* 77: 377–407.

Stephen, Lynn. 1991. *Zapotec Women.* Austin: University of Texas Press.

———. 1998. The Cultural and Political Dynamics of Agrarian Reform in Oaxaca and Chiapas. In *The Future Role of the Ejido in Rural Mexico,* ed. Richard Snyder and Gabriel Torres, pp. 7–30. La Jolla, Calif.: Center for U.S.-Mexican Studies.

Stuart, James W. 1990. Maize Use by Rural Mesoamerican Households. *Human Organization* 49:135–39.

Suárez Argüello, Clara Elena. 1997. *Camino Real y Carrera Larga: La Arriería en la Nueva España durante el Siglo XVIII.* Mexico City: Centro de Investigaciones y Estudios Superiores en Antropología Social.

Suárez Jácome, Cruz. 1978. Petición de Lluvia en Zitlala, Guerrero. *Boletín del Instituto Nacional de Antropología e Historia, Tercera Epoca* 22:3–13.

Super, John C. 1981. Miguel Hernández: Master of Mule Trains. In *Struggle and Survival in Colonial America,* ed. David G. Sweet and Gary B. Nash, pp. 298–310. Berkeley: University of California Press.

Tax, Sol. 1937. The Municipios of the Midwestern Highlands of Guatemala. *American Anthropologist* 39:423–44.

———. 1941. World View and Social Relations in Guatemala. *American Anthropologist* 43:27–42.

———. 1953. *Penny Capitalism: A Guatemalan Indian Economy.* Smithsonian Institution, Institute of Social Anthropology, Publication 16. Washington, D.C.

Thomson, Guy. 1989. *Puebla de los Angeles: Industry and Society in a Mexican City, 1700–1850.* Boulder, Colo.: Westview Press.

Thünen, Johann Heinrich von. 1966. *Von Thünen's Isolated State.* Oxford: Pergamon Press. Originally published 1826.

Torre Villar, Ernesto de la. 1995. *Las Congregaciones de los Pueblos de Indios, Fase Terminal: Aprobaciones y Rectificaciones.* Mexico City: Universidad Nacional Autónoma de México.

Van Young, Eric. 1981. *Hacienda and Market in Eighteenth Century Mexico: The Rural Economy of the Guadalajara Region, 1675–1820.* Berkeley: University of California Press.

Velázquez, Gustavo G. 1981. *El Rebozo en el Estado de México.* Mexico City: Biblioteca Enciclopédica del Estado de México.

Ventura, Carol. 2002. The Ikat Rebozos of Central Mexico. *Shuttle, Spindle, and Dyepot* 33 (4): 41–48.

Vieyra-Odilon, Leticia, and Heike Vibrans. 2001. Weeds as Crops: The Value of Maize Field Weeds in the Valley of Toluca, Mexico. *Economic Botany* 55: 426–43.

Villaseñor y Sánchez, José Antonio de. 1746. *Theatro Americano: Descripción General de los Reynos, y Provincias de la Nueva-España, y sus Jurisdicciones; Dedicala al Rey Nuestro Señor el Señor d. Phelipe Quinto, Monarcha de las Españas.* Mexico City: Imprenta de la viuda de d. J. Bernardo de Hogal.

Vogt, Evon Z. 1969. *Zinacantan: A Mayan Community in the Highlands of Chiapas.* Cambridge, Mass.: Harvard University Press.

Warman, Arturo. 1980. *We Come to Object: The Peasants of Morelos and the National State.* Baltimore, Md.: Johns Hopkins University Press.

Weitlaner, Robert, and Irmgard Weitlaner. 1943. Acatlán y Hueycantenago, Guerrero. *El México Antiguo* 6:140–204.

West, Robert. 1948. *Cultural Geography of the Modern Tarascan Area.* Smithsonian Institution, Institute of Social Anthropology, Publication 7. Washington, D.C.

Wilk, Richard R. 1991. *Household Ecology: Economic Change and Domestic Life among the Kekchi Maya in Belize.* Tucson: University of Arizona Press.

Wilken, Gene C. 1987. *Good Farmers: Traditional Agricultural Resource Management in Mexico and Central America.* Berkeley: University of California Press.

Winning, Hasso von. 1941. Un Viaje al Sureste del Estado de Guerrero. *México Antiguo* 5:329–36.

Wolf, Eric. 1956. Aspects of Group Relations in a Complex Society: Mexico. *American Anthropologist* 58:1065–78.

——. 1957. Closed Corporate Communities in Mesoamerica and Central Java. *Southwestern Journal of Anthropology* 13:1–18.

Yaworsky, William. 2002. *Nongovernmental Organizations in the Highlands of Guerrero, Mexico.* Ph.D. dissertation, University of Oklahoma, Norman.

——. 2005. At the Whim of the State: Neoliberalism and Nongovernmental Organizations in Guerrero, Mexico. *Mexican Studies* 21:403–27.

INDEX